International Financial Markets

An Overview

Second Edition

BY

Peter E. Koveos

Syracuse University

George C. Philippatos

University of Tennessee –Knoxville

cognella

SAN DIEGO

Bassim Hamadeh, CEO and Publisher
Carrie Montoya, Manager, Revisions and Author Care
John Remington, Executive Editor
Abbey Hastings, Production Editor
Jess Estrella, Senior Graphic Designer
Alexa Lucido, Licensing Coordinator
Natalie Piccotti, Director of Marketing
Kassie Graves, Vice President of Editorial
Jamie Giganti, Director of Academic Publishing

Printed in the United States of America.

cognella® | ACADEMIC PUBLISHING
3970 Sorrento Valley Blvd., Ste. 500, San Diego, CA 92121

Contents

Introduction

The book was written because we are both committed to the study of international finance and believe that all students must understand the international financial environment and its implications. Whether you major in finance, accounting, economics, or any other field, knowing how our financial system works is necessary for survival. Our global economy does not give you any other options.

International Finance is a fascinating subject. It borrows themes and concepts from finance, economics and accounting. It also shares issues with international relations, law, and other disciplines. Furthermore, it is not a topic that will lose its relevance tomorrow! As long as countries, banks, companies, and individuals want to trade or invest across national borders, the theories and methodologies of international finance will serve as useful tools.

To better understand the nature and role of international finance, you must go beyond the textbook. By their nature, most textbooks are outdated between the time they are written and the time they are published. Events take place in rapid fashion! In international finance, a year can feel like a decade and a decade like a century! You should therefore be aware of current developments and of other information that can help you appreciate the richness of the field.

A country's financial institutions and markets perform a variety of functions within its national boundaries, thus enhancing the efficiency of its economic system. The orderly operation of financial markets in converting savings into investment is both the generator and the hallmark of advanced economic development. Access to these markets is essential for participants in a dynamic environment if they are to build on their competitive advantages.

As national economies interact with each other to an increasingly greater extent, developing new markets presents new opportunities and new risks for a variety of constituents. For the individual firm, international markets may mean access to new sources of funds. For the investor, they may present the opportunity to diversify portfolio holdings. For governments, these new markets constitute both an opportunity and a special challenge as these markets have historically evaded regulations and grown beyond government control. International financial markets indeed have widespread and pervasive influence in today's interconnected world.

International financial markets perform functions similar to those of their domestic counterparts. The environment, however, is very different. Differences in the economic, regulatory, technological, and political environment present both rewards and challenges as goods, services, and capital flows across national or regional borders. Appreciating the nature of these differences and acting on their implications is a fundamental prerequisite for survival in our complicated and competitive global economy.

The first chapter of the book introduces us to the largest global financial market, the foreign exchange market. The chapter describes the structure, conduct, and performance of the foreign exchange market. It explains the functions of the market, the major participants, and the major pricing methods of the market. Chapter 1 primarily covers the spot market component of the foreign exchange market, while Chapter 2 describes the nature of the market's derivative instruments (forward, futures, options and swaps).

International finance is founded on a rich theoretical framework. The third chapter shows us how dependent individual financial markets are on each other. It also exposes us to the principal theories and concepts in international finance: market efficiency, Purchasing Power Parity, Interest Rate Parity Theorem, Forward Rate Theory of Exchange Rate Expectations, and the International Fisher Effect.

One of the critical issues in global financial markets is identification and understanding of the forces that are behind the value of currencies. The system within which currencies attain their value, the international monetary system (IMS), is the subject of the fourth chapter. The Chapter examines the various forms that the IMS has taken over the years and the distinguishing elements of each form. It also describes the principal agencies and agreements supporting international trade and finance. Finally, it discusses important developments of the system and their implications.

Chapter 5 expands on what we learned in Chapter 4 by presenting us with the various variables that move exchange rates from one equilibrium position to the next. These variables provide the foundations for the formulation of various theoretical frameworks. The chapter examines the various exchange rate determination theories. It also examines the dynamic relationships between exchange rates and macroeconomic variables.

Forecasting exchange rates is one of the most challenging tasks of the international financial manager. Chapter 6 discusses various forecasting approaches available and shows how they can be applied to alternative exchange rate systems. It also explains several measures for evaluating forecasts and notes some managerial implications of forecasting.

The currency world has experienced a great deal of volatility during the post-Bretton Woods period. This volatility has generated a new risk environment for market participants. Chapter 7 describes the risks posed by exchange-rate volatility and the strategies available to deal with them. The chapter discusses the concepts of exchange risk and exchange exposure, explaining the ways managers can identify, measure, and manage exposure.

In addition to the foreign exchange market, this book includes a description of other international financial markets. The last chapter of the book, Chapter 8, presents us with the major characteristics of financial markets operating across borders: the Eurocurrency, Medium-Term Note (MTNs), international bond, and international equity markets. These and related markets are integral to the operation of the international financial system as they perform the critical function of channeling international capital from savers to borrowers.

We hope that the book will help you appreciate the complicated and fascinating world of international financial markets. Although we provided you with an overview, you must realize that to better understand the dynamic nature of these markets means that you have to keep up with current developments. We also suggest that, as you do that, you make an effort to connect these developments with what you learned from reading this book.

Thank you for your confidence in us!

Peter E. Koveos
Syracuse University
George C. Philippatos
University of Tennessee – Knoxville

Chapter 1

The Basics of the Foreign Exchange Market

Overview of Chapter Material

As national borders open to international transactions, monies originated in other countries become relevant in individual and firm-level consumption and investment decisions. These foreign monies, or currencies, are traded in the foreign exchange market. This chapter offers an introduction to the structure, conduct, and performance of the foreign exchange market. It explains the functions of the market, the major participants, and the major pricing methods of the market.

After Studying This Chapter, You Will Be Able To

- Understand the nature, importance, and functions of the foreign exchange market
- Identify the different components of the foreign exchange market
- Discuss the implications of the foreign exchange market for its participants

Chapter Outline

I. Definition and Functions of the Foreign Exchange Market
II. Classifying the Currency Market
III. The Spot Market
IV. Foreign Exchange Market Participants
V. Exchange Rate Indices and Effective Exchange Rates
VI. Summary

I. Definition and Functions of the Foreign Exchange Market

1. What is the Foreign Exchange Market?

In simple terms, the foreign exchange market is the market where one currency is exchanged for another. Just like in any other market, buyers and sellers come together in the foreign exchange (or currency) market to exchange their products (in this case, currency) at a price called the (foreign) exchange rate. The exchange rate, then, is the price of one currency expressed in terms of units of another currency. If you need 2 US dollars to buy one British pound sterling, the exchange rate between dollars and pounds is 2 to 1.

As we will see later in this chapter and the rest of the book, there are two types of market transactions: outright and swap. An outright transaction involves buying/selling one currency for another. When the exchange of these two currencies takes place immediately, the transaction is called a spot transaction. When the parties agree to make the exchange at some time in the future, the transaction is called a forward. In addition to the initial exchange of the two currencies, a swap transaction involves a re-exchange of the currencies at an agreed upon exchange rate and time in the future.

To facilitate currency trading, each currency is represented by a three-letter code designed by the International Organization for Standardization (ISO 4217). Accordingly, USD is the code for the US dollar; JPY is for the Japanese yen, and CNY for the Chinese yuan. The yen/dollar exchange rate is usually shown as the number of yen that buys you one dollar, or USD/JPY. In this case, USD is termed the *base* currency, while the JPY is termed the *counter*, or *quote*, currency; the USD is quoted against the JPY. Other notable currency codes are EUR for euro, GBP for Great Britain pound, CAD for Canadian dollar, and CHF for Swiss franc. The Chinese currency, the renminbi, presents an interesting case of dual notation that can be confusing. The terms "renminbi" and "yuan" have sometimes been used interchangeably, but they have a slightly different meaning. The first name, renminbi, simply refers to the official name of the currency. Yuan, on the other hand, is a currency unit. If you travel to China and wish to exchange your 100 US dollars for an appropriate amount of Chinese currency, and if the exchange rate is CNY6.3=USD1, you will receive 630 yuan (CNY), not renminbi (RMB). In this book, the Chinese currency is quoted as CNY, so the exchange rate with the dollar will be USD/CNY. A list of selected currencies with their ISO code and symbol is shown in Table 1.1. Note that certain symbols are shared by multiple currencies. In this book, we will use either the ISO code or the symbol for some of the well-known and frequently traded currencies (US dollar, British pound, the euro). For other currencies, we will just use the ISO code to avoid confusion.

The foreign exchange currencies and currency pairs are also known by the nicknames given to them by traders and other foreign exchange market participants. The US dollar, for example, is also known as the greenback or the buck; the Canadian dollar is the loonie; the GBP/USD pair is the cable. A list of some of the nicknames is provided in Table 1.2.

Country	ISO	Symbol
Argentine Peso	ARS	$
Australian Dollar	AUD	$
Brazilian Real	BRL	R$
British Pound	GBP	£
Canadian Dollar	CAD	$
Chinese Yuan	CNY	¥
Danish Krone	DKK	kr
Hong Kong Dollar	HKD	$
Indian Rupee	INR	₹
Indonesian Rupiah	IDR	Rp
Israeli Sheqel	ILS	₪
Japanese Yen	JPY	¥
Malaysian Ringgit	MYR	RM
Mexican Peso	MXN	$
Russian Rouble	RUB	руб
Singapore Dollar	SGD	$
South African Rand	ZAR	S
South Korean Won	KRW	₩
Swedish Krona	SEK	kr
Swiss Franc	CHF	CHF
Thai Baht	THB	฿
US Dollar	USD	$

Table 1.1 Selected Currency ISO Codes and Symbols.

Source: http://www.exchangerates.org.uk/currency-symbols.html. Accessed May 15, 2015.

Currency/Pair	Symbol	Nickname
US Dollar	USD	Greenback or Buck
British Pound	GBP	Sterling*
Euro	EUR	Fiber
Canadian Dollar	CAD	Loon or Loonie
Swiss Franc	CHF	Swissy

Table 1.2 Currencies, Currency Pairs, and Their Nicknames.

Downloaded from http://forexillustrated.com/currency-nicknames-secret-handshake-traders/. Accessed December 22, 2017

**Note: Sterling is not a nickname in the sense of the other nicknames listed. It can be better viewed as an abbreviation of the currency's official name: British Pound Sterling.*

Currency/Pair	Symbol	Nickname
Australian Dollar	AUD	Aussie or Ozzie
New Zealand Dollar	NZD	Kiwi
Norwegian Krone	NOK	Nockie
Swedish Krona	SEK	Skokie
British Pound/US Dollar	GBP/USD	Cable
US Dollar/Russian Rubble	USD/RUB	Barnie
Euro/Russia Rubble	EUR/RUB	Betty
Euro/British Pound	EUR/GBP	Chunnel
US Dollar/Japanese Yen	USD/JPY	Ninja

Table 1.2 *(Continued)*

2. Exchange Rate Changes

Currency values move as a result of a number of economic and non-economic events. Exchange rates, especially between the major currencies, may change from day to day or from one trade to the next. For example, today's exchange rate between the USD and the EUR is US$1.2000 per one euro. The next day, it changes from US$1.2000 per €1 to US$1.2100 per €1. We conclude that the US dollar has depreciated versus the euro. That is, the US dollar's value has fallen against the euro, or the euro has increased in value versus the dollar. Putting it yet another way, it takes more US dollars to buy one euro. To measure the extent of the depreciation, we can use the following expression:

$$(S_1 - S_0)/S_0 = (1.2100 - 1.2000)/1.2000 = .0083$$

Where S_0 is the initial exchange rate, 1.2000, and S_1 is the new exchange rate, 1.2100; we can state that the US dollar depreciated versus the euro by 0.83%.

If, alternatively, the exchange rate changed from US$1.2000=€1 to US$1.1700=€1, we state that the dollar has appreciated versus the euro; the price of the US dollar versus the euro has increased. Using the same kind of expression as above:

$$(S_1 - S_0)/S_0 = (1.1700 - 1.2000)/1.2000 = -0.025$$

The price of the US dollar has increased by 2.5 % (0.025 × 100) against the euro.

As the US dollar fluctuates vis-à-vis the euro, it may also fluctuate vis-à-vis other currencies, but not necessarily in the same direction and to the same extent. The US dollar's value may increase versus the Japanese yen while simultaneously staying the same against the British pound sterling and decreasing against the Canadian dollar. The exchange rate we read about in the financial newspapers is a bilateral rate. It indicates the price of one currency against another specific currency, not against all currencies. To gain a perspective on how a currency fares against all other currencies, we can use indices of exchange rate movements (we will discuss indices later in this chapter).

We use the terms "depreciation" and "appreciation" to show changes in the price of a currency generated primarily by market forces. On the other hand, we use "devaluation" and "revaluation" to indicate changes in the price of a currency resulting from government action. For example, the Chinese government may wish to readjust the price of its currency from CNY6.0000 per USD to CNY6.2500 per USD; that action would constitute a devaluation of the Chinese renminbi versus the US dollar.

3. What Does the Foreign Exchange Market Do?

As the saying goes, "money is what money does." Within the domestic economy, money performs a number of functions, including

- providing a medium of exchange,
- serving as a standard of value (or unit of account),
- offering a store of value, and
- facilitating deferred payments (credit).

The foreign exchange market provides the instruments through which these functions are performed on a cross-border basis. It also allows for transactions that are unique because of their international nature. In particular, the foreign exchange market may provide the framework for:

A. Transfer of purchasing power. Consumption plays a central role in every economy. The foreign exchange market enables consumers to purchase goods and services originating in countries other than their own. Exports and imports are possible because companies know they can buy and sell their products and services by exchanging their country's currency for another country's currency in the foreign exchange market. An ability to buy foreign goods expands the potential consumption basket and allows for greater consumer satisfaction, or utility. Parties to transactions exchange goods for currency that they can eventually convert into another currency.

As an example, assume that a US manufacturer exports medical equipment to a Canadian customer. The US exporter may accept payment in US dollars or in Canadian dollars. In the former case, the Canadian importer will either pay in US dollars that were accumulated through past transactions using the foreign exchange market or purchase them with Canadian dollars in the foreign exchange market within the period allowed for payment. If the importer pays in Canadian dollars, the US exporter will in turn need to convert the Canadian dollar proceeds into US dollars in the foreign exchange market in order to buy goods domestically.

B. Unit of account. As a consumer, you want to be able to state prices of various goods and services in terms of your home currency. Therefore, if a European car dealer quotes you a price of €30,000, and if the exchange rate is USD1.20=EUR1, then you calculate the price of the car as $36,000 (including all charges). The foreign exchange market, then, gives you the information to calculate the price of the car in terms of US dollars.

C. Facilitation of credit. The existence of the foreign exchange market allows firms and individuals to carry receivables from foreign clients. A US exporter may allow a Swiss customer to pay for the shipment of goods in Swiss francs at any time within a specified period. The exporter knows that the Swiss francs received in sixty days are easily exchangeable for US dollars in the foreign exchange market.

D. Store of value. The foreign exchange market allows local residents to buy and sell currencies with the expectation that they will profit from future currency value fluctuations. A Japanese investor who expects the dollar to rise in relation to the yen can buy dollars (or dollar-denominated bonds) and hold them until the appropriate time for conversion back to yen.

E. Medium of exchange-risk management. Holding and dealing with currencies entails the risk that their value will fluctuate in an adverse fashion. Participants in the foreign exchange market can alleviate at least a portion of that risk by using the appropriate market instruments, which include futures, forward, and options contracts.

F. Economic and political indicator. Movements in a currency's value may reflect the influence of economic variables such as prices or interest rates. A currency's movements may also signal the level of confidence that international markets have in the domestic economy. If international investors believe that the US economy is stable and the country is a safe place in which to invest, they will convert their local currency denominated assets into US dollar-denominated assets, thus strengthening the dollar.

G. Reserve asset. Governments enter the foreign exchange market to buy or sell currencies that will serve as their official reserves. Governments hold reserves (currencies and gold) for different reasons and in different amounts. Motivation to hold reserves may be rooted in precautions that countries take to protect themselves from unforeseen capital flows. They may also build up their foreign exchange reserves to be able to enter the foreign exchange market to protect the value of their own currencies. Holdings of reserves may be facilitated by a country's revenue influx from increased exports or foreign investment. Foreign exchange reserves are also useful in determining a country's ability to repay its debt.

4. Why Should We Care About Exchange Rates?

The foreign exchange market is the fundamental component of international trade and capital flows. Indeed, the foreign exchange market performs many valuable functions. What does this imply, specifically? Well, both the level of and changes in exchange rates, whether they are anticipated or not, affect international businesses, policy makers, and individuals in a variety of ways. We offer some examples:

1. On April 1, Ms. Price, a US citizen, decides to visit Paris. On April 1, the euro/US dollar exchange rate (€/$, or EUR/USD) is at $1.1000 = €1. To prepare for the trip, Ms. Price puts aside $11,000.00. However, by June 1, when Ms. Price departs for Paris, the

exchange rate has changed to $1.21500 = €1. The same vacation amenities, then, will now cost $12,150.00. Ms. Price was not prepared for the change. She will now either have to dig into his savings and spend more US dollars than she originally planned to spend or forego some of the fun she had planned to have in Paris.

2. USMed, an American company, just sold medical equipment to a German customer. USMed usually sells one of its products to this customer for $30,000. Since the current exchange rate is $1.100 = €1, the company bills its customer for €27,272.72. According to the sales contract, the client has sixty days in which to make payment. However, by the time payment is made, the US dollar has depreciated versus the euro; it is now $1.1500 = €1. By converting its euro receivables in to US dollars, the company ends up with $31,363.63, a full $1,363.63 more than it had expected.
3. BDCF, a Spanish company is interested in buying up Toto Cement of Bellefonte, Pennsylvania. In December, 2018, the asking price for Toto is US$400m. At the exchange rate of $1.2000 = €1, this amount is approximately equivalent to €333.33 million. BDCF decides to act on the opportunity in early April, 2019. By that time, however, the exchange rate had changed to $1.1500 per €1. Buying the American company would now cost about €347.83 million. Waiting for a few months made the acquisition a more expensive proposition and BDCF decides not go through with the acquisition.

The importance of changes in currency values became evident during the rise in the value of the US dollar during late 2014 and the early months of 2015. For example, on May 1, 2014, the US dollar/euro rate was about $1.39 per €1. On May 1, 2015, the exchange rate was $1.12 per €1. The dollar also strengthened against the British pound and the yen, among other currencies. The dollar's strength has repeatedly been blamed for contributing to the decline in US exports, the widening of the US trade deficit, and the slowdown of the US economy. The rise in the value of the US dollar even prompted President Trump to declare in April 2017 that the "dollar is too strong" and to state his support for a "weak" dollar. At the micro level, a strong dollar certainly benefits US citizens traveling abroad, but it cuts into the earnings of exporters, whose goods and services become less competitive globally, and multinationals, whose foreign currency earnings and assets decrease in dollar value as the greenback flexes its muscles. Some sectors have been traditionally hit particularly hard by the rise in the value of the dollar. United States automakers and their suppliers face increasing competition from European and Asian firms, whose products become cheaper in the US market. To deal with the effects of a strong dollar, they have in the past adopted several strategies, such as point-of-sale pricing adjustments and currency hedging, to deal with the situation.

On the other hand, of course, exporting firms from countries and regions whose currencies have depreciated against the dollar have reaped the benefits of their weaker currency. For example, according to a Wall Street Journal report (Fujikawa, 2015), Japanese exporters reported record profits in 2014. Toyota and Nissan showed especially strong gains. The weaker yen also brought more tourists to Japan, increasing All Nippon Airways Co.'s profits.

Exchange rates also affect the economy as a whole. For example, when the value of a country's currency falls, the country's goods become cheaper to the world; aggregate demand will then increase, leading to an increase in the country's GDP. Of course, imports will now be more expensive. Depending on what else is going on in the economy, the increase in the price of imports may lead to an increase in the general level of prices, or inflation.

The important point to keep in mind is that exchange rates and foreign exchange markets matter! They are important to individual economic agents as well as to the policy makers. We must therefore understand the world of foreign exchange and appreciate its importance to the rest of the economy.

5. Currency Wars!

Do policy makers really care about the international value of their country's currency? The unequivocal answer is yes! They care enough to go to war! Currency war, that is.

Currency wars are manipulations of a currency by the government. In essence, they are competitive devaluations in which countries engage, especially during periods of unfavorable balance of payments and overall economic performance (Rickards, 2011). According to the US Department of the Treasury (May, 2019), three criteria are used to classify a country as a currency manipulator: "(1) A significant bilateral trade surplus with the United States of at least $20 billion; (2) a material current account surplus of at least 3 percent of GDP; and (3) persistent, one-sided intervention when net purchases of foreign currency are conducted repeatedly and total at least 2 percent of an economy's GDP over a 12 month period." The Treasury Department also compiles a "monitoring watch list," which includes countries that are in danger of inclusion in the manipulator risk. China, Germany, South Korea, Japan, and Singapore are among the countries featured in the watch list.

A currency war may start with one country devaluing its currency in order to increase domestic production, jobs, and demand for its products. Other countries, however, may not take this action sitting down, and they may respond in kind! They want to protect their own economic interests and so they devalue their own currency. It is the old "beggar thy neighbor" policy. If left unchecked, currency wars can erupt into trade wars or general economic wars.

According to Joseph Gagnon of the Peterson Institute (2013), currency manipulation or aggression has been the principal factor affecting trade surpluses and deficits, with fiscal policy a distant second. According to his research findings, the current account balance increases by 65 cents for every dollar attributed to currency manipulation. No wonder some countries rely so much on aggressive currency positions to fix their economies!

Aggressive currency policies were in fashion during the Great Depression of the 1930s, as countries attempted to adjust their currencies and thus improve their balance of payments situation at the expense of their trading partners. The practice, however, remained in effect long after the Depression ended. In 2010, for example, Brazil's Finance Minister, Guido Mantega, declared the existence of a new currency war. Two years later, in December 2012, the change in government policies in Japan resulted in double-digit fall in the value of the JDY versus the USD. Japanese exporters were, to say the least, very appreciative of this development. Smaller countries may be even worse offenders, since they are generally more vulnerable to global economic downturns. On November 7, 2013, the Czech National Bank announced that it is increasing its foreign exchange reserves by 14% by buying foreign currency through the printing of new korunas. The bank's objective was to provide a stimulus to the economy by bolstering exports (Carney, 2013).

Will currency wars ever end? It is probably safe to say that, as long as some governments see these wars as benefitting their cause, history will keep on repeating itself.

6. Market Size and Activity

The foreign exchange market is the world's largest financial market. It operates on a 24-hour basis. According to the Bank for International Settlements (BIS) 2019 Triennial Bank Survey, the average daily turnover in the foreign exchange market has reached $6.590 trillion at April 2019 exchange rates, an increase of $1.632 trillion from 2016 and $1.763 trillion from 2013. Figure 1.1 below shows the growth of foreign exchange turnover since 2001.

Table 1.3 shows the distribution of OTC foreign exchange turnover by selected currencies. The US dollar is the dominant currency used in currency trades,

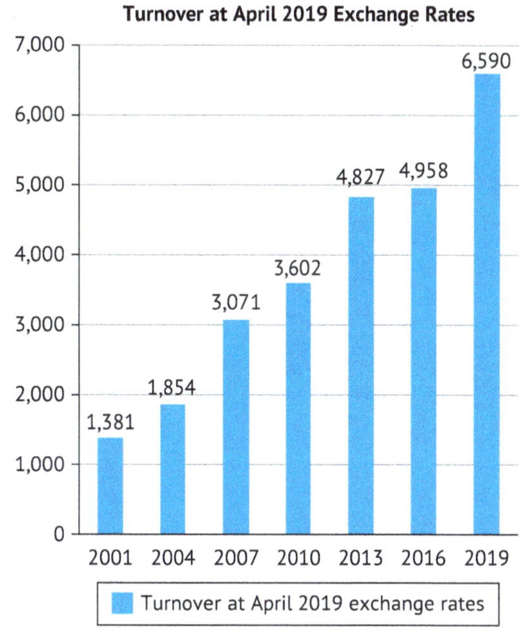

Figure 1.1 Turnover at April 2019 Exchange Rates.
Generated from Bank of International Settlements. *Triennial Central Bank Survey of foreign exchange and derivatives market activity in 2019*. Accessed at https://www.bis.org/statistics/rpfx19_fx.pdf, on October 12, 2019.

Currency	2004		2007		2010		2013		2016		2019	
	Share	Rank	Share	Rank	Share	Rank	Share	Rank	Share	Rank	Share	Rank
USD	88.0	1	85.6	1	84.9	1	87.0	1	87.6	1	88.3	1
EUR	37.4	2	37.0	2	39.0	2	33.4	2	31.4	2	32.3	2
JPY	20.8	3	17.2	3	19.0	3	23.0	3	21.6	3	16.8	3
GBP	16.5	4	14.9	4	12.9	4	11.8	4	12.8	4	12.8	4
AUD	6.0	6	6.6	6	7.6	5	8.6	5	6.9	5	6.8	5
CAD	4.2	7	4.3	7	5.3	7	4.6	7	5.1	6	5.0	6
CHF	6.0	5	6.8	5	6.3	6	5.2	6	4.8	7	5.0	7
CNY	0.1	29	0.5	20	0.9	17	2.2	9	4.0	8	4.3	8
HKD	1.8	9	2.7	8	2.4	8	1.4	13	1.7	13	3.5	9
NZD	1.1	13	1.9	11	1.6	10	2.0	10	2.1	10	2.1	10

Table 1.3 Currency Distribution of OTC Foreign Exchange Turnover; Top 10 Currencies.

Net-net basis, 1 percentage shares of average daily turnover in April of the given year

Generated from Bank of International Settlements. *Triennial Central Bank Survey of foreign exchange and derivatives market activity in 2019*. Accessed at https://www.bis.org/statistics/rpfx19_fx.pdf, on October 12, 2019.

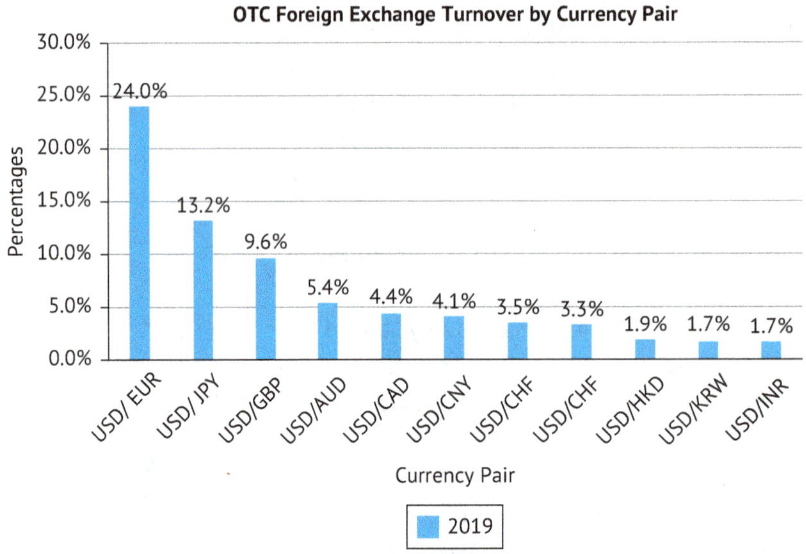

Figure 1.2 OTC Foreign Exchange Turnover by Currency Pair: Top Pairs.
Generated from Bank of International Settlements. *Triennial Central Bank Survey of foreign exchange and derivatives market activity in 2019.* Accessed at https://www.bis.org/statistics/rpfx19_fx.pdf, on October 12, 2019.

accounting for 88.3% of one side of all deals. The US dollar's share declined around the financial crisis (2007–2010), but afterwards recovered to its pre-crisis share. Since 2010, the share of some of the other frequently traded currencies (euro, yen, Swiss franc) has slightly declined. On the other hand, there has been a significant rise in the trading of the Chinese renminbi. China only recently started appearing on the top-10 currency trading tables, but we should expect its presence to increase considerably as the country has become a global economic superpower.

The US dollar also dominates the market in currency-pair trading activity. As the Bank for International Settlements (BIS) data show (Figure 1.2), the USD/EUR currency pair has the highest amount of turnover, followed by the USD/JPY and USD/GBP currency pairs. The USD/CNY currency pair did not materialize until 2010. Its share increased from 0.8% in 2010 to 2.1% in 2013, 3.8% in 2016, and 4.1% in 2019. Of the trades not using the USD, the most frequently used currency pairs are EUR/GBP, at 2.0% in 2019, and EUR/JPY at 1.7% (not shown in the Figure).

Although the dollar is the dominant currency used in deals, London is the dominant center of market activity (43.1%, or USD3,576 billions), followed by New York (16.5%, or USD1,370 billions), Singapore (7.6%), Hong Kong (7.6%), Tokyo (4.5%), and Switzerland (3.3%). The geographical distribution of foreign exchange centers shown in Table 1.4 illustrates the 24-hour nature of the foreign exchange market. London's dominance is a result of many factors that influenced its global position over the years, including regulatory (following the 1979 market deregulation), historical, and geographical. London has also engaged in aggressive campaigns

Country	% of total
United Kingdom	43.1
United States	16.5
Singapore	7.6
Hong Kong	7.6
Japan	4.5
Switzerland	3.3
Rest of World	17.4

Table 1.4 Geographical Distribution of OTC Foreign Exchange Turnover, 2019[1]. Net Gross basis[2], daily averages, in percentages.

Generated from Bank of International Settlements. *Triennial Central Bank Survey of foreign exchange and derivatives market activity in 2019*. Accessed at *https://www.bis.org/statistics/rpfx19_fx.pdf*, on October 12, 2019.

[1]Data may differ slightly from national survey data owing to differences in aggregation procedures and rounding.

[2]Adjusted for local inter-dealer double-counting (i.e., net gross basis).

in order to become the financial center of choice for trading in emerging market currencies (China) and new products (for example, Dim Sum Bonds). The initial uncertainty generated from the UK's exit from the European Union (Brexit) seems to have faded, bringing foreign exchange market activity back to London.

Concept Questions

1. What is the foreign exchange rate?
2. What is the difference between currency depreciation and appreciation?
3. What is the difference between currency depreciation and devaluation?
4. What are the functions of the foreign exchange market?
5. What are currency wars? Why do countries engage in these wars?

II. Classifying the Currency Market

1. Market Components

The foreign exchange market is large, ubiquitous, and operates around the clock; it is also multifaceted and fascinating for observers and participants. It offers a number of instruments, each having its own unique market, but with these markets also overlapping and reinforcing each other's functions. We can understand better the basic characteristics of each market by referring to the definitions offered by the Bank for International Settlements (https://www.bis.org/statistics/rpfx19_fx.pdf; downloaded October 12, 2019):

- *Spot Transactions*: single outright transactions involving the exchange of two currencies at a price (exchange rate) determined on contract day for delivery in two or three days. The date on which delivery is actually made is called the value date. This practice is denoted as t + 2 or t + 3, where t stands for the trade date and t + 2, t + 3 are the value dates.
- *(Outright) Forwards*: exchange of specified amount of two currencies at a price (rate) determined on contract day for delivery (value) at an agreed upon time in the future. The forward market also offers a number of other instruments, such as forward exchange agreements and non-deliverable forwards.
- *Currency and Foreign Exchange Options*: contracts that give the right to buy or sell a specified amount of a currency with another currency at a predetermined exchange rate within or at the conclusion of a specified period.
- *Currency and Foreign Exchange Swaps*: these two types of swaps are very similar in that both serve currency-hedging purposes. The difference is that *currency swaps* represent an exchange of (fixed or floating) interest payments in two currencies during the duration of the contract. Principal amounts, based on initial spot rate, are exchanged at the beginning and end of the contract. *Foreign exchange swaps* are an exchange of specified amounts of two currencies on a specified date at a price (rate) agreed to at the time of the contract, followed by a reverse exchange of these two currencies on a future date at a rate agreed to at the time of the contract.

According to the Bank of International Settlements (2019), foreign exchange swap transactions show the highest turnover ($3.202 tr.), followed by spot ($1.987 tr.) and outright forwards (about $1 tr.). The composition of the foreign exchange market by instrument is shown in Table 1.5.

Instrument	2019 (trillions $)
Spot Transactions	1.987
Outright Forwards	999
Foreign Exchange Swaps	3.202
Currency Swaps	108
Options and Other Products	294

Table 1.5 Global Foreign Exchange Turnover by Instrument, April 2019.

Generated from Bank of International Settlements. *Triennial Central Bank Survey of foreign exchange and derivatives market activity in 2019*. Accessed at https://www.bis.org/statistics/rpfx19_fx.pdf, on October 12, 2019.

2. Market Characteristics

We can classify the foreign exchange market in various ways according to its many characteristics. We briefly discuss some characteristics of the market below.

i. The pricing principle to which they adhere:
   Spot pricing refers to transactions made in the spot market; forward pricing refers to transactions made in the forward, futures, options, and swap markets.
ii. The maturity of the currency instrument:
   Exchanges of currencies in the spot markets have immediate maturity, at least theoretically. Forward and other transactions, however, mature in the future. Some forward contracts may mature in 30 days, others in 40.
iii. The degree of control exerted by government:
   Some governments allow their currency to change according to market conditions, while others control the official price and movement of its currency.
iv. The marketability and convertibility of the currency:
   Currencies of the major industrialized economies (the USD, JPY, GBP, EUR, and CHF among them) have a ready worldwide market. In general, a currency is considered convertible if it can be freely exchanged at the market exchange rate into a major reserve currency or another currency. Internal convertibility implies that residents may hold foreign assets domestically but cannot make payments abroad or hold assets that either are located in a foreign country or represent claims against nonresidents. Convertibility is an important aspect of a currency. Individuals and companies doing business in other countries need to know whether they can convert their foreign currency earnings into their own currency. An Italian company doing business in the US and generating revenues in USD knows that it can at any time convert its US dollars into euros since both currencies are freely convertible into each other. Other countries, however, may impose controls on holdings of their currency by foreigners and, as a result, do not allow conversion of their currency into other currencies; their currencies, thus, are termed "non-convertible." The Chinese currency, for example, was non-convertible for decades. Some countries allow convertibility of their currency for purposes of trade-related transactions (current-account convertibility) but may not allow convertibility for moving funds in and out of the country (capital-account convertibility).
v. Trading in organized exchanges:
   Selected currencies are also traded on organized exchanges, such as the Chicago Mercantile Exchange (futures contract) and the Philadelphia Options Exchange (options contracts). Other currencies may be traded in the over-the-counter (OTC) market or informally.
vi. The consideration of price changes (nominal versus real):
   Observers of the foreign exchange market may be interested in the purchasing power of a certain currency. To determine its purchasing power, we adjust a currency by the inflation of its economy, thus generating the real exchange rate (as opposed

to the nominal exchange rate). Similarly, we can calculate the real exchange rate index or real effective exchange rate using weights for both currencies and price variables. Economists have always been interested in the relationship between exchange rates and prices. This relationship is further examined in Chapter 3.

Concept Questions

1. What are the components of the foreign exchange market? Which of these components is the largest?
2. What are the various characteristics of the foreign exchange market?

III. The Spot Market

As noted above, currencies may be priced according to spot or forward-pricing principles. Spot transactions involve agreement on the terms of a given transaction and exchange of a good or service for immediate delivery. An example may be a traveler from the United States going to a bank in London to exchange dollars for pounds. The parties transact according to the terms agreed upon at that time (through the bank's listing of its foreign exchange quotations). Often, the transaction can be completed right then and there (on the spot). This specific transaction is a cash transaction. However, spot transactions, such as the transfer of currencies from one bank to the other, may involve adjustments in bank accounts taking perhaps one or two days depending on characteristics of the transaction (such as the type of currencies involved and the size of the transaction).

An example will illustrate the nature of a spot transaction. On January 19, The Bank of Manhattan buys one million euros with US dollars from Banque de Paris at $1.1315 per euro. January 19 is the trade date. The actual transfer of the currencies takes place on January 21, referred to as *value date* or *settlement date*. When the transfer materializes, the transaction will show on the books of both banks.

1. Direct and Indirect Spot Quotations

Exchange rates may be depicted in two ways. The quotation expressing the number of home-currency units required to buy one unit of the foreign currency is referred to as the *direct quotation*. For example, a spot market quote of USD0.145 = CNY1 (as in Table 1.5 this is a direct quotation for the dollar amount required to buy one yuan in the United States). An *indirect quotation*, on the other hand, is stated in terms of the number of foreign currency units necessary to buy one unit of the local currency. An example of this arrangement for the dollar is CNY6.8982 = USD1. If we have one of these quotations, we can generate the other, since:

$$\text{Direct Quotation} = 1/\text{Indirect Quotation}$$
$$\text{Or } 0.145 = 1/6.8982$$

Note that the rates shown in the table are for wholesale transactions at one point in time (the 30 seconds prior and up to 4 p.m. in this case). The rate generated is called a "fix." Individuals for the most part operate in the retail market, which implies a less favorable rate than the fix.

US-Dollar Foreign Exchange Rates in Late New York Trading

	IN US$		US$ VS. % CHG		PER US$	
	WED	TUES	1-DAY	YTD	WED	TUES
Americas Argentina peso	0.0158	0.0158	0.2	5.6	63.24	63.114
Brazil real	0.1958	0.1996	1.97	27.1	5.1075	5.0089
Canada dollar	0.6893	0.7041	2.14	11.7	1.4507	1.4203
Chile peso	0.00115	0.00118	2.32	17.4	868	848.3
Colombia peso	0.00024	0.00025	4.06	26.8	4161	3998.5
Ecuador US dollar	1	1	**unch**	**unch**	1	1
Mexico peso	0.0422	0.0436	3.32	25.3	23.713	22.952
Uruguay peso	0.02249	0.023	2.28	19.7	44.46	43.47
Asia-Pacific Australian dollar	0.5773	0.5998	3.9	21.6	1.7322	1.6672
China yuan	0.1419	0.1427	0.58	1.2	7.0475	7.0072
Hong Kong dollar	0.1288	0.1289	0.04	−0.4	7.7638	7.7608
India rupee	0.01341	0.0135	0.66	4.5	74.55	74.063
Indonesia rupiah	6.6E-05	6.6E-05	0.32	9.6	15218	15170
Japan yen	0.00925	0.00929	0.37	−0.5	108.07	107.67
Kazakhstan tenge	0.00225	0.00229	1.51	16.2	443.52	436.93
Macau pataca	0.12504	0.12491	−0.1	−0.3	7.997	8.006
Malaysia ringgit	0.2286	0.2298	0.52	6.9	4.3735	4.351
New Zealand dollar	0.5739	0.5935	3.42	17.3	1.7425	1.6849
Pakistan rupee	0.00631	0.00631	0.08	2.3	158.5	158.38
Philippines peso	0.0194	0.0193	−0.12	1.9	51.67	51.73
Singapore dollar	0.6934	0.6999	0.94	7.1	1.4422	1.4288
South Korea won	0.0008	0.00081	1.35	8.8	1256.5	1239.8
Sri Lanka rupee	0.00539	0.00541	0.37	2.4	185.67	184.99
Taiwan dollar	0.03293	0.0331	0.52	1.5	30.37	30.21
Thailand baht	0.03066	0.0311	1.46	9.6	32.62	32.15

Table 1.6 Snapshot of Exchange Rates

NY trading at closing; March 18, 2020. Downloaded from The Wall Street Journal/Markets Section. *http://www.wsj.com/public/page/news-currency-currencies-trading.html. Accessed on March 19, 2020.*

	IN US$		US$ VS. % CHG		PER US$	
	WED	TUES	1-DAY	YTD	WED	TUES
Vietnam dong	4.3E-05	4.3E-05	0.03	0.3	23246	23238
Europe Bulgaria lev	0.55822	0.56275	0.81	2.8	1.791	1.777
Croatia kuna	0.1436	0.145	0.97	4.9	6.9615	6.8945
Czech Rep. koruna	0.03932	0.04049	2.99	12.2	25.433	24.696
Denmark krone	0.146	0.1472	0.78	2.8	6.8477	6.7946
Euro area euro	1.0916	1.0998	0.75	2.7	0.9161	0.9093
Hungary forint	0.00309	0.00316	2.47	9.7	324.03	316.21
Iceland krona	0.00718	0.00713	-0.75	15	139.26	140.31
Norway krone	0.0886	0.0954	7.72	28.6	11.289	10.48
Poland zloty	0.2424	0.2459	1.44	8.7	4.1252	4.0668
Romania leu	0.2243	0.2267	1.08	4.4	4.4579	4.4103
Russia ruble	0.01234	0.01326	7.41	30.6	81.031	75.441
Sweden krona	0.0974	0.1012	3.85	9.6	10.265	9.8838
Switzerland franc	1.033	1.0406	0.74	0.1	0.9681	0.961
Turkey lira	0.1542	0.1563	1.39	9	6.4859	6.3971
Ukraine hryvnia	0.0366	0.0368	0.54	15.3	27.307	27.16
U.K. pound	1.1615	1.2055	3.79	14.2	0.861	0.8295
Middle East/Africa Bahrain dinar	2.6488	2.6483	-0.02	0.1	0.3775	0.3776
Egypt pound	0.0635	0.0635	0.01	-1.8	15.752	15.75
Israel shekel	0.2656	0.2614	-1.59	9	3.765	3.8258
Kuwait dinar	3.2237	3.2298	0.19	2.3	0.3102	0.3096
Oman sul rial	2.59602	2.59757	0.06	0.1	0.39	0.38
Qatar rial	0.2769	0.2746	-0.81	-0.9	3.612	3.6416
Saudia Arabia riyal	0.2664	0.2664	0.01	0.1	3.7538	3.7536
South Africa rand	0.0585	0.0604	3.25	22.1	17.095	16.557

Table 1.6 *(Continued)*

Source: Tullett Prebon.

2. American and European Terms

Related to direct and indirect quotations are the terms "American" and "European." A quotation expressed in American terms shows the price of one unit of foreign currency in terms of the US dollar. For example, the exchange rate between the US dollar and the euro is stated as EUR/USD, or EURUSD, and indicates the number of USD to be exchanged for one EUR.

The euro here is quoted in terms of the dollar. If the rate is equal to USD1.2000, it will take \$1.2000 to buy 1 euro. In this expression, the euro, as the dominant currency, is the "base" currency and appears in the denominator. The dollar, appearing in the numerator, is the "rates" or the "quote" currency.

An expression of the value of another currency versus the US dollar is simply termed "European." For example, the exchange rate between the Japanese yen and the US dollar may be stated as USD/JPY, or dollar-yen. That is, it may take JPY110 to buy one USD. The dollar is being valued in terms of the yen. When using European terms, the dollar is the base currency and the other currency, the yen in the above example, is the quote currency.

The convention is for the dominant currency to be in the numerator. The euro, representing currencies of many countries, is the most dominant. It is followed by the GBP and affiliated currencies due to tradition, and then by the USD. Since the dollar is recognized as the dominant currency, the convention is for exchange rates to be expressed in European terms. Exceptions are made in the cases of the euro (EUR), the British pound (GBP), and associated currencies: the Australian dollar (AUD) and the New Zealand dollar (NZD). So, the usual quotations are: EUR/USD, or EURUSD; GBP/USD, or GBPUSD; AUD/USD, or AUDUSD; NZD/USD, or NZDUSD; EUR/GBP, or EURGBP; USD/JPY, or USDJPY; USD/CAD, or USDCAD; USD/MXN, or USDMXN (also see Table 1.2 above).

3. Cross Rates

Table 1.6 above shows the exchange rates between various currencies and the US dollar. The EUR/USD rate is \$1.0916, and the JPY/USD rate is \$0.00925. From these two exchange rates we can calculate a third rate, or cross rate, as shown in Table 1.7. The EUR/JPY rate may then be thought of as the composite of two transactions, one of euros for dollars and the other of dollars for yen (or the other way around). In simple terms, then, the cross rate is:

$$\begin{gathered} EUR/JPY = [(EUR/USD)][(USD/JPY)] \\ (1.0916)(108.07) = 117.97 \end{gathered} \tag{1.1}$$

The result is slightly different from the number in Table 1.7 due to rounding errors. In addition, we should point out that this calculation produces an approximate value for the actual cross rate used by the market, since conversion of euros into yen can be more accurately described as a two-step process. The first step involves conversion of euros into dollars at the bank's bid rate for swiss franc; the second step involves conversion of dollars into yen at the bank's offer rate for yen. Cross-rate tables may be found in the *Wall Street Journal*, *Financial Times*, or other financial print and electronic publications. As the relative importance of currencies such as the yen, euro and yuan increase, interest in the cross-currency market also increases. Most of the cross-rate trading takes place in London, although New York and Tokyo are financial centers with significant cross-rate activity.

	Dollar	Euro	Pound	Sfranc	Peso	Yen	Cdndlr
Canada	1.448	1.5458	1.673	1.4684	0.0597	0.0131	—
Japan	110.5	117.96	127.63	112.02	4.5521	—	76.28
Mexico	24.28	25.913	28.037	24.61	—	0.2197	16.757
Switzerland	0.986	1.053	1.1395	—	0.0406	0.0089	0.681
U.K.	0.866	0.9238	—	0.8776	0.0357	0.0078	0.5977
Euro	0.937	—	1.0821	0.9496	0.0386	0.0085	0.6469
U.S.	—	1.0676	1.1552	1.0139	0.0412	0.0091	0.6905

Table 1.7 Key Currency Cross Rates

Snapshot of Foreign Exchange Cross Rates at 5 p.m. Eastern time, March 18, 2020. Downloaded from The Wall Street Journal/Markets Section. http://www.wsj.com/public/page/news-currency-currencies-trading.html. Accessed on March 19, 2020.

Concept Questions

1. Distinguish between direct and indirect Quotes.
2. Distinguish between European and American Quotes.
3. What are Cross Rates?

IV. Foreign Exchange Market Participants

The foreign exchange market is ubiquitous; you may be able to find somebody exchanging one currency for another practically anywhere in the world. Many of us have already participated in the market directly or indirectly. We have traveled to other countries or have bought a car imported from another country. For convenience, we identify the following major groups of market participants: banks, central banks, individuals, and firms.

1. Banks

Banks are the dominant foreign exchange market participant. The largest share of trading takes place between banks through electronic networks in the so-called interbank market. Banks trade foreign exchange on their own account and for their customers as dealers. The numerous and important roles banks play in the foreign exchange market are reflected in the survey of the *World's Best FX Providers* published by the magazine *Global Finance* (2019; Table 1.8). The criteria used for the selection of these banks included transaction volume, market share, scope of global coverage, customer service, competitive pricing, and innovative technologies.

Global Awards	
Best Global Foreign Exchange Bank	Citi
Best FX Provider For Corporates	Société Générale
Best FX Provider For Emerging Markets Currencies	Standard Chartered Bank
Best Liquidity Provider	State Street
Regional Awards	
North America	Citi
Latin America	BBVA
Western Europe	HSBC
Central & Eastern Europe	Société Générale
Middle East	National Bank of Kuwait
Africa	Standard Bank
Asia-Pacific	DBS Bank
Foreign Exchange Research & Analysis	
FX Research	BNY Mellon
Fundamental Analysis	BNP Paribas
Technical Analysis	Goldman Sachs
Forecasts	CIBC Capital Markets
Best Bank FX Trading Technology	
Best Bank Platform (Overall)	Citi Velocity
Most Innovative Bank Platform	Shinhan SOL
Best Platform For Corporations	Sherbank Markets
Best Execution Algorithms	Société Générale
Best Transaction Cost Analysis	BNP Paribas
Best Big-Picture View Of Positions	Citi Velocity's Command Centre
Best End-To-End Processing	JP Morgan's Execute

Table 1.8 The World's Best Foreign Exchange Providers 2019: Financial Institutions

Source: Global Finance. January 2019, p. 20

The banks included in Table 1.8 are very large, multinational institutions that have become known worldwide for their impact on the global economy. Smaller, local banks, however, also participate in the foreign exchange market. Of course, local banks do not have either the knowledge or the resources to offer a full line of foreign exchange services; they instead rely upon the services of a large bank with which they have established a correspondent relationship. As banks exchange currencies with their customers and with each other, they "make the market." In this capacity, banks maintain the continuity of the market by standing ready to buy and sell excess quantities of currencies. Bank foreign exchange operations have both marketability (liquidity) and price effects. International transactions become feasible when participants know that their foreign currency proceeds can be converted into local currencies or, alternatively, when they are assured that they can acquire foreign currencies through their bank (marketability effect). Bank foreign exchange activities tend to eliminate price differentials among currency markets in the various financial centers (price effect).

1.1. Arbitrage: Definition and Taxonomy

The process of elimination of return differentials through the flow of funds from one financial institution or financial market to another is referred to as arbitrage. The concept of arbitrage is one of the foundations of many theoretical frameworks in finance and financial economics. If we view the global financial system as a connected group of markets, arbitrage implies that market participants search for, identify, and exploit the most favorable market opportunities at least for as long as these opportunities are present. If the transfer of funds entails no additional risk, arbitrage is call *pure. Risk arbitrage,* on the other hand, entails pursuit of higher returns accompanied by higher risk; the extent of the trade-off is a function of the investor's risk-averse nature.

Three types of pure arbitrage are the most frequently encountered in the foreign exchange market: triangular, locational (or space), and interest-rate arbitrage. In all cases below, we assume that transactions costs and taxes are zero.

A. Triangular arbitrage: Triangular arbitrage occurs when currency prices are not mutually consistent within the same market. Refer to the old axiom of transitivity: If A=B and B=C, then A=C. What if A=B, B=C, but A is not equal to C? Market participants see this as an opportunity to act to take advantage of the inconsistency. For example, what if USD1=EUR1 and EUR1=GBP1, but USD1.20=GBP1 in the New York market? You can exchange USD1 for EUR1, then buy GBP1 with your euro and subsequently exchange your GBP1 for USD1.20. You just made yourself a tidy USD0.20 profit per each US dollar you start with! That was so easy!

B. Locational (space) arbitrage: Currency prices should also be consistent from one market to the other. Whether you want to buy euros in New York or in London, you should have to pay with the same amount of dollars. But what if we observe different prices for the same currency in these two markets? That is, what if USD1=EUR1 in the New York market, but

USD1.10=EUR1 in London? Then you buy euros in New York with your dollars and convert your euros back to dollars in London. Another profit made, this time ten cents per dollar! Fantastic! Why doesn't everybody do the same thing?

C. Interest-rate arbitrage: Interest-rate arbitrage is the movement of funds between currencies in order to take advantage of favorable relationships among spot currency markets, forward markets, and domestic and foreign interest rates. A fuller analysis of Interest Rate Arbitrage is presented in Chapter 3.

1.2. Direct/Dealer Transactions

Banks trade foreign exchange with each other directly and through brokers. Foreign exchange dealings can be a considerable source of profits for a bank. One interesting aspect of bank dealings is the manner in which rate quotes are given. In response to a request from another bank to trade US dollars and British pounds, Gladovia National may quote the GBP/USD "spread" as 1.3745/47. The first number, 1.3745, also referred to as the "bid" rate, indicates that the dealer/bank is ready to buy USD (the quote currency) for one GBP (the base currency). The second number, 47, is shorthand for 1.3747, which is the "offer" or "ask" rate. The bank stands ready to offer, or sell, USD at USD1.3747/GBP. The customer, on the other hand, buys British pounds sterling at 1.3747USD and sells for 1.3745USD.

The difference between the two rates is the "bid-ask spread" or just the "spread." In the example above, from the dealer's/bank's viewpoint, the spread is 0.0002USD or 2 "pips." A particular spread reveals the risk that the bank associates with a particular currency market. For the bank, this risk may arise from the liquidity of the currency, the size of the transaction, and even the time of the day the transaction takes place. If the bank can convert a particular currency into a major currency easily and without a loss, the spread is small. If the deal is a large one, the bank may charge a higher spread because of the chance of greater loss. Since currencies are traded in different time zones, a transaction that takes place in New York when European markets are closed may be associated with greater risk. The greater the risk, the greater the concern of the bank about its ability to convert the currency it holds without a loss and the wider the spread that the bank would require.

Dealer trades are important in terms of setting the tone of the entire market. These trades are the primary determinant of the so-called foreign exchange "fix." As we already noted, a fix is a benchmark of the exchange rate used in a particular trade and therefore impacts all market participants. Currency fixes are determined by actual trading taking place in London 30 seconds before and 30 seconds after 4 p.m.

Since 2013, the foreign exchange market has been beset by accusations of fix manipulation against some of the major banks. The foreign exchange market, because of such characteristics as size and geographic ubiquity, is very difficult to manipulate. However, according to the G20's Financial Stability Board, New York's Department of Financial Services, the FBI, and other authorities, traders from major banks colluded to rig the fix in their favor. To do so, they placed large orders during the 60-second window of the 4 p.m. fix, thus affecting the benchmark. The result was significant profits for the traders and their banks. To ensure secrecy, these traders communicated with each other in chat rooms with interesting names (The Bandits, Mafia, Semi-Grumpy Old Men, and such). By February 2019 EU/UK, Swiss, and US regulators had levied heavy fines against the manipulators (Bank of America, Barclays, Citigroup, HSBC, JPMorgan Chase, RBS, UBS, Deutsche Bank, and others). In addition, new regulations were enacted to enable the authorities to supervise the market more closely. For example, in February 2015, the fix window was enlarged from 1 minute to 5 minutes in order to make it more difficult for traders to manipulate the market.

1.3. Broker Transactions

Banks also participate in the market by arranging transactions through foreign-exchange brokers. Brokers do not buy and sell currencies for themselves but instead accept bid and offer requests from banks and relate them to other interested banks. As long as the particular currency has an active market, using a broker presents certain advantages over direct dealing. The bank has less pressure to make the market and keeps a lower profile in the market.

Currency trading can be a very profitable as well as challenging activity for banks. Their revenues from foreign exchange trading are impacted by many factors, including the global macroeconomic and regulatory environments, automation, algorithmic trading, and currency market conditions. For example, during the first quarter of 2013, total revenues from foreign exchange trading amounted to $2bn for the top ten banks. That represented a 10% decline from a year ago and a 60% drop from the third quarter of 2008.

1.4. Foreign Exchange Trading and Settlement Risk

Foreign exchange transactions involve a number of risks for banks and other participants. For example, market traders (and investors) are subject to business risk associated with global macroeconomic fluctuations. The European Debt Crisis caused a slowdown in foreign exchange trading and profits. Settlement risk, on the other hand, arises from counterparty default, operational problems, and other factors. It is "the risk of loss when a bank in a foreign exchange transaction pays the currency it sold but does not receive the currency it bought" (Bank for International Settlements, 2008). As in other cross-border transactions, a number of things may happen that diminish the value of a foreign exchange transaction. For example, the principal may not be received, or it may be received late; the amount of foreign exchange paid/received may be different from the one agreed upon in the contract. Settlement risk, then, should not be ignored.

Settlement risk is also known as "Herstatt risk." Bankhaus Herstatt was a medium-sized German bank that was actively operating in foreign exchange transactions. On June 26, 1974, the bank was declared insolvent and as a result closed by the German authorities. By closing time, the bank had already received Deutsche Mark from its customers and was supposed to complete the transaction by delivering US dollars. However, because of the difference in time zones, Herstatt's collapse meant that the US customers never received their payment.

As an example of settlement risk, consider the case of a UK bank that needs to exchange pounds for euros. The UK bank sends £100,000 to a French bank and expects to get back €120,000 as settlement of the transaction. If the French bank does not have the funds to meet its obligation, then the UK bank loses the full amount of £100,000. To eliminate settlement risk, CLS (Continuous Linked Settlement), a US financial institution established in 2002, serves as a clearinghouse. Using the above transaction as an example, CLS would act as a trusted third party between the two banks making sure that both sides of the transaction are settled at the same time (payment-for-payment approach). The two banks are CLS members and as such have multicurrency accounts with CLS Bank, part of the CLS Holding Company. If the French bank fails to make payment, CLS will return the payment to the UK bank. CLS has contributed to the decrease of settlement risk by settling about two-thirds of transactions as of the beginning of 2013. As the foreign exchange market changes in structure with the introduction of emerging country currencies and operation though technology, CLS is facing many challenges ahead (Economist, 2013).

2. Central Banks

Central banks operate in the foreign exchange market in various capacities. In their role as their governments' bankers and agents for domestic and international payments, central banks hold the currency reserves accumulated for international payments.

Another key function of a central bank is to bring about a targeted exchange rate movement through its intervention. The central bank operates on behalf of the country's treasury department or for its own account to influence the market value of the currency. This foreign exchange market intervention is distinct from payments operations, which take place as frequently as necessary with very little, if any, effect on currency values. We discuss the effect of intervention in more detail in Chapter 4.

3. Individuals and Firms

An individual or a firm needing foreign currency also participates in the foreign exchange market. Individuals may include travelers, speculators, hedgers, relatives sending foreign currency to those in another country, or students enrolled in an academic program abroad. Firms include non-bank financial institutions such as investment managers and hedge funds, exporters and importers, multinationals, and public, semi-public, or private enterprises or institutions operating both on the demand and supply sides of the market for a currency.

Concept Questions

1. In what ways do commercial banks participate in the foreign exchange market?
2. In what capacities do central banks operate in the foreign exchange market?
3. Differentiate between pure and risk arbitrage.
4. What are the three forms of arbitrage explained in this chapter?
5. What is settlement risk?

V. Exchange Rate Indices and Effective Exchange Rates

Our discussion so far has centered on bilaterally calculated exchange rates. Observers of the dollar, for example, may not be in a position to offer a simple description of the path of the currency with respect to another single currency: if, say, its value goes up with respect to the British pound by 10%, the Canadian dollar by 8%, and the Thai baht by 15% while it goes down against the Japanese yen by 7% and the Swiss franc by 11%. But what if we want to see how the dollar has fared against many currencies as a group? One approach is to express the performance of the dollar through the construction of an effective exchange rate. An effective exchange rate is simply a weighted exchange rate: It is an exchange rate index. It shows how one currency moves against a group of other currencies. The use of indices has been popularized in other sectors of the economy, such as the stock market (Dow-Jones Industrial Index, S&P500, and others) and prices of goods and services (such as the Consumer Price Index). Construction of any index faces several theoretical and methodological issues, including selection of the currencies comprising the index and weight in which each currency enters the index (Cox, 1987; Labuszewski, 2013).

Some international financial institutions, such as the Bank for International Settlements (BIS) and the International Monetary Fund (IMF), have been constructing such indices for decades. BIS, for example, constructs its Effective Exchange Rate (EER) index using weights derived from a country's trade importance to the home currency. Two basket compositions are calculated: the Broad Index and the Narrow Index, comprised of sixty-one and twenty-seven currencies, respectively. These measures are presented both in their Nominal and Real (price-adjusted) form.

The Fed constructed the US Dollar Index in 1973, following the abandonment of the Bretton Woods Agreement that we will discuss in Chapter 4 of this text. The Index is now calculated by the InterContinental Exchange (ICE). Using 1973 as the base year, the index shows how the value of the dollar changes vis-à-vis the basket of other currencies included in the calculation of the index. For example, a value of 163 in 1985 tells us that the dollar appreciated by 63% versus the other currencies. A value of 72 in 2008 tells us that the dollar depreciated by 28% versus those other currencies. By the way, these values represent the all-time high and low, respectively, for the Index. Table 1.9 shows the currencies tracked by other dollar indices. The *Wall Street Journal* reports on the values of the WSJ Dollar Index and the ICE/US Dollar index on a daily basis.

Index	Currencies Tracked	Weighting for Currency Pairs
WSJ Dollar	AUD, CAD, CHF, EUR, GBP, JPY, SEK	Based on total FX trading volume as measured by BIS
ICE	CAD, CHF, GBP, EUR, JPY, SEK	Based on international trade data as of 1973
Dow Jones FXCM	AUD, EUR, GBP, JPY	Equal weights for all pairs
FTSE Curex USD.G8	AUD, CAD, CHF, CNH, EUR, GBP, JPY, NZD	Equal weights for all pairs

Table 1.9 US Dollar Indices

Sourse: DJ/FX Trader. www.dowjones.com/pressroom/smprs/WSJDollarIndex.asp. Accessed on November 29, 2013.

VI. Summary

The growth of international business has bolstered the development of the foreign exchange market; in turn, the development of the foreign exchange market has greatly facilitated the conduct of international business. The market serves many useful functions, including transfer of purchasing power across national borders, facilitation of credit internationally, standard and store of value, management of exchange risk, and performance as an economic indicator.

Participants in the foreign exchange market include commercial banks, central banks, non-bank financial institutions, firms engaged in international trade, multinationals and individuals as consumers, traders, hedgers, or speculators. Foreign exchange markets are differentiated in terms of their various characteristics, such as their pricing principle and the degree of control exerted by governments.

Exchange rates can be expressed on a bilateral or multilateral basis. In the latter case, a weighted or effective exchange rate is calculated. The use of these rates allows for an evaluation of the performance of a single currency compared to multiple currencies, rather than to other single currencies.

Key Terms and Concepts

In the order in which they are presented in the text.

Foreign exchange market: The market where one currency is exchanged for another. Just like in any other market, buyers and sellers come together in the foreign exchange (or currency) market to exchange their products (in this case, currency) at a price called the (foreign) exchange rate.

Exchange rate: It is the price of one currency expressed in terms of units of another currency. If you need 2 US dollars to buy 1 British pound sterling, the exchange rate between dollars and pounds is 2 to 1.

Outright transaction: It involves buying/selling one currency for another. When the exchange of these two currencies takes place immediately, the transaction is called a spot transaction. When the parties agree to make the exchange at some time in the future, the transaction is called a forward.

Swap transaction: A swap transaction involves an initial exchange of two currencies followed by a re-exchange of the currencies at an agreed upon exchange rate and time in the future.

ISO4217: To facilitate currency trading, each currency is abbreviated by a three-letter code designed by the International Organization for Standardization (ISO4217).

Base currency and counter or quote currency: When an exchange rate of a certain currency versus the dollar, say, the yen, is expressed as JPY/USD. In this case, USD is termed the *base* currency, while the JPY is termed the *counter*, or *quote*, currency, The USD, that is, is quoted against the JPY.

Depreciation/appreciation: A currency X is said to depreciate versus a currency Y when X's value falls versus Y. It now takes more units of X to buy one unit of Y. On the other hand, X is said to appreciate versus Y when it takes fewer units of X to buy one unit of Y. These changes in the values of X and Y take place as a result of market forces.

Devaluation/revaluation: Analogous to the use of terms depreciation/appreciation, the terms devaluation/revaluation are used to indicate changes in the value of a currency resulting from government action.

Functions of the foreign exchange market: The foreign exchange market transfers purchasing power across national borders, provides a unit of account and a store of value, facilitates credit, serves as a medium of foreign exchange risk management, signals the economic and political stability of a country, and allows countries to build their foreign exchange reserves.

Currency wars: Manipulations of a currency by the government. They are competitive devaluations in which countries engage, especially during periods of unfavorable balance of payments and overall economic performance.

Spot transactions: Single outright transactions involving the exchange of two currencies at a price (exchange rate) determined on contract day for delivery in two or three days. The date on which delivery is actually made is called the value date. This practice if denoted as t + 2 or t + 3, where t stands for the trade date and t + 2, t + 3 are the value dates.

Outright forwards: Exchange of specified amount of two currencies at a price (rate) determined on contract day for delivery (value) at an agreed upon time in the future. The forward market also offers a number of other instruments, such as forward exchange agreements and non-deliverable forwards.

Currency and foreign exchange options: Contracts that give the right to buy or sell a specified amount of a currency with another currency at a predetermined exchange rate within or at the conclusion of a specified period.

Currency and foreign exchange swaps: Currency swaps represent an exchange of (fixed or floating) interest payments in two currencies during the duration of the contract. Principal amounts, based on initial spot rate, are exchanged at the beginning and end of the contract.

Foreign exchange swaps are an exchange of specified amounts of two currencies on a specified date at a price (rate) agreed to at the time of the contract, followed by a reverse exchange of these two currencies on a future date at a rate agreed to at the time of the contract.

Currency marketability and convertibility: A convertible currency can be freely (easily and at a fair price) exchanged at the market exchange rate into a major reserve currency or another currency. Internal convertibility implies that residents may hold foreign assets domestically but cannot make payments abroad or hold assets that either are located in a foreign country or represent claims against nonresidents. Current account convertibility means that a country allows convertibility of its currency for trade-related transactions. Capital account convertibility means that a currency is convertible for the purposes of moving funds across national borders.

Nominal versus real exchange rate: The real exchange rate is the value of one (nominal) currency adjusted by inflation against another inflation-adjusted currency.

Direct versus indirect quotations: A direct quote is one expressed in terms of the number of home currency units required to buy one unit of the foreign currency. An indirect quote indicates the number of units of the foreign currency required to buy one unit of the home currency.

American versus European terms: A quote expressed in American terms shows the value of the US dollar in terms of one unit of foreign currency. For example, it takes $1.2000 to buy one euro. An expression of the value of another currency versus the US dollar is simply termed "European." For example, EUR0.8333/$ implies that it takes 0.8333 euros to buy one US dollar.

Cross rates: A cross rate is the exchange rate between two currencies, say the euro and the Japanese yen, calculated through their individual relationship to the US dollar. For example, if the exchange rate between the euro and the dollar is $1.2000/€, and the exchange rate between the yen and the dollar is $0.0100/¥, then the cross rate between the euro and the yen is ¥120.00/€. The term cross rate is thus used to express the exchange rate between currencies other than the US dollar.

Arbitrage: The process of elimination of return differentials through the flow of funds from one financial institution or financial market to another is referred to as arbitrage. If the transfer of funds entails no additional risk, arbitrage is called *pure*. *Risk arbitrage*, on the other hand, entails pursuit of higher returns accompanied by higher risk; the extent of the trade-off is a function of the investor's risk-averse nature.

Triangular arbitrage: Triangular arbitrage occurs when currency prices are not mutually consistent within the same market.

Locational or space arbitrage: Locational arbitrage occurs when currency prices are not consistent between markets.

Interest rate arbitrage: Interest rate arbitrage is the movement of funds between currencies in order to take advantage of favorable relationships among spot currency markets, forward markets, and domestic and foreign interest rates.

Bid-ask spread or spread: The difference between the bid and the ask quotes of the price of a currency.

Foreign exchange trading and settlement risk: Foreign exchange trading risk is the business risk associated with global macroeconomic fluctuations. Settlement risk, on the other hand, arises from counterparty default, operational problems, and other factors.

Exchange rate indices and the effective exchange rate: An effective exchange rate is simply a weighted exchange rate; it is an exchange rate index. It shows how groups of currencies move together. A single currency's movements, then, is analyzed against movements of the entire group.

Web Exercises

W1. Refer to the IMF's site: https://www.imf.org/external/np/fin/data/rms_mth.aspx?SelectDate=2019-05-31&reportType=REP

Click on the "Exchange Rate Archives" tab and find the exchange rate numbers for January 2019 and December 2019. Calculate the changes in the exchange rate versus the dollar for the following currencies: UK pound, euro, yen, Chinese renminbi/yuan, Australian dollar, and the South African rand. Comment on the exchange rate changes you calculated. How did the dollar fare against these currencies during calendar year 2019?

W2. Refer to the official site of the Bank for International Settlements: www.bis.org. Construct one graph of the nominal US dollar narrow effective exchange rate and one for the real US dollar narrow rate. Comment on the relationship between the two graphs.

Questions and Problems

1. Have you ever participated in the foreign exchange market? Under what circumstances? What specific service/function did the market serve for you? What challenges did you face, if any? Discuss.
2. On May 29, 2020, the Wall Street Journal reported the following rates: GBP/USD= 1.2343 and USD/CHF=0.9619

   You want to exchange British pounds for Swiss francs.

   a. What is the GBP/CHF exchange rate?
   b. Now assume that the Swiss franc depreciated 20% against the US dollar. What is the new GBP/CHF exchange rate?

3. In order to give its goods a competitive advantage in the international markets, the country of Slabovia devalued its currency, the Slab, about a year ago. However, a year later, the action has not made any significant change to its exports. Can you produce a scenario in which the Slabovian action did not bring about the desired results?
4. A US company buys GBP with USD in order to pay its British suppliers. What type of foreign exchange market transaction does this exchange of GBP for USD represent? Outright spot? Outright forward? Swap? Explain.
5. A US company agrees to buy GBP from a British company in exchange for USD right now. The two companies also agree to re-exchange the two currencies one month from now at a specific exchange rate. Is this an outright spot, outright forward, or swap transaction? Explain.
6. The exchange rate between the EUR and the USD is given as EUR0.8 per USD1. Which currency is the base currency? The quoted currency?
7. The USD/MXN rate changed from MXN20=USD1 to MXN25=USD1. By how much did the MXN change? In which direction (appreciate or depreciate vs. the USD)? By how much did the USD change? In which direction?
8. You just arrived in Paris from London and need to convert your GBP into EUR. You go to the currency exchange counter and read the sign; "GBP: Bid €1.20; Ask €1.10."

   a. How many euros are you going to get in exchange for your £100.00?
   b. On your way back to London, you still have €50.00 left over. Assuming that the exchange rate has remained the same as when you arrived and that there are no transaction costs, how many GBP would you receive in exchange for your euros?

9. Yesterday's exchange rate between the Japanese yen and the US dollar was JPY96=USD1. Today, the two currencies trade at JPY92=USD1. Which currency appreciated? By how much?
10. When the market opened, you bought euros at $1.1234 and sold at the end of the day at $1.1294. What was your profit/loss?
11. The exchange rate between the dollar and the euro is EUR/USD=1.20. The exchange rate between the dollar and the yen is USD0.0125=JPY1. What is the exchange rate between the euro and the yen? Show your work.
12. On June 6, 2017, the exchange rate between the USD and the Mexican peso was USD0.0548/MXN. On the same day, the exchange rate between the USD and the Swiss franc was 1.0395. One month later, the exchange rate between the Mexican peso and the US dollar was 18.2572; the exchange rate between the Swiss franc and the US dollar was 0.9640.

    a. What is the cross rate between the CHF and the MNP on June 6? On July 6?
    b. What is the extent of appreciation or depreciation of the dollar versus the Peso and the franc during this period?
    c. What is the extent of appreciation or depreciation of the CHF versus the MXN during the period?

13. Why is currency convertibility important? What are its implications for governments and domestic and foreign-based firms?
14. What do we mean by a "strong" dollar? Do you think that the US should strive to have a strong dollar? Should Japan strive to have a strong yen? Who benefits and who loses when a currency is strong or weak?
15. Assuming no transactions costs, do you see any opportunities for arbitrage in these following quotations? check

New York	London
USD/1.3000GBP	180JPY/GBP
75JPY/CHF	1.5CHF/USD
2.8CHF/GBP	

16. The First Bank of Syracuse quotes sterling as $1.7220/38 and the Swiss franc $0.7075/92.

    a. Explain what these quotes mean. What is the rate at which the Bank sells sterling? Buys franc?
    b. As a bank customer, at which rate would you sell sterling? Buy franc?

Selected References

Bank for International Settlements. 2019. *Triennial Bank Survey. Triennial Central Bank Survey of foreign exchange and derivatives market activity in 2019.* Downloaded at https://www.bis.org/statistics/rpfx19_fx.pdf. Downloaded October 12, 2019

Carney, S. 2013. Czech National Bank Goes Large for FX Intervention. *The Wall Street Journal Online.* http://blogs.wsj.com/moneybeat/2013/11/25/czech-fx-reserves-jump-on-central-bank-intervention/tab/print/. Downloaded July 31, 2014.

Cox, W. M. 1987. A Comprehensive New Real Dollar Index. *Economic Review.* Federal Reserve Bank of Dallas, March 1987, 1–14.

Fujikawa, M. 2015. Weak Yen Fuels Record Profits in Japan. *The Wall Street Journal,* May 19, 2015. Downloaded from www.wsj.com May 19, 2015.

Gagnon, J. E. Currency Wars. 2013. *Milliken Institute Review, January 2013.*

Global Finance, 2019. Best Financial Institution Foreign Exchange Awards 2019: A Bumpy Ride in Fracturing Markets. https://www.gfmag.com/magazine/january-2019. Downloaded February 13, 2019.

Labuszewski, J. W.2013. Inter-Market Stock Index Spreads. Chicago: CME Group, August 14, 2013.

Rickards, J. *Currency Wars: The Making of the Next Global Crisis.* New York: Penguin, 2011

US Department of the Treasury. 2019. *Macroeconomic and Foreign Exchange Policies of Major Partners of the United States.* May 2019. https://home.treasury.gov/news/press-releases/sm696. Downloaded 5/28/19.

Credits

Table 1.1: Source: http://www.exchangerates.org.uk/currency-symbols.html.
Fig. 1.1: Source: https://www.bis.org/statistics/rpfx19_fx.pdf.
Table 1.2: Source: http://forexillustrated.com/currency-nicknames-secret-handshake-traders/.
Fig. 1.2: Source: https://www.bis.org/statistics/rpfx19_fx.pdf.
Fig. 1.3: Source: https://www.bis.org/statistics/rpfx19_fx.pdf.
Table 1.3: Source: https://www.bis.org/statistics/rpfx19_fx.pdf.
Table 1.4: Source: https://www.bis.org/statistics/rpfx19_fx.pdf.
Table 1.5: Source: https://www.bis.org/statistics/rpfx19_fx.pdf.
Table 1.6: Source: http://www.wsj.com/public/page/news-currency-currencies-trading.html.
Table 1.7: Source: http://www.wsj.com/public/page/news-currency-currencies-trading.html.
Table 1.8: Source: Global Finance.
Table 1.9: Source: www.dowjones.com/pressroom/smprs/WSJDollarIndex.asp.

Chapter 2

Foreign Exchange Derivatives

Forwards, Futures, Options, and Swaps

Overview of Chapter Material

This chapter extends our discussion of the basics of the foreign exchange market by examining the major derivative products and markets. Following a brief introduction to derivatives, Chapter 2 covers the markets for currency forward, futures, options and swaps. These contracts are priced in accordance with the forward pricing principle introduced in Chapter 1.

After Studying This Chapter, You Will Be Able To

- Understand the nature and composition of the foreign exchange derivatives market
- Identify the various types and functions of foreign exchange derivatives
- Differentiate among forward, futures, options and swaps

Chapter Outline

I. Foreign Exchange Market Derivatives
II. Forward Markets and Forward Pricing
III. The Futures Market
IV. Currency Options Markets
V. Swaps
VI. Final Note on Derivatives
VII. Summary

I. Foreign Exchange Market Derivatives

A derivative is a security whose price is *derived from* an underlying asset, or even a group of assets. Stocks, bonds, currencies, commodities, interest rates and market indices are some of the assets used as underlying assets. Derivatives contracts may be traded over-the-counter (OTC) or on organized exchanges.

Derivatives serve a number of functions in their respective markets and the economy in general. In an increasingly risky global economic environment, participants have found it necessary to seek ways with which they can deal with risks. Derivatives enable market participants to transfer risks, a practice called hedging. They also enable market participants to engage in transactions principally aimed at generating a profit, a practice called speculation. We will be discussing these two concepts later in this chapter and in subsequent chapters. Derivatives also provide the market with more information about the underlying asset, increasing liquidity and helping with the price determination process. As we will also see in this chapter, derivatives provide leverage, since a relatively small change in the value of the underlying asset can be associated with a large swing in the value of the derivative contract. In addition to providing benefits, then, using and trading derivatives entails risks that need to be identified and addressed effectively.

As we discussed in Chapter 1, the foreign exchange market encompasses several components. Spot exchange rates are the underlying asset, while forward, futures, options and swaps markets are markets for derivatives. We now turn our attention to learning more about the characteristics of these interesting and important markets.

II. Forward Markets and Forward Pricing

A forward contract is an agreement between two parties to exchange currencies at a future time (beyond the two days required for settlement of a spot transaction) and at an exchange rate agreed upon today. Thus, if on July 10, 2017, you buy Mexican pesos thirty days forward, you are making a commitment to accept a certain amount of pesos thirty days from that date at an exchange rate agreed today between you and your bank or broker. We find examples of forward pricing in the foreign exchange market in forward and futures contracts. Participants in these markets include traders (importers/exporters), hedgers, speculators, and multinational firms.

1. Characteristics of the Forward Market

The forward market, like the spot market, is not located in one particular place. Each transaction is formulated in a manner suiting the immediate participants, with the size and maturity negotiated to accommodate the particular needs of the parties involved. Transactions in the forward market are not subject to formal regulation.

1.1. Forward Quotations

Let us examine Table 2.1. It reproduces the foreign exchange market quotations from the *Wall Street Journal* of March 9, 2013. It shows spot and forward rates versus the US dollar for

Country/Currency	in US $	per US $
Australian (Dollar)	1.0371	0.9642
1-mos forward	1.0346	0.9666
3-mos forward	1.0301	0.9707
6-mos forward	1.0235	0.9771
Japan (Yen)	0.010263	97.44
1-mos forward	0.010264	97.43
3-mos forward	0.010268	97.39
6-mos forward	0.010275	97.32
Switzerland (Franc)	1.0759	0.9295
1-mos forward	1.0762	0.9292
3-mos forward	1.077	0.9285
6-mos forward	1.0782	0.9275
UK (pound)	1.5533	0.6438
1-mos forward	1.5529	0.6439
3-mos forward	1.5524	0.6442
6-mos forward	1.5518	0.6444

Table 2.1 NY Market Closing Quotations (1m+).

Source: The Wall Street Journal, May 1, 2013

Downloaded from http://www.wsj.com/public/page/news-currency-currencies-trading.html/Markets. Accessed on 5/20/2013

some of the most frequently traded currencies, AUD, JPY, CHF, and GBP. The *Wall Street Journal* discontinued the posting of forward rates in 2014, but the data shown can still be useful for illustrative purposes. On the table, forwards are shown as having maturities of 1 month, 3 months, and 6 months. As the table suggests, not all currencies have active forward markets. Market activity and specific contract characteristics may be dependent on the global trade environment or a particular country's trade activity. In some cases, the relationship between the two parties, such as the bank and the exporter, may also shape the nature of the contract.

When the forward rate is quoted as the price of the contract (120 or 150 in Table 2.2), it is called the outright rate. Forward rates may also be quoted in relation to the respective current spot rate. The difference between forward and spot rates is called "points." When the trader refers to the number of points by which the forward rate is greater or smaller than the spot, that number is referred to as the swap rate, which is simply the cost involved in exchanging one currency for the other for the period indicated by the maturity of the contract. When points are positive (added to the spot to arrive at the forward rate), a currency is said to be at a premium. When points are negative (subtracted from the spot rate to arrive at the forward) a currency is said to be at a discount vis-à-vis another currency. How do we know if we should add these points to the spot rate or subtract them from it? As we will see in the next chapter, interest rate differentials between two countries have a lot to do with the

	Bid	Ask
Spot	120	150
Points for:		
30-day forward	5	10
90-day forward	15	25
180-day forward	25	35
Outright Quotations		
30-day forward	125	160
90-day forward	135	175
180-day forward	145	185

Table 2.2 Spot and Forward Quotations.
Examples of Spot and Forward Quotations (USD/JPY)

sign and size of these points. Once these points are set, they send a signal to the market as to the expected spot exchange rate.

The swap rate also figures in an important activity of commercial banks: currency trading that involves both spot and forward contracts. For example, when the Bank of New York has an immediate need for yen, it might exchange US dollars for yen now with the Bank of Zurich and agree to pay back a specific amount of yen for dollars in twenty days at a given exchange (or *swap*) rate. The swap is an alternative to borrowing yen in the spot market and entering a contract to buy yen forward to repay the loan. The relationship between forward and spot rates also may be expressed in terms of bid and ask rates. Consider again the scenario shown in Table 2.2:

In Table 2.2, we calculate the 1-month, 3-month, and 6-month forward rates by adding the respective points to the spot rate. For the bid, then, the outright quotations are 125, 135, and 145, respectively. For the ask quotation, they are 160, 175, and 185. In this case, the dollar is at a premium vis-à-vis the yen, since it takes more yen to buy one dollar for future delivery than it takes to buy one dollar right now. If, instead, the ask points were 0, 5, and 10, the bank would subtract these increases from the spot to arrive at the forward. The yen would then be at a premium vis-à-vis the dollar. In other words,

$$\text{Forward Rate} - \text{Spot Rate} = \text{Forward Points}$$

Or

$$\text{Spot Rate} + \text{Forward Points} = \text{Forward Rate}$$

1.2. Forward Discount or Premium

We can also calculate the relationship between spot and forward rates by expressing the forward points as the percentage of the discount or premium. Assume that the yen to dollar spot rate is JPY98=USD1 using the indirect quote, or USD0.0102=JPY1 using the direct quote; the one-year forward rate is JPY102=USD1, or USD0.0098=JPY1.

The indirect quotes for the dollar tell us that it takes 98 yen to buy one dollar today, but it will take 102 yen to buy one dollar in the future. Since the dollar is more expensive in the future than it is now, the dollar is trading at a "forward premium." On the other hand, the yen is trading at a forward discount (it is not worth as much in the future as it is now, at least in terms of the dollar).

We now calculate the forward premium or discount as the percentage difference between the two rates, the spot and the forward.

Using the indirect quote in USD, we calculate the forward premium or discount as:

$$\begin{aligned}\text{Forward Premium/Discount} &= [(\text{forward rate} - \text{spot rate})/(\text{spot rate})] \times 100 \\ &= [(102 - 98)/98] * 100 = 4.1\% \text{ approximately}\end{aligned} \quad (2.1)$$

The US dollar is at a premium by 4.1% versus the yen.

If, instead of the one-year maturity, the quoted forward rate has a 3-month maturity, we can calculate the forward premium or discount on an annualized basis as:

$$\begin{aligned}&\text{Annualized Forward Premium/Discount} = \\ &[(\text{forward} - \text{spot rate})/\text{spot rate})] * (12/n) * 100\end{aligned} \quad (2.2)$$

Where n = the number of months to maturity; in the example above, n = 3.

Using the same numbers as above, the 3-month premium would be the following on an annualized basis is:

$$\text{Annualized Forward Premium/Discount} = [(102 - 98)/98] * 4 * 100 = 16.4\ \% \quad (2.3)$$

We can also calculate the premium or discount using the direct quote:

$$\text{Forward Premium/Discount} = [(\text{spot rate} - \text{forward rate})/(\text{forward rate})] * 100 \quad (2.4)$$

In this case, the one-year forward premium/discount is equal to:

$$\text{Forward Premium/Discount} = [(.0102 - .0098)/(.0098)] * 100 = -4.1\% \quad (2.5)$$

The yen is at a discount versus the dollar.

1.3. Additional Forward Products

Forward contracts are structured to address specific needs and concerns of the buyer, and so their characteristics can deviate from the traditional forward contract we have been discussing so far. Some of the variations of the forward contract include:

a) The Window Forward.
   The window forward enables the buyer to make and accept payment from the contract during an agreed period prior to (or even after) the contract's expiration. It offers the protection of the traditional forward contract but also the flexibility

with respect to the timing of payment. For example, I may enter into a forward contract to deliver £10,000 to my bank in exchange for $12,000 in ninety days. If the contract includes a thirty-day window, and if I receive payment from my customer prior in seventy days, I may want to make the exchange before the ninety days are up depending on the exchange rate. Similarly, if the window extends to thirty days after the ninety-day original expiration date, I may delay payment if I expect the exchange rate to change to my advantage.

b) The Non-Deliverable Forward Contract (NDF).
NDFs allow the seller and the buyer of the forward contract to settle it without a physical exchange of funds. There is no delivery of the foreign currency. Instead, at maturity, there is a transfer of net funds in US dollars or another convertible currency amounting to the difference between the forward rate and the spot rate. The advantage of the NDF versus the traditional forward, in addition to offering the same protection against risk, is that the NDF can include currencies whose governments do not allow currency convertibility.

The existence of additional forward products, such as the window forward and the NDF, offers a glimpse into the ability of the financial services sector to address practically any risk preference among participants. Obviously, there is a price for everything!

Concept Questions

1. What is the underlying asset of a currency derivative contract?
2. What is the forward rate?
3. What is the difference between outright and swap rate?
4. Define the terms "forward premium" and "forward discount."
5. What is the window forward?
6. What is the NDF?

III. The Futures Market

The foreign exchange futures market is the market for currency futures contracts. A futures contract is conceptually similar to a forward contract; it represents a commitment to deliver or to accept delivery of a certain quantity of a specific currency at a specified time in the future and at an exchange rate determined right now. In practice, however, there are several differences between forward and futures markets. For example, while transactions in the forward market are not formally regulated or standardized, transactions in the futures market are subject to regulation and standardized to the extent that participants trade contracts of specific size and maturity and follow common trading rules. In the US, regulations are established by the Commodity Futures Trading Commission, the appropriate regulatory body in the exchange's home state, and the Exchange. Currency futures contracts are traded on exchanges other than the Chicago Mercantile's International Monetary Market (IMM; see Melamed, 1986), including the MidAmerica Commodity, the New York Cotton Exchange, and the London International Financial Futures Exchange (LIFFE).

We will now examine how currency futures contracts are quoted and explain their characteristics.

1. Currency Futures Market Quotations and Characteristics

We can find futures contract quotations for currencies listed on the Chicago Mercantile Exchange, in many financial papers, including the *Wall Street Journal,* and online. See, for example, Table 2.3, taken from the *WSJ*, May 29, 2019 print edition. Quotations for the euro contracts include the opening price of each contract for the day, the highs and the lows for the trading day and for the entire life of each contract, the settlement price for the day, and the open interest for each contract.

	Open	High	Low	Settle	Change	Open Interest
Japanese Yen (CME) – ¥12,500,000; $ per 100¥						
June	0.915	0.9171	0.9136	0.9148	−0.0011	163,824
Aug	0.9214	0.9214	0.919	0.9194	−0.0011	2,075
British Pound (CME) – £62,500; $ per £						
June	1.2692	1.2761	1.2662	1.2668	−0.0059	198,046
Sept	1.2753	1.2812	1.2721	1.2726	−0.0059	5,919
Euro (CME) – €125,000; $ per €						
June	1.1213	1.1235	1.1177	1.1184	−0.0043	499,533
Sept	1.1299	1.132	1.1263	1.1269	−0.0043	29,694

Table 2.3 Currency Futures Prices.

Source: Wall Street Journal, May 29, 2019, p. B8

We can now explain some of the characteristics of a typical futures contract: the contract's size, expiration, settlement price, margin, and open interest.

Size: Each futures contract is traded in specified units. The size of the euro contract, for example, is fixed at €125,000.00 and is expressed as the number of USD needed to buy one EUR. Similarly, the GBP trades in contracts of GBP125,000.00; the JPY contract is JPY12,500,000.00. When we buy or sell futures contracts, we do so in multiples of the established contract sizes.

Expiration: Currency futures contracts expire in specific months (on the third Wednesday of the month): March, June, September, and December. Contracts of different maturities, say, March EUR and September EUR, are theoretically different financial assets. When we trade

EUR contracts, we therefore need to specify the exact maturity month. So, we should say March EUR rather than simply EUR.

Settlement price (exchange rate): Denotes the price at which the contract "settles" at the end of the day. This price is important because it determines the value of futures contracts at the end of the trading day. In the futures market, the value of a contract changes according to the current market price; it "marks-to-market." If the market is active, the settlement price will most likely be the price of the last trade of the day or the average price of the last few trades. Otherwise, the Exchange's settlement committee establishes its level. That level must be reasonable and fair, as it will determine what has to be paid to settle a contract and what will happen to the **margin**. The margin is the amount of money the buyer and seller must deposit before they can trade on the contract. It is usually a fraction of the total value of the contract.

The margin has two parts: the initial margin and, its subset, the maintenance margin. The initial margin is the amount of cash that buyers and sellers need to open their account; the magnitude of the margin in currency futures markets may vary from .25% to 3–5%; the exact value of the initial margin depends on the daily price movement limits set for the contract and on the individual broker. Any losses incurred during the day's trading activity, however, must be covered by the customer (you). The broker requires that at least a portion, perhaps 80%, of the initial margin be always on deposit. This portion is the maintenance margin. At the end of each day, the contract is marked to market; that is, its value is determined based on the settlement price. If the market has turned against the value of a position, additional margin must be deposited to replenish the required margin. This margin, which is equal to the change in the value of the contract, is called the variation margin.

Let us look at an example. Mr. Jones wants to buy a currency futures contract. The current value of the contract is $100.00; he must put down a deposit (initial margin) of $5.00. Ms. Smith is selling the same contract at $100.00, and she put down a margin of $5.00. In both cases, the maintenance margin is set at $4.00. At the end of the day, the settlement price has increased; the contract marks-to-market and its value now is $102.00. Mr. Jones bought the contract for $100.00; he now has a contract valued at $102.00; he has gained $2.00, which is added to his account bringing his margin to $7.00. On the other hand, Ms. Smith has lost $2.00, since she sold for $100.00 something that is valued at $102.00. Her margin is now $5.00-$2.00 = $3.00, which is below the maintenance margin. She must replenish her account by putting up another $2.00 (the variation margin).

The last column, **Open Interest**, refers to the number of contracts not liquidated as of that date. For example, as a market participant sells a contract of June euro, open interest increases by one. The open interest number, which fluctuates during the life of the contract, is indicative of future activity in the particular market. Since about 98% of the contracts do not involve actual delivery, traders with a buy or sell position will have to reenter the market and close their position prior to the expiration of the contract. Ordinarily, open interest is low in the early stages of the contract, increases to maximum probably a few weeks before maturity, and then declines as the contract nears expiration.

2. Futures, Spot, and the Basis

2.1 Futures Positions

The positions taken in the currency futures market are similar to those observed in other futures markets. For example, market participants may take long, short, or combined positions (such as spread or saddle). In the case of the euro, then, a "long" position indicates that the investor buys a euro contract, thereby accepting delivery of a specified amount of euros during a specified delivery month.

Futures contracts in the IMM are expressed in terms of positions taken by participants vis-a-vis the US dollar. Thus, a (net) long position in Japanese yen indicates that the buyer of the contract expects an increase in the value of the yen in terms of the dollar. A short position in Canadian dollars, on the other hand, reveals an expectation that the Canadian dollar will fall in reference to the US dollar. A spread involves simultaneous long and short positions. It can be accomplished on an intra-currency or inter-currency basis. The former involves taking opposite positions (long and short) on contracts of the same currency with different maturity months, say, long on March Yen and short on June Yen. On an inter-currency basis, the buyer enters long and short contracts for different currencies maturing the same month. These spreads allow traders to develop strategies reflecting expectations of movements in currencies other than the US dollar. For example, an expectation that the euro will rise in value in relation to the Canadian dollar may imply going long on March euro and short on March Canadian dollar futures.

2.2. An Example of a Futures Transaction: Futures, Spot, and the Basis

We should now go over a simple example of a futures transaction to understand how the spot and futures market interact.

JR, a young entrepreneur from New York City, designed a line of "glow-in-the-dark" yoyos. Although the domestic market was going up and down, he managed to make his first international sale to a British customer on August 20. In accordance with the sales agreement, JR's British customer will pay him GBP62,500.00 in sixty days. Since JR does not want to speculate in the foreign exchange market, he wants to protect himself against any unexpected changes in the GBP/USD rate.

His best friend, a recent finance graduate from a nearby institution, explains to him that he has a number of options, including hedging through the futures market. That is, JR could take a position in the futures market that is opposite to his spot market position. JR still did not understand how the futures market works, so his friend had to explain further: since you will be receiving GBP in the future, you are long in the spot market; to protect yourself against a change in the exchange rate, you should take a short (sell) position in the futures market. Following his friend's advice, JR enters the futures market by selling one December GBP contract, which is the contract whose maturity is closest to the time of the anticipated receipt of GBP62,500.00. JR now has an open short position in GBP futures. If JR does not want to make delivery of GBP when the contract expires, he must eventually close his position by going long on (buying) GBP.

JR is still confused, so, his friend gives him an example.

Let us assume that:

Today's spot rate: USD1.24=GBP1
Today's December GBP futures price: USD1.26=GBP1
Today's Basis: Futures-Spot=0.02

On October 10, JR receives the amount owed by his customer. On that day, the spot rate is USD1.20=GBP1, and the futures rate is USD1.22=GBP1. He can now convert his GBP receipts into US dollars in the spot market and close his short position in the futures market by buying GBP at the current futures rate. How did he make out?

Date	Spot	Futures	Basis	Net Gain (Loss)
August 10	USD1.24=GBP1	USD1.26=GBP	0.02	
October 10	USD1.20=GBP1	USD1.22=GBP1	0.02	
Gain (Loss)	(0.04)	0.04		0

According to the example, the hedge taken through the futures market turned out to be perfect, resulting in zero net position. JR was able to offset his loss in the spot market through the gain in the futures market. Naturally, JR's friend structured the example so that the difference between futures and spot prices, called the basis, remain constant. The behavior of the basis during the life of the contract indicates whether hedges will generate a profit or a loss. As market conditions change, so will the relationship between spot and futures markets. Hedges, therefore, are not usually perfect. By going through with the hedge, however, JR could sleep at night because he knew that fluctuations in currency values would not affect him as adversely as if they might have in the absence of hedging.

2.3. The Speculator's Viewpoint: Return on Futures Positions

The above example also illustrates the difference between a hedger and a speculator. JR is a hedger because he counteracts his position in one market, the spot market, by taking an opposite position in the other market, the futures market. A speculator, on the other hand, would only operate on one side of the market, in this case the futures. If a speculator had gone short on GBP futures on August 10 and liquidated her position on October 10, she would have generated a profit.

For a typical investment position, we express the rate of return as

Rate of Return = (payoff − investment)/investment

If we buy a share of a common stock purchase, ignoring dividends, the return is

Rate of Return = (selling price − purchase price)/(purchase price) (2.6)

By contrast, in the futures market the initial deposit represents only a fraction of the total face value of the contract. Consider the case of an investor (speculator) who enters the market by buying a futures contract; the investor is long in the market. The investor can now calculate the approximate return earned on the investment in futures as:

$$R(\text{long}) = (P_1 - P_0)/m \qquad (2.7)$$

Where:

R(long) is the return on the long position;
P_0 is the price paid per contract, or per unit of currency at time 0;
P_1 is the price per contract at time 1;
m is the amount of margin on deposit.

If we now go back to Mr. Jones and Ms. Smith, we can arrive at Mr. Jones's rate of return by inserting the numbers from the example:

$$P_0 = \$100;\ P_1 = \$102;\ m = \$5$$

Giving a rate of return of

$$R = (102 - 100)/5 = 40\%$$

His rate of return, then, is a whopping 40%! This rate is even higher if Mr. Jones decides to get out of the market and receives a reimbursement for his deposit. The bad news, of course, is that Ms. Smith's return is −40%, a huge loss. The example illustrates both the attraction and the risks associated with futures markets. Buyers and sellers enter the market with a highly leveraged position. As we know from our basic finance course, leverage can be a good thing when circumstances are favorable to us; it can be quite a burden when markets turn against us.

If the investor sells a futures contract, taking a short position, the rate of return would be

$$R(\text{short}) = (P_0 - P_1)/m \qquad (2.8)$$

For the intra-currency spread, we can show the return as

$$R(\text{spread}) = (P_{1i} - P_{0i}) + (P_{0j} - P_{1j})/m_d \qquad (2.9)$$

Where

P_{1i},P_{0i} are the buying and selling prices on the long position contract at the indicated times;
P_{0j}, P_{1j} are the selling and buying prices associated with the short contract;
m_d is the margin on the spread.

2.4. Arbitrage and the Differences Between Futures and Forward Markets

IMM member firms monitor the futures and forward markets continuously in search of arbitrage opportunities between the two markets. If a profit is possible when prices are out of sync, even if briefly, traders may simultaneously purchase a contract in a given currency futures market and sell an equivalent amount of the currency forward.

The appearance of arbitrage opportunities on paper, however, does not imply that these opportunities are realized. As we already noted, forward and futures markets show many differences. These differences may stand in the way of arbitrage activities.

One major difference between forward contracts and futures contracts is the role of the Exchange. In futures contracts, the Exchange plays the role of the clearinghouse of transactions. The Exchange guarantees completion of the contract for each of the participants (buyer, seller). There is no counterparty risk! In the forward market, on the other hand, counterparty risk may surface if, for example, my British customer does not come through with the payment of the promised number of GBP for the products I sold to her. Since I did not receive payment, I do not have the necessary GBP to exchange for USD as stipulated in the forward contract with the bank. The bank, naturally, still wants to receive the contracted amount of GBP. In order to honor my side of the contract, I need to convert USD to GBP at the current exchange rate.

Some additional differences between forward and futures markets in currencies include

- **Primary objective:** Forward contracts are primarily used for hedging purposes. Futures contracts may also be used for hedging, but speculation is also an important objective.
- **Contract structure:** Forward contracts are structured according to the specific requirements of the buyer. Futures contracts, on the other hand, are standardized in terms of their size and maturity.
- **Primary risk:** Forward contracts are subject to counterparty risk. Futures contracts listed on organized exchanges are settled through a common clearinghouse, the Exchange. The Exchange, in essence, is the counterparty to the transaction. Therefore, payment is guaranteed. Futures contracts, however, are subject to "basis" risk. As we noted above, the basis is the difference between the futures price of the contract and the spot price at any given time. If the basis remains the same, hedgers neither lose nor profit from their futures position. If, on the other hand, the basis changes, the hedger may profit or lose by entering the futures market.
- **Delivery:** When a US exporter sells GBP forward, settlement of the contract will take place through delivery of the stated amount of GBP at the specified time and agreed upon exchange rate. Contrary to the forward market practice, futures contracts are usually (about 98 percent) settled prior to maturity and do not involve delivery of the underlying asset. For example, you buy a June 2017 GBP contract at $1.30 on April 23, 2017. You now have an open long position (at which point the contract's open interest number increases by 1). Your intention, however, is not to deliver the GBPs but to hopefully profit from changes in the market price of the contract. On May 10, you see that the contract price has risen to $1.35; you decide to sell the contract, thus closing your position (with open interest decreasing by 1). This is a paper transaction, with no physical assets changing hands. There is no delivery!

- **Payment:** Forward contracts generally require no upfront payment; depending on the relationship between the seller of the contract (the bank) and the buyer (the exporter, for example) some banks may require a small upfront deposit for issuing the contract. Futures contract require an upfront deposit (margin).
- **Price behavior/contract value:** The value of the forward contract is indicated in the contract. It remains constant throughout its life. On the other hand, the value of the futures contract changes every day as each contract "settles" at the end of the day.
- **Secondary market:** The standardization of the characteristics of futures contracts makes them amenable to resale at a fair price. Futures contracts have marketability and liquidity. Forward contracts, because of their customized nature, have very limited secondary market.

Concept Questions

1. What is a currency futures contract? What are its characteristics?
2. What is the nature of a long position in futures markets? How does it differ from a short position?
3. What is the nature and significance of the basis?
4. Define the margin. What is its importance to the workings of the futures market?
5. In what ways is the futures contract similar to the forward contract? In what ways is it different?
6. If you are a speculator in the currency futures market, what types of positions would you take? How would you know if these positions are profitable?

IV. Currency Options Markets

An important foreign exchange market has developed through the extension of options trading to currencies. The volume of trading in the options market has been increasing by an impressive rate. Every student of economics and finance must understand the nature and importance of options in the financial system.

1. The Options Contract

Options on currencies are based on the same principles pertaining to options on stocks or commodities (for an excellent treatment of the options market, see Hull, 2012). An options contract calls for the parties to exchange the right to buy or sell a certain amount of currency during some specified period at an agreed-upon exchange rate. This exchange rate is called the exercise or strike price or rate. The agreement may be exercised any time within the period, in which case the option is termed American; a European option may be exercised only at a specified date at the end of the period. The listing of an options contract, an example of how an option is quoted, and a description of a contract are shown in Tables 2.4 and 2.5. Both tables refer to the Euro options.

	Calls		Puts	
Strike	Bid	Ask	Bid	Ask
108	1.5	6.5	0.01	0.09
109	0.5	5.5	0.06	0.15
110	2.18	2.29	0.16	0.25
111	1.39	1.49	0.37	0.44
112	0.78	0.86	0.74	0.83
113	0.38	0.45	1.33	1.42
114	0.16	0.25	2.1	2.21
115	0.05	0.15	0.5	5.5
116	0.01	0.09	1.5	6.5

Table 2.4 Euro Currency Options Detail.
Option Chain for PHLX U.S. Dollar-Settled Euro-Currency, May 30, 2019

Source: http://www.nasdaq.com/aspxcontent/optionsWC.aspx?symbol=^XDC&qm_page=10490&qm_symbol=^XDC#ixzz3a8tRXEuS.

Accessed May 31, 2019

Description: Euro currency options are quoted in terms of US dollars per unit of the underlying currency, and premium is paid and received in US dollars.

Contract Size: 10,000 euros

Trading Symbol: XDE

Settlement Value Symbol: EPW

CUSIP Number: 69336Y

Exercise Style: European

Expiration Date: The third Friday of the expiration month.

Expiration Cycle: Quarterly on the March cycle plus two additional near-term months (six months at all times).

Settlement: US dollars

Settlement Value for Expiring Contracts: The spot price at 12:00:00 Eastern Time (noon) on the expiration date. The settlement value is disseminated under the symbol EPW. Consult PHLX Rule 1057 for further information.

Last Trading Day for Expiring Contracts: The third Friday of the expiration month.

Table 2.5 Euro Options Contract Description.

Source: FX Options Product Specification. http://www.nasdaqtrader.com/micro.aspx?id=phlxwcoproductspecs#cd. Downloaded 5/18/17

Contract Point Value: \$100 (i.e., .01 × 10,000)

Exercise (Strike) Price Intervals: The Exchange shall determine fixed-point intervals of exercise prices. Generally, the exercise (strike) price interval shall be set at half-cent intervals. Consult PHLX Rule 1012 for further information.

Premium Quotation: One point = \$100. Thus a premium quote of 2.13 is \$213. The minimum change in a premium is .01= \$1.00.

Position Limits: 1,200,000 contracts on the same side of the market. Hedge exemptions are available. For more information consult PHLX Rules 1001 and 1002.

Trading Hours: 9:30 a.m. to 4:00 p.m. (Eastern Time)

Issuer and Guarantor: The Options Clearing Corporation (OCC)

Table 2.5 *(Continued)*

The two principals in options contracts are the buyer and the writer (seller) of the option. The buyer of the contract pays the writer a price (called the premium) for the right to exercise the option, that is, to buy or sell the agreed-upon amount of currency at the agreed exchange rate on the date dictated by the options contract. By having the right, rather than the obligation, to exercise the option, the buyer will do so only when s/he can generate profit or minimize losses. The writer does not have the same choice; the buyer's request to exercise the option must be honored regardless of the loss implications to the writer. As compensation, of course, the writer receives the premium. To understand the structure and implications of an options contract for the two parties, we can examine the basic market positions available in options trading.

The primary characteristics of the option contract are its

- type (call or put, for example),
- expiration (maturity) date,
- expiration or strike price (exchange rate), and
- price (premium).

2. Basic Options Types

The principal options types are the call and the put. Because of their relatively simple nature, these two types of options are called vanilla options. The market positions represented by the vanilla options form the basis upon which more complicated market positions can be taken.

2.1. The Call

A call option (Figure 2.1) offers the buyer the right to buy (call) from the writer a certain quantity of foreign exchange at the exercise price during a specified period. The buyer of the option will have a long position in the currency. In exchange for offering the buyer this right, the writer receives a certain payment (the premium). The premium, then, is the price of the option.

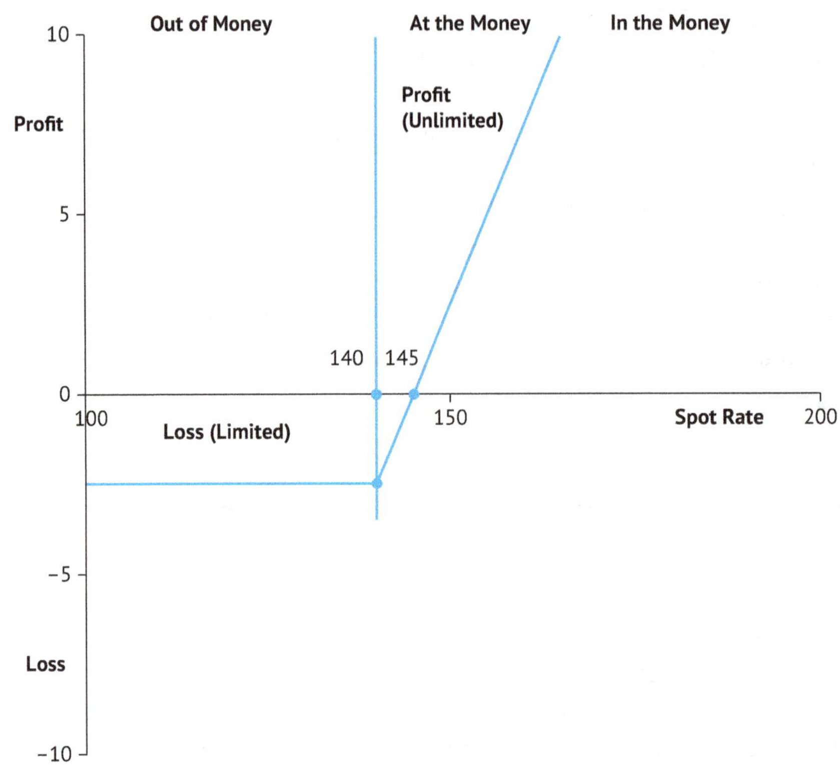

Figure 2.1 Call Option: Profit and Loss for Buyer (US. Cents/GBP)

The ramifications of the call option are shown in Figure 2.2, which illustrates the possible outcomes of a European option from the viewpoint of the buyer. To make things simpler, we assume that there are no transactions costs. The horizontal axis represents the spot exchange rate at the time the option expires, while the vertical axis depicts the profit or loss incurred by the buyer under alternative currency market values. For example, assume that the exercise or strike price is $1.40/£ and that the premium is $.05. As long as the current market (spot) exchange rate is below the strike price, the buyer of the call can buy GBP at a lower price in the market; the option is "out-of-the-money." If, say, the contract is exercised when the market price at expiration is $1.20/£, the buyer would incur a loss of $0.25 ($1.20 − $1.40 − $0.50). Better not to exercise it at all and, instead, accept a loss equivalent to the premium, $0.50. When the spot rate is equal to the exercise price, the buyer is indifferent with respect to exercising the option; the option is "at-the-money." The buyer now becomes a net loser by the amount of the premium. As soon as the spot exchange rate exceeds the exercise price, exercising the option becomes feasible. The option becomes "in-the-money." The buyer does not make a net profit if the market rate is between $1.40/£ and $1.45/£, but exercising the option at least minimizes the buyer's losses. If the market exchange rate is above $1.45/£, exercising the option enables the buyer to recoup the premium and earn a net profit.

The call option buyer's profit/loss position can then be shown as:

Call Buyer Profit (Loss) = Market Rate − (Exercise Price + Premium)

The diagram shows that the premium is the maximum loss incurred by the buyer. The buyer, then, is protected from downside risk. The writer does not receive the same assurance. For the writer, the maximum profit is delineated by the premium. The writer's maximum loss is not known, however, until maturity. Thus, if option is not exercised:

Call Writer Profit = Premium

If option is exercised:

Call Writer Profit (Loss) = Premium + Exercise Price − Market Rate

The call option writer's profit/loss opportunities are shown in Figure 2.2.

2.2. The Put

A put option allows the buyer the opportunity to sell (put) to the writer a certain amount of currency during some period before or at expiration date at an agreed upon strike price. Ignoring transactions costs, the buyer will exercise the option as long as the current exchange

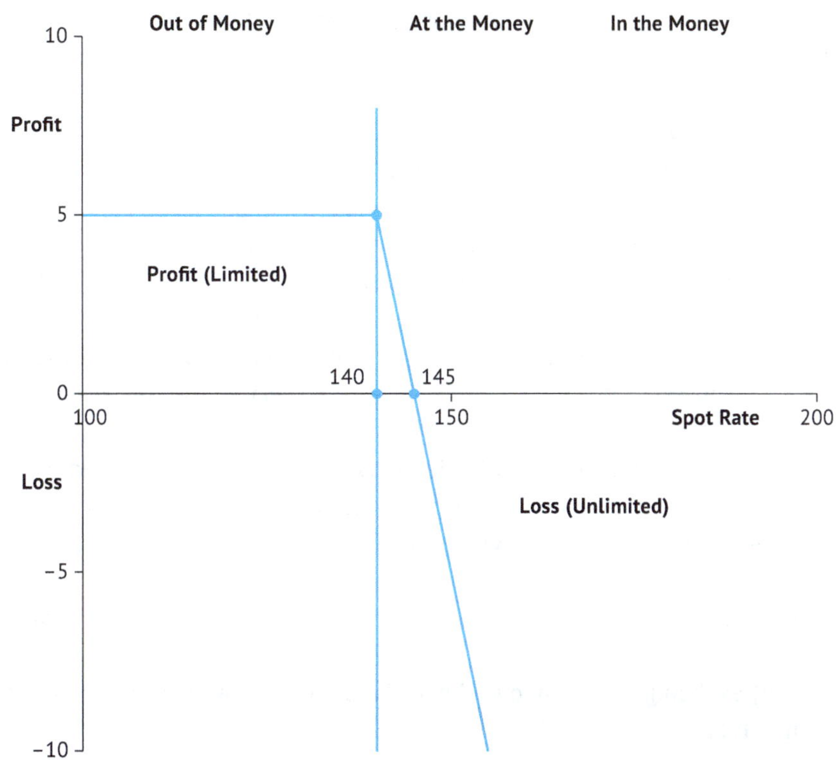

Figure 2.2 Call Option: Profit and Loss for Writer (Seller) (US. Cents/GBP)

rate is below the strike price (in-the-money). If the exchange rate is above the strike price, the option will not be exercised (out-of-the-money) and the buyer will incur the loss of the premium. Thus,

Put Buyer Profit (Loss) = Exercise Price – (Current + Premium)

For the writer of the put, the premium represents the maximum profit. The maximum loss is the strike price minus the premium, which occurs when the current rate is at its theoretical low, zero. Thus,

If the option is not exercised

Put Writer Profit = Premium

If the option is exercised

Put Writer Profit (Loss) = Premium + Current Rate – (Strike Price)

The relationship between the strike and futures price can be described in the same manner we examined in the relationship between strike and spot exchange rates: That is, if the strike price is the same as the underlying futures price, the option is referred to as at-the-money. In the case of a call, the option is referred to as in-the-money if the strike price is less than the futures price. In the case of put, the option is in-the-money when the strike price is greater than the futures price.

2.3. The Straddle and the Strangle

Simply buying or selling a put or a call, as well as going long or short on a forward or a futures contract, is called taking naked or uncovered positions. Covered positions, by contrast, represent the combination of two or more uncovered and opposite positions, such as the straddle. Buying a straddle involves the simultaneous purchase of a put and a call at the same exercise price. The buyer will profit from a straddle as long as the current exchange rate deviates significantly from the strike price. The writer, conversely, profits as long as the exchange rate observed during the period does not deviate from the strike price by more than the amount of the premium.

The profitability scenario of the straddle depends on whether it is exercised or not and, if it is exercised, whether the buyer exercises its call or its put component. If the current exchange rate is below the strike price, the buyer will exercise the put. The buyer's profit will be equal to

Straddle Buyer Profit (Loss) = Strike Price – (Current Rate + Premium)

If the current exchange rate is above the strike price, the call will be exercised, and the buyer's profit will be

Straddle Buyer Profit (Loss) = Current Rate – (Strike Price + Premium)

For the writer, on the other hand, the profit generated is equal to

Straddle Writer Profit (Loss) = Premium − | Strike Price − Current Rate |

The strangle is an options market strategy that is similar to the straddle. It is a simultaneous purchase or sale of a put and a call of the same currency at the same expiration date. Unlike the straddle, however, a strangle has a different exercise price for each side of the contract (put and call). As in the case of the straddle, the buyer of the strangle benefits from high volatility in the underlying asset. A long strangle involves purchase of an out of money call and an out-of-money put with the same expiration date. Usually, but not always, the call exercise price is higher than the put exercise price. As in the long straddle, the buyer hopes to take advantage of high market volatility.

Option positions can become about as complicated and innovative as the trader desires. They come with colorful names, too. Straddles and strangles may be further combined to form butterflies. Near-the-money strangles and out-of-money straddles are called condors. Other options are given names related to geography. Bermuda, for example, is somewhere between the US and Europe. A Bermudian option, then, has characteristics of American and European options. This option gives the buyer the right to exercise the option prior to expiration, but at discreetly spaced times. (Can you identify the American and European characteristics of this option?)

Besides entering standard contracts available within the options markets, investors can design strategies that combine options with instruments in other markets. Positions in the options markets can be combined with positions in the forward market. Such a combination is sometimes referred to as a "synthetic" position. Buying a put and simultaneously buying a currency forward is equivalent to a synthetic (buy) call position. Similarly, buying a call and selling a put result in a synthetic forward purchase.

3. Options Intrinsic and Time Values

The difference between the strike price and the underlying price is called the intrinsic value of the option. For example, if the spot rate is USD2=GBP1 and the exercise price for a call is USD1.5=GBP1, the intrinsic value is USD0.50. Because the intrinsic value is positive, the option is in-the-money. If the futures rate turned out to be USD1=GBP1, the option would be out-of-the-money. The option premium is made up of the intrinsic value and the time premium. The option's intrinsic value is generated according to how much the option is in-the-money. The time value of such is the value of the option derived by the movement of price between now and the time of the option's expiration and of the option's volatility. Greater option time premium is associated with longer time to expiration and greater volatility. When the option is first issued, it has no intrinsic value. It does, however, have time value, since investors believe that the option will become more profitable with time. As it nears expiration, its intrinsic value increases, while its time value decreases. Other things equal, the higher the premium, the greater the probability that the writer will profit from underwriting the option—not a surprising conclusion, since the premium goes to the writer.

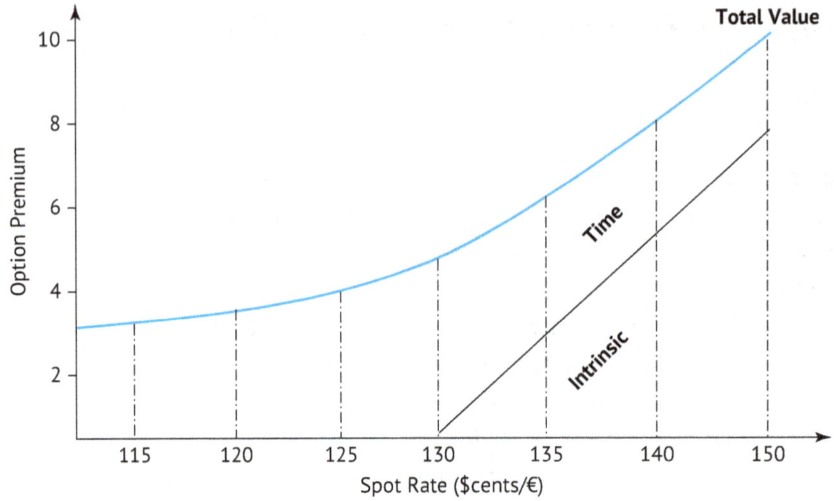

Figure 2.3 Total Value of Option: Intrinsic Value and Time Value: Call Option on Euro with a Strike Price of 130 (US Cents per GBP)

4. Factors Affecting the Option Premium

A variety of factors determine the premium for currency-related options. Some of them are analogous to the factors determining the premium for options on equity instruments. There are some differences, however, arising from the cross-border nature of currencies.

1. Expected volatility of the underlying currency.
   Volatility is a critical issue in pricing options. Volatility may be expressed in historical terms (historical volatility) or expected terms (expected or implied volatility, or IV). Measures of implied volatility are usually viewed as forecasts of the volatility of the option. As the expected volatility of the currency increases, so does the option premium. In issuing a straddle, for example, the writer will profit as long as the premium is large enough to counteract the effects of a volatile spot exchange rate.
2. Time to maturity.
   The longer the time left to expiration, the higher the premium. This relationship, of course, has some connection with the relationship between time to expiration and volatility. If the currency right now is fluctuating in value considerably, a near expiration date may be associated with a high premium; if volatility is expected to decrease in the future, a distant option may be associated with a lower premium.
3. The price of the underlying asset (spot or futures).
   The current relationship between the spot or futures exchange rate and the strike price may also determine the premium. For a call option, the higher the spot exchange rate relative to the strike price, the greater the chance that the buyer will profit from exercising the option, and the greater the chance that the writer will incur a loss. To compensate for this occurrence, the writer will demand a higher

premium. For a put option, the same relationship between spot and strike price would be associated with a lower premium, since the buyer will probably not be exercising the option.

4. Other variables.
   As we will discuss in Chapter 5, the determination of the premium for a currency-option differs from the determination of an equity option premium because of the former's relationship to additional factors, such as domestic and foreign interest rates. These factors are unique to the determination of currency options and reflect the bilateral characteristic of the exchange rate measure.

5. Options on Spot Versus Options on Futures

Options on currencies may be taken out on the spot rate or on the futures. Options on foreign exchange futures have certain advantages over options on the spot rate.

1. Options on futures are easier and less expensive to exercise than options on spot. Exercising an option on the spot requires putting up the entire amount of the strike price, while exercising an option on futures necessitates only payment of the premium plus the margin differential between the futures and the strike price at exercise time.
2. Options on futures give investors arbitrage opportunities with the futures market. That is, buyers of options on futures are in a position to profit from differences between the market price of futures contract and the exercise price on the respective option.

6. Beware of Greeks Bearing Letters: Delta, Gammas, Theta, and Vega

Hedgers, investors and traders in options must understand the behavior of the options contract and the factors influencing that behavior. Several useful measures have been developed to explain the behavior of the option premium and its relationship to the underlying asset, which in this case is the pertinent exchange rate.

Delta (δ) is the simple change in the option price associated with a certain change in the spot exchange rate (the underlying asset). Its value varies between −1 and +1. If we look at Table 2.6, the delta for the call option with exercise price 110 is 0.51. So, if the spot exchange rate goes up by 10 cents ($0.10), the premium will increase by [δ × (exchange rate change)] = 0.51 × $0.10 = $0.051. The delta of the put option at the same exercise price is −0.53. So, the premium for the put option will decrease by $0.053 if the exchange rate increases by $0.10. Another implication of the delta relates to hedging. A delta of 0.51 for the long call implies that one call options contract can be hedged by selling an amount of currency equal to [(1 contract) × (δ)]. The investor's position is said to be delta neutral.

Gamma (Γ) is the rate of change in delta associated with the change in the price of the currency. It shows the rate of change of delta. As expiration date comes near, long options experience an increase in gamma. Hedging then becomes more difficult. To illustrate, if

	Calls						Puts					
Strike	Delta	Gamma	Rho	Theta	Vega	IV	Delta	Gamma	Rho	Theta	Vega	IV
108	1	0	0.14	−0.07	0	0.03	−0.05	0.03	0	0	0.04	0.09
109	1	0	0.14	−0.07	0.01	0.13	−0.16	0.07	−0.02	0	0.1	0.09
110	1	0	0.14	−0.07	0	0.01	−0.2	0.11	−0.02	0	0.1	0.09
111	0.76	0.06	0.11	−0.08	0.12	0.01	−0.32	0.2	−0.02	0	0.12	0.09
112	1	1	7.75	−2.89	0	0.01	−0.57	0.25	−0.02	0	0.12	0.09
113	0.99	0.09	0.15	−0.08	0.05	0.05	−0.83	0.21	0	0	0	0.13
114	0.79	0	0.12	−0.06	0.18	0.03	−1	0.08	0	0	0	0.13
115	0.41	0	0.06	−0.04	0.21	0.07	−0.92	0.09	0	0	0	0.13
116	0.21	0	0.03	−0.2	0.12	0.5	−1	0.5	0	0	0	0.13

Table 2.6 Greeks FOR PHLX U.S. Dollar-Settled Euro Currency, July 19, 2019 Contracts.

Source: http://www.nasdaq.com/aspxcontent/optionsWC.aspx?symbol=^XDC&qm_page=10490&qm_symbol=^XDC#ixzz3a8tRXEuS Downloaded 5/31/2019

delta is 0.51 and gamma is 0.02, then an increase in the exchange rate by $0.10 will change the delta by 0.02 to 0.53. Gamma tells us that delta changes as the exchange rate changes. Trading strategies, then, should also change in order to achieve the trading objective.

Options have definite life. As the expiration date approaches, their price also changes. The change in the option price with respect to time is called **theta** (Θ). If theta is −0.03 per given period, say a day, the option price will decrease by .03 units (cents) every day.

Finally, **vega** (v) shows the change in option price due to a change in volatility of the currency.

7. Listed Futures and Options and OTC Markets

Options can be bought and sold at an organized exchange or over-the-counter (OTC). Exchange-listed options provide market participants with a number of benefits:

- Information. Listed futures and options derivatives are usually the most active ones. Information about them is publicly available.
- Anonymity. OTC transactions require the trader's position to be known by the other party directly involved, usually a bank. In the case of Exchanges-traded options, only the broker knows the position.
- Liquidity. As noted above, listed derivatives are usually associated with more active trading. Positions, then, are a lot easier to liquidate. In addition, trading through exchanges makes it possible to participate in a limited or extensive way.
- The guaranty given by the nature of the exchange as the clearinghouse. OTC options, of course, can be customized. Listed and OTC options, however, are not always viewed as substitutes. When a bank writes an option for a customer, it may decide to offset the risk it incurs by entering the exchange traded market.

Concept Questions

1. What is an options contract? What are its components?
2. What is an American option? How does it differ from a European option?
3. What is a call option? A put option? A straddle? A strangle?
4. What is the relationship between the time and intrinsic value of the option?
5. State the factors affecting the option premium. Briefly explain the nature of the relationship between each of these factors and the premium.
6. What is delta? Who are the other Greeks (in options)?

V. Swaps

The final component of the FX market discussed in this chapter is the foreign exchange and currency swaps market. In general, a swap entails the exchange of a series of cash flows with certain characteristics (currency, interest rate) for another series of cash flows with different characteristics. The two major types of swaps are interest rate and foreign exchange/currency swaps. An example of an interest rate swap is the exchange of the cash flows (interest and principal) of a fixed interest rate series with cash flows associated with a floating interest rate series. As we mentioned in Chapter 1, there are technically two types associated with the foreign exchange market: the currency swap and the foreign exchange swap.

A currency swap is the exchange of cash flows in one currency for cash flows in another currency. Cash flows involved are the principal of the transaction and the appropriate interest rate. A British firm, for example, may issue euro-denominated bonds. At the same time, a German firm may issue GBP-denominated bonds. Since the British firm needs GBP and the German firm euros, the two firms exchange the proceeds of their issues and service each other's debt.

Conceptually, at least, we can view the currency swap as consisting of three steps. The first step involves the exchange of the original principals, the amount raised by each firm in the debt market. The second involves payment of interest charges associated with each issue; in this case, we assume that the UK interest rate is 7% and the German interest rate is 5%. Finally, the two firms re-exchange the principal of the loan so that payment can be made to the original issuers. The example above illustrates the case of a fixed-to-fixed swap; the interest rate is fixed. More usual are the fixed-to-floating swaps, where the floating interest rate is based upon the London Interbank Offer Rate (LIBOR).

Most of the activity in the exchange rate swaps market takes place in foreign exchange swaps. A foreign exchange swap involves an exchange of specified amounts of two currencies on a specified date at a price (rate) agreed to in the contract, followed by a reverse exchange of these two currencies on a future date at a rate agreed to at the time of the contract. We can think of the swap as a combination of a spot and a forward contract. First, you buy euros; second, you sell euros forward. The first date of the transaction is called the near date, while the second date, when the re-exchange takes place, is called the far date; these two dates are the swap's value dates.

Why do firms engage in swaps? The basic economic principle of comparative advantage comes into play here. In our example, the German firm is relatively more efficient than the British firm in raising GBP funds, while the British firm is relatively more efficient in securing loan terms in EUR than the German firm. In addition, the exchange of stated cash flows eliminates risks arising from currency fluctuations. Swaps, however, still entail risks depending on the nature of the transaction. If one of the sides of the currency swap is based on a floating interest rate, the firm will be subject to interest rate risk and could even not be in a position to pay its obligations. Credit risk also exists. The art and science of putting together a swap agreement, as always, is to correctly price all risks involved.

Swaps have existed for a long time in one form or another. The predecessors of the swap include the back-to-back loan agreement. For example, a US firm has a subsidiary in Japan; the subsidiary needs local currency financing. At the same time, the subsidiary of a Japanese company in the US needs USD financing. In this case, the two parents may extend loans to the other company's in-country subsidiary. Settlement will take place in the local currency, thus overcoming any possible capital controls and eliminating exchange risk. Although there were no upfront costs in entering into such an agreement, search costs and counterparty risk could be substantial.

Today's swap market dates back to August, 1981 and involved the World Bank and IBM. At the time, IBM had already issued Swiss franc and Deutsche Mark debt maturing in 1986. The World Bank, on the other hand, could raise funds more easily in the US than in Switzerland, where the Bank had hit its debt limit. The World Bank issued a USD bond and assumed IBM's Swiss franc and German mark payments, whereas IBM assumed the World Bank's USD payments. The deal was the brainchild of Salomon Brothers. The firm acted as a broker for the swap and formulated the appropriate terms of the transaction.

Thanks primarily to the 1985 establishment of the International Swaps and Derivatives Association (ISDA), markets have become both safer and more efficient. Through the operations of the ISDA's member swap brokers and dealers that facilitate the market, counterparty risk has been decreased, transparency has increased, and the overall infrastructure of the market has improved substantially, resulting in lower transactions costs.

Concept Questions

1. What are the two major types of swaps?
2. What is a currency swap?
3. What is a foreign exchange swap?

VI. Final Note on Derivatives

Derivative markets have been very popular but, at the same time, very controversial. As is well-known by now, in the Berkshire-Hathaway 2002 Annual Report, Warren Buffet likened derivatives to financial weapons of mass destruction. According to Buffet:

> I view derivatives as time bombs, both for the parties that deal in them and the economic system. Basically these instruments call for money to change hands at some future date, with the amount to be determined by one or more reference items, such as interest rates, stock prices, or currency values. (Boyd, 2015)

Not everybody agrees with Buffet, of course. The difference of opinion on derivatives stems primarily from the fact that many casual observers consider these markets to exist for solely speculative purposes. While speculation is one of the motives for market participation, and while the practice of trading derivatives has featured a number of abuses through the years (Jacque, 2015), these markets also perform an extremely useful role by assisting participants in hedging their currency risks and contributing to the price discovery process of the underlying security.

VII. Summary

Chapter 2 built on the coverage of the foreign exchange market that was included in Chapter 1 by examining the major foreign exchange derivative markets and products. Our coverage began with the characteristics of the forward market and important concepts, such as the forward premium/discount associated with forwards. We then discussed the futures currency market, which is similar to the forward market in theory, but differs in practice by offering contracts with standardized characteristics.

We followed by examining the currency options market. Options contracts differ significantly from forward and futures contracts since options call for an exchange of the right to buy/sell, rather than an obligation to do so. Our discussion pertained to the primary characteristics of options contracts: type, expiration date and price, and premium. We also examined other concepts associated with options contracts, such as time value, intrinsic value, and the Greeks.

Foreign exchange and currency swaps were the last topics we discussed in this chapter. As we noted, a swap is generally defined as the exchange of a series of cash flows with certain characteristics, such as currency and interest rate, for another series of cash flows with different characteristics.

Key Terms and Concepts

In the order in which they are presented in the text

Derivative: A derivative is a security whose price is *derived from* an underlying asset, or even a group of assets. Stocks, bonds, currencies, commodities, interest rates, and market indices are some of the assets used as underlying assets. Derivatives contracts may be traded over-the-counter (OTC) or on organized exchanges.

Forward contract: A forward contract refers to an agreement between two parties to exchange currencies at a specified future time (beyond the two days required for settlement of a spot transaction) at an exchange rate agreed upon today.

Outright, points, and swap: When the forward rate is quoted as the price of the contract (120 or 150 in Table 2.2), it is called the outright rate. Forward rates may also be quoted in relation to the respective current spot rate. The difference between forward and spot rates is called "points." When the trader refers to the number of points by which the forward rate is greater or smaller than the spot, that number is referred to as the swap rate, which is simply the cost involved in exchanging one currency for the other for the period indicated by the maturity of the contract.

Forward premium/discount: We can also calculate the relationship between spot and forward rates by expressing the forward points as the percentage of the discount or premium. Assume that the yen to dollar spot rate is JPY98=USD1 using the indirect quote, or USD0.0102=JPY1 using the direct quote; the one-year forward rate is JPY102=USD1, or USD0.0098=JPY1. The forward premium or discount is the percentage difference between the two rates, the spot and the forward.

Window forward: The window forward enables the buyer to make and accept payment from the contract during an agreed period prior to (or even after) the contract's expiration. It offers the protection of the traditional forward contract, but also the flexibility with respect to the timing of payment.

Non-deliverable forward contract (NDF): NDFs allow the seller and the buyer of the forward contract to settle it without a physical exchange of funds. There is no delivery of the foreign currency. Instead, at maturity, there is a transfer of net funds in US dollars or another convertible currency amounting to the difference between the forward rate and the spot rate.

Futures contract: A futures contract is conceptually similar to a forward contract; it represents a commitment to deliver or to accept delivery of a certain quantity of a specific currency at a specified time in the future and at an exchange rate determined right now.

Futures contract characteristics:

> **Size**: Each currency futures contract is traded in specified number of units.
>
> **Expiration:** Currency futures contracts expire in specified months: March, June, September, and December.
>
> **Settlement price (exchange rate):** Denotes the price at which the contract "settles" at the end of the day. This price is important because it determines the value of futures contracts at the end of the trading day (marks-to-market).

Margin: The margin is the amount of money the buyer and seller must deposit before they can trade on the contract. It is usually a fraction of the total value of the contract. The margin has two parts: the **initial margin** and, its subset, the **maintenance margin**. The broker requires that at least a portion, perhaps 80 percent, of the initial margin be always on deposit. This portion of the margin is termed the maintenance margin. If, when the market settles, the total margin falls below the maintenance margin, additional margin must be deposited. This is the **variation** margin.

Open interest: The number of futures contracts not yet liquidated.

Differences between forward and futures contracts: Differences include the primary objective for each contract, the payment required, the primary risk, the expiration and size of the contracts, the regulation in each market, the setting of transaction terms, the contracts price behavior during its life, and the general availability of these contracts for each currency.

Options: An options contract calls for the parties to exchange the right to buy or sell a certain amount of currency during some specified period at an agreed-upon exchange rate. This exchange rate is called the **exercise or strike** price or rate. The agreement may be exercised any time within the period, in which case the option is termed **American**; a **European** option may be exercised only at a specified date at the end of the period.

Call option: A call option offers the buyer the right to buy (call) from the writer a certain quantity of foreign exchange at the exercise price during a specified period. The buyer of the option will have a long position in the currency. In exchange for offering the buyer this right, the writer receives a certain payment (the premium). The premium, then, is the price of the option.

Put option: A put option allows the buyer the opportunity to sell (put) to the writer a certain amount of currency during some period before or at expiration date at an agreed upon strike price.

Straddle: The simultaneous purchase or sale of a put and a call of the same currency at the same exercise price and expiration date.

Strangle: Similar to straddle (simultaneous purchase or sale of a put and a call of the same currency at the same expiration date) but with different exercise price for each.

At-the-Money, In-the-Money, Out-of-the-Money Options: If the strike price is the same as the underlying futures price, the option is referred to as at-the-money. In the case of a call, the option is referred to as in-the-money if the strike price is less than the futures price; if the strike price is greater than the exercise price, the option is out of-the-money (it will not be exercised).

Intrinsic and time value of option: The total value of the option is the sum of its intrinsic value and its time value. Intrinsic value is the value of the option when exercised. It is the difference between the strike price and the underlying price. The time value of the option is the premium paid over and above its intrinsic value. It is a function of the time to expiration and the volatility of the option.

Factors affecting the option premium: The factors affecting the value of the currency option include the volatility of the currency, time to maturity, the spot exchange rate, the domestic interest rate, and the foreign interest rate.

The Greeks:
Measures developed to explain the behavior of the option premium and its relationship to the underlying asset.

Delta (δ) is the change in the option price associated with a certain change in the spot exchange rate (the underlying asset).

Gamma (Γ) is the rate of change in delta associated with the change in the price of the currency. It shows the rate of change of delta.

Theta (Θ) is the change in the option price with respect to time.

Vega (v) shows the change in option price due to a change in volatility of the currency.

Swaps: In general, a swap entails the exchange of a series of cash flows with certain characteristics (currency, interest rate) for another series of cash flows with different characteristics.

Currency Swaps: The exchange of (fixed or floating) interest payments in two currencies until the end of the contract. Principals, based on initial spot rate, are exchanged at the beginning and end of the contract.

Foreign exchange swaps: An exchange of specified amounts of two currencies on a specified date at a price (rate) agreed to at the end of the contract; it is followed by a reverse exchange of these two currencies on a future date at a rate agreed to at the time of the contract.

Web Exercises

W1. Refer to the FX options link shown in the chapter. Comment on the relationship between bid and ask prices for calls and puts on the euro and the respective strike price.

W2. Refer again to the FX options link shown in the chapter. Click on the "Greeks" tab. Comment on the numerical values of the individual Greeks.

Questions and Problems

1. Compare forward, futures, and options markets in terms of the upfront investment necessary to participate in each.
2. Contrast the benefits and costs of listed and OTC options.
3. Go back to the futures market example in the chapter (Section 2.2). What if the futures price on October 10 was USD1.22 per GBP1? What if it was USD1.28 per GBP1? Recalculate the basis and explain the implications in each case.
4. The spot rate for the GBP/USD rate is $1.2600=£1. The 30, 90, and 180-day forwards are $1.2900, $1.3400, and $1.365, respectively. Find the forward discount/premium for each pair of rates.
5. The following are quotations for the Swiss franc futures market:

	May 23	June 23
June	$0.7000	$0.7100
September	0.7100	0.7150
December	0.7200	0.7220

   a. Find the basis for each contract, assuming that the spot rates are $0.6950 for May 23 and $0.6975 for June 23.
   b. Explain the relationship between changes in the basis and the net effects of hedging for each contract.

6. Assume that on March 21 the rate for September Swiss franc is $0.6975 and for December franc $0.6965. On June 20, the rates are $0.7067 and $0.7063 respectively.

Let the margin be $.02 per SF for all transactions. If the positions are liquidated on 6/20, what is the profit (loss) and rate of return on the following positions?

a. Going long on each futures contract
b. Going short on each futures contract
c. Combining September long and December short contracts

Comment on the performance of these positions during the above period.

7. You bought an option (European) on the British Pound. The exercise price is $1.30 and the premium is $0.15. If the spot price at the time of exercise is $1.40, what is the option buyer's profit (loss) if the option is a call? If it is a put?
8. You wrote an option (European) on the euro. The exercise price is $1.10 and the premium is $0.10. If the spot price at the time of exercise is $1.25, what is the writer's profit (loss) if the option is a call? If it is a put?
9. Graphically illustrate and comment on the following combinations

a. Short put and long call (the exercise price is the same for both)
b. Short call and long put (the exercise price is the same for both)

10. A call option on the euro has an exercise price of $1.10. When the spot exchange rate changed to $1.30, the premium went up by $0.05. What is delta?
11. A put option on the euro has an exercise price of $1.00 and a delta of −0.20. If the spot exchange rate increases to $1.10, by how much will the premium increase (decrease)?

Selected References

Boyd, T. 2015. Warren Buffett still says derivatives are "weapons of mass destruction." *Financial Review* (June). Downloaded from: http://www.afr.com/markets/derivatives/warren-buffett-still-says-derivatives-are-weapons-of-mass-destruction-20150617-ghpw0a. Accessed on July 22, 2017.

Hull, J.C. 2012. *Options, Futures, and Other Derivatives*. Prentice-Hall/Pearson: Boston, 2012.

Jacque, L. L. 2015. *Global Derivative Debacles: From Theory to Malpractice*. Second edition. Singapore: World Scientific.

Melamed, L. 1986. Evolution of the International Monetary Market. *Cato Journal* 8 (2): 393–404.

Credits

Table 2.5: Source: http://www.nasdaqtrader.com/micro.aspx?id=phlxwcoproductspecs#cd.

Table 2.6: Source: http://www.nasdaq.com/aspxcontent/optionsWC.aspx?symbol=^XDC&qm_page=10490&qm_symbol=^XDC#ixzz3a8tRXEuS.

Chapter 3

Exchange Rates, Interest Rates, and Prices in Equilibrium

Overview of Chapter Material

In the first two chapters, we explained the basics of the foreign exchange market and described each of its major components. Individual market components, however, are not independent of each other. The behavior of markets for spot currencies is connected to that of the markets for forward currencies. Similarly, the foreign exchange market as a whole is related to the workings of markets for other financial assets, such as bonds and short-term marketable securities. Financial markets in turn can be viewed in terms of their relationship to the rest of the markets in the economy, such as markets for goods and services.

This chapter explains the interrelationships among the different markets. In the process, it presents concepts that have been fundamental to the study of international finance: market efficiency, Purchasing Power Parity, interest-rate parity, forward discount/premium, forward-rate expectations, and the International Fisher Effect.

After Studying This Chapter, You Will Be Able To

- Describe the concepts of market efficiency and equilibrium in foreign exchange markets
- Recognize interrelationships between foreign exchange and other markets
- Explain the relationship among forward rates, spot rates, inflation rates, and interest rates
- Derive the implications of rate relationships for individuals, firms, and governments

Chapter Outline

I. Market Efficiency and the Foreign Exchange Market
II. Implications of Efficiency for Foreign Exchange Markets
III. The Purchasing Power Parity Doctrine
IV. Interest Rate Parity Theorem
V. The Fisher and International Fisher Effects
VI. Forward Market Theory of Exchange Rate Expectations
VII. Integrating the Equilibrium Conditions
VIII. Summary

I. Market Efficiency and the Foreign Exchange Market

The concept of market efficiency is basic to finance and economics. Financial markets, especially secondary markets for securities and the foreign exchange market, are usually analyzed in terms of their informational efficiency. According to this concept, a market is efficient if prices of traded assets fully reflect all information contained in the relevant set. Depending on the information set considered, markets may be called weak form, semi-strong form, or strong form efficient.[1]

1. Weak Form Efficiency

A market is efficient in the weak form if current prices reflect all available information contained in past prices and volume traded of the same asset. Weak form efficiency in the euro/dollar market would imply that today's rate reflects every piece of information contained in exchange rates of previous periods. In other words, examining past information on the euro and its volume of trading will not yield any evidence that would consistently allow an investor a profit over and above what would be earned by following a simple buy-and-hold strategy. Today's exchange rate, that is, has already incorporated all past price and volume information.

2. Semi-strong Form Efficiency

The foreign exchange market is semi-strong efficient if currency values reflect, in addition to past market values, every other related public information item. Government involvement in the foreign exchange market, changes in monetary policy, or other developments are appropriately reflected in today's exchange rate. The only other avenue available to consistently extract greater profits than those yielded by a buy-and-hold strategy, then, is to trade based on privately held information.

---

1 Investment texts provide further explanation of the concept, forms, and implications of market efficiency. One example is Francis, J. C. *Investments*. New York: McGraw-Hill Book Company, 1986, especially Chapter 19.

3. Strong Form Efficiency

If a market is efficient in the strong form, there is no way to earn excess profits; rates reflect all available information, both public and private. In the stock market, for example, we may be able to analyze the behavior of those considered insiders within a firm through their reported trades. In the foreign exchange market, however, there are no firms issuing currency shares and consequently no insiders in the traditional sense. Still, there are people or organizations with special knowledge of the circumstances likely to affect a particular currency, such as interest rates and money supplies.

We should again remind ourselves that, for an analysis of market efficiency to be meaningful, profits in excess of buy-and-hold need to be earned on a consistent basis. These earnings should also be adjusted for risk and for costs associated with analyzing the performance of the currency or acquiring the currency.

Concept Questions

1. Explain the three forms of market efficiency.
2. A financial market has been identified as efficient in the semi-strong sense. Is the same market also efficient in the weak form? Explain.
3. What is the relationship between market efficiency and market profits?

II. Implications of Efficiency for Foreign Exchange Markets

Market efficiency has certain important implications for market participants and observers. Our discussion of efficient foreign exchange markets is organized along the lines suggested by Brealy and Myers[2] while exploring the implications of market efficiency for the stock market.

1. Markets Have No Memory

Weak form efficiency implies that past movements in the exchange rate do not provide any clues about future movement. The dollar's fall against the yen yesterday does not enable us to say that the dollar will fall farther tomorrow. It is futile to try to forecast tomorrow's rate based on today's rate. Similarly, if we collect daily data over a two-month period and find that the dollar has fallen over that period, we cannot draw any conclusions about the dollar's path over the next two-month period. Conclusions on the efficiency of foreign exchange markets must take account of other aspects of the market, such as the international monetary system. Markets may have memory, for example, if the exchange-rate system in effect features fixed rates or pegging.

---

2 Brealey, R. and S. Myers, *Principles of Corporate Finance*. New York: McGraw Hill Book Company, Second Edition, 1984, Chapter 13.

2. Trust Foreign Exchange Market Rates

Exchange rates observed in an efficient market can be counted on to reflect all available information that contributed to this particular value in the first place. Market participants, then, cannot consistently earn excess returns. Assume, for example, that a bank hires a foreign exchange trader. In an efficient market, the trader will not generate profits for the bank over and above the costs incurred and the risks undertaken.

3. You Can Rely on the Quotations

In an efficient market, all information about payments to foreigners and receipts from foreigners, money supply, interest rates, and other variables considered influential to a currency's value are incorporated in the exchange rate. Therefore, the only thing that an analyst needs to do to assess the relationship between external payments and receipts, or the state of the money account, is to pay attention to the exchange rate. Why worry about other international financial statistics when the ultimate statistic, the exchange rate, is available? Exchange rate quotations will not reflect any irrelevant information.

The quoted GBP/USD rate, then, would present an accurate reflection of all information about economic developments in the two countries. Say that investors formulate expectations on June 15 about a certain action by the Fed or the Bank of England. The exchange rate will adjust accordingly at that time. Three weeks later, however, when the action is taken, the market does not react. Why? The market had already made its adjustment on June 15! Any further reaction would be superfluous and even potentially misleading.

4. All Currencies Are Alike

Participants in the foreign exchange market play no favorites! International investors are indifferent between holding securities denominated in euros and holding similar securities denominated in Japanese yen as long as each currency has the appropriate risk/return characteristics. Firms are indifferent between issuing debt in Swiss francs or British pounds as long as the decision regarding the currency in which the debt is denominated is compatible with the principle of value maximization.

Examples of this attitude may be found in the approaches many private and public organizations have followed in order to raise funds in the international capital markets. As we will see in Chapter 8, the Italian State Utility, ENEL, in 1970 issued bonds that were denominated in US dollars, not in lira.

5. The Homemade Alternative

In an efficient market, participants should not have to pay for services they can perform themselves. One of the benefits, for example, of international operations for a firm is the ability to diversify fund sources across national borders. If the firm's assets and liabilities are not diversified in terms of their currency denomination, individual investors wishing to attain currency diversification may simply accomplish it on their own through borrowing or lending in the desired currencies.

Concept Questions

1. What are the implications of market efficiency for foreign exchange market participants?
2. Let us assume that the US dollar/Canadian dollar market is weak form efficient. What does today's quotation reveal about tomorrow's rate?

III. The Purchasing Power Parity Doctrine

The Purchasing Power Parity (PPP) Doctrine is one of the oldest frameworks in international finance. As far back as the early 1800s, economists of such fame as Henry Thornton (1760–1815) were exploring the basic tenet of PPP: a relationship between exchange rates and prices. The work of Gustav Cassel brought the doctrine into the twentieth century, giving it a formal name and framework. Since that time (1916), various versions of PPP have been put forth, and a seemingly endless debate has developed around its theoretical validity and empirical applicability.[3]

1. The Law of One Price

PPP is based on the so-called Law of One Price. That is, the "international price" of goods is the same in all countries. The international price is simply the domestic price adjusted by the appropriate exchange rate. Other costs associated with the product reaching the market may also be added—transportation costs, for example.

An example may serve to illustrate the Law of One Price. Assume that a resident of the United States is visiting Germany and needs to decide whether to buy a car there and have it delivered back home or wait to buy the car upon return to the United States. The price of the car in Germany is EUR20,000. The exchange rate between the two currencies is $1.3000=€1. Assuming that taxes, transportation, and other such costs are zero; a US resident would be indifferent between the two buying points if the price of the car in the United States is $26,000. If the price in the United States is less than $26,000, the consumer

3 Officer, L. H. (30–33) traces the origin of PPP to the sixteenth century to the Spanish scholars of the University of Salamanca. Among the scholars mentioned are Azpilcueta de Navarro (1556), who also made original contributions to the Quantity Theory of Money, Domingo de Báñez (1594), and Juan de Lugo (1642). Officer also reports on the contributions of other schools, such as the Swedish Bullionists, particularly Pehr Niclas Christiernin. Like Henry Thornton (1760–1815), Christiernin offered a version of PPP that assumed that foreign prices did not adjust. See Officer, L. H. *Purchasing Power Parity and Exchange Rates*. Greenwich, Connecticut: JAI Press Inc., 1982. Also see Humphrey, T. M. and R. E. Keleher, *The Monetary Approach to the Balance of Payments, Exchange Rates, and World Inflation.* New York: Praeger Publishers, 1982, Chapter 11.

will have an incentive to buy the car in the US, and so will other German and American consumers. Assuming that the exchange rate remains at \$1.3000=€1, and the price of the car is \$24,000, more cars will be bought in the US and fewer cars will be bought in Germany; prices in the two countries will move closer together until there is no more incentive to buy the car in the United States.

In the PPP framework, prices of goods and values of currencies adjust to eliminate any differences between buying power of the currencies in the two countries. Any incentive to purchase the car in either country will disappear through commodity arbitrage, and a new market equilibrium will be reached. We can express the international equilibrium condition as:

$$S = P_{\text{United States}}/P_{\text{Germany}} \tag{3.1}$$

where S is the exchange rate expressed as the number of US dollars needed to buy one EUR, and P is the price of the individual commodity in each country (region) expressed in terms of the local currency.

2. Absolute Purchasing Power Parity and the Real Exchange Rate

From the Law of One Price, we derive the Purchasing Power Parity relation by aggregating across all commodities in each country. We will then get the equilibrium relation

$$S = P_{\text{United States}}/P_{\text{Germany}} \tag{3.2}$$

where S is the exchange rate as stated above and P now refers to the respective aggregate price levels for the two countries (it is assumed here that Germany's price level and inflation are the same as the entire European Union's).

How does PPP work? Let us assume that prices in the US increase, while prices in Germany stay the same. US goods would then become less competitive (more expensive) in the German market, while German goods would become more competitive (less expensive) in the US market. US consumers would need to convert more US dollars into euros, whereas German consumers would not need as many US dollars as they did before the US price increase. As a result of these two developments, the US dollar will depreciate. Let's start with both countries' Price Index being 100; for PPP to hold, the exchange rate would be \$1=€1. If, now, US prices increase by 5%, moving the US Price Index to 105, while German prices and the German Price Index remain the same, the dollar will depreciate, with the new exchange rate being \$1.05=€1. The implication of relation (3.2) is that individual countries cannot gain an advantage for their products in the international markets by lowering their prices. Any time they try to change their domestic prices, the exchange rate will adjust accordingly by moving to a level necessary to make (3.2) hold.

Relation (3.2) represents the Absolute Version of Purchasing Power Parity, because the variables included are stated in terms of level magnitudes observed at a particular time.[4]

---

4 The absolute PPP has come in for considerable criticism. For example, Bresciani-Turroni concludes that the absolute version is mis-specified. The appropriate equilibrium condition should state that the

The relation can be used to illustrate the absolute version of the real exchange rate (ARX), which is equal to:

$$ARX = P_{\text{United States}}/(P_{\text{Germany}}{}^{*}S) \tag{3.3}$$

Equation (3.3) indicates that, if PPP holds, ARX is equal to 1. So, if, let's say the US Price Index is 130 and the German Price Index is 100, for PPP to hold, the exchange rate must be $1.3000=€1. What if prices and the exchange rate (S) are such that ARX in (3.3) is not equal to 1? In that case, PPP does not hold; either prices or the exchange rate have not adjusted appropriately. For example, let us say that the dollar appreciates from $1.3000=€1 to $1.2000=€1, while prices in both the US and Germany remain the same. ARX now is greater than 1 (it is 130/120=1.0833). According to the PPP framework, the dollar is now overvalued. If we go back to the Law of One Price and to our car example, the dollar price of the car in the US (still $26,000) will be higher than the price in Germany (now equivalent to $24,000). More consumers, then, will want to buy the car in Germany than in the US. If we generalize, we conclude that US products are relatively more expensive; the country has suffered a loss in its competitive position vs. Germany. This loss in competitiveness and sales of domestic products means that funds invested in US industry will generate lower returns; investment will then move out of the US in search of higher returns.

3. Relative PPP and the (Relative) Real Exchange Rate

The relative version of PPP deals with price changes instead of levels; it states that, over a period of time, percentage changes in the exchange rate should be equal to the inflation differential between the two countries considered. According to the relative version of PPP,

$$\Delta S_t = \Delta I_t \tag{3.4}$$

Where $_t$ stands for the current period, ΔS_t is the percentage change in the exchange rate between time periods t_1 and t; and ΔI_t stands for the differential between the continuously compounded inflation rates in the two countries.

If we rearrange the variable in (3.4) we get the deviation from PPP, d_t, stated as:

$$d_t = \Delta S_t - \Delta I_t = 0 \tag{3.5}$$

---

exchange rate equals PPP multiplied by the terms of trade, relative obstacles to trade, and relative internal price structures. The presence of these other factors may cause persistent deviations from PPP. If these other factors remain constant, relative PPP holds. See Humphrey and Keleher, pp. 332–35, from "Report from the Select Committee on the High Price of Gold Bullion" (Bullion Report)(No.349) III, 1810, quoted in Constantino Bresciani-Turroni, "The Purchasing Power Parity Doctrine," L'Egypte Contemporaine 25 (May 1934), 433–64; reprinted in *Saggi di Economia* (Milan: Giuffre, 1961), 91.

If the relative version of PPP holds, the deviation, d_t, equals zero. Expression (3.5) may be rewritten as:

$$d_t = [(S_t - S_0)/S_0] - [I_{US} - I_G] \tag{3.6}$$

where I_{US} and I_G are the inflation rates for the United States and Germany respectively. When PPP holds, d_t is equal to zero, since

$$[(S_t - S_0)/S_0] = I_{US} - I_G \tag{3.7}$$

For example, if the US inflation rate in a given year is 10%, and the German inflation rate is 7%, relative PPP suggests that the dollar will depreciate by 3% in relation to the euro.

We can now illustrate the concept of the real exchange rate, which is compatible with relative PPP. By rearranging (3.7), we get:

$$1 = (I_{US} - I_G)/[(S_t - S_0)/S] \tag{3.8}$$

If relative PPP holds, the Real Exchange Rate (RRX) in accordance with relative PPP is equal to 1. An observed increase in RRX implies that the inflation differential increased faster than the adjustment in the exchange rate. Due to a relatively higher inflation in the home country, US goods now become less attractive to German consumers.

The variables and relationships included in (3.3) and (3.4) form the basis for distinguishing between two versions of PPP: the classical and efficient-market versions.

3.1. Classical Version of PPP

The classical version of the PPP doctrine may be stated in terms of relation (3.4). ΔI_t, that is, completely offsets ΔS_t. Changes in the differences between inflation rates of the two countries are offset exactly by percentage changes in the exchange rate. If (3.4) holds, d_t, the deviation from PPP, is zero.

3.2. Efficient Markets and PPP

If markets are efficient in the semi-strong sense, the exchange rate should reflect any changes in the inflation differential beween the two countries. Today's spot rate, then, includes all information available to forecast next period's spot rate, adjusted for any anticipated inflation.

The efficient-market version of PPP has implications for the observed deviations from parity. In contrast to the classical version, where deviations are viewed as cumulative and interconnected from one period to another, efficient-market PPP posits that over a long period deviations should be equal to zero and that these deviations should be independent of each other, period to period.

In general, tests of the Classical and Efficient Markets versions of PPP conducted by various analysts indicate that the efficient-market approach offers an appropriate framework for examining the doctrine. Of course, numerous tests of PPP have been conducted. In order for the results of these tests to be interpreted meaningfully, however, analysts must consider the conceptual and empirical issues involved. We now turn to a discussion of some of these issues.

3.3. Conceptual and Empirical Issues Surrounding PPP

Even though we formulate PPP through the use of a relatively simple concept, there is plenty of disagreement regarding its theoretical validity and practical application. The debate about PPP usually centers on the following issues:

3.3.1. Is PPP a "Full Theory" or a Mere Shortcut?

PPP, according to some, does not provide a full-fledged theoretical framework. It does not explain, for example, whether exchange rates respond to changes in prices or whether prices respond to exchange rates. Furthermore, the relationship by itself ignores the fact that both exchange rates and prices are shaped by the influence of other variables that are not included in this simple framework.

3.3.2. Is PPP a Bilateral or a Multilateral Framework?

Countries conduct business with multiple trade and investment partners. Therefore, any analysis of the relationship between prices and exchange rates should incorporate prices and currencies of all trading partners. The exchange rate used, then, should be a multilaterally derived rate, and the foreign country price index used should be a weighted average. Calculating a weighted average of all national price indices, of course, presents its own conceptual and methodological challenges.

3.3.3. What is the Appropriate Price Index?

In aggregating across commodities to arrive at relation (3.2), we need to decide on the commodities that we want to include. Some analysts use all goods and services produced in a country. Others use only traded goods and services. Yet others use the Consumer Price Index, or the Wholesale Price Index, or the Labor Cost Index.

3.3.4. What About Transportation Costs and Obstacles to Trade?

Individual or groups of countries impose numerous add-ons to the "sticker" price on goods, making the delivery price to the consumer different from one country to the other. These potential add-ons include taxes, transportation costs, import duties, and quotas, and may serve as impediments to attaining PPP.[5]

---

5 See Roll, R. "Violations of Purchasing Power Parity and their Implications for Efficient International Commodity Markets," in M. Sarnat and G. Szego (eds.), *International Finance and Trade*, Vol. 1, Cambridge, MA: Ballinger, 1979, 133–176. Also see Koveos, P. and B. Seifert, "Purchasing Power Parity and Black Markets." *Financial Management*, Autumn 1985, pp. 40–46. For further empirical work, see Katseli-Papaefstratiou, L. "The Reemergence of the Purchasing Power Parity Doctrine in the 1970s."

3.4. The Economist's *Big Mac Index*

Since 1986, *The Economist* has been putting the Law of One Price to test by examining the global price of the popular Big Mac sandwich. The question: is the Big Mac's price the same everywhere when adjusted for the exchange rate? Furthermore, is the price of the Big Mac the same around the world when we adjust for the exchange rate as well as the purchasing power of the country's currency? According to the *Economist's* findings, the average price of the Big Mac in the US in January 2020 was $5.67. In China, it was RMB21.5. With the exchange rate of RMB6.8885=USD1 at the same time, the U.S dollar equivalent price of the Big Mac in China was $3.12. The Chinese RMB is then undervalued by 44.93% versus the US dollar. How did we arrive at 44.93%? Simply by calculating what the price of the Big Mac should be in China if the Law of One Price held; it should be 39.04 yuan (6.885 × 5.67). In other words, the actual price of 21.5 yuan is 55.07% of what the price should be if the Law Of One Price held. We conclude that the RMB is 44.93% of the level at what it should be, or that it is undervalued by 44.93% [(1−0.5507) = 0.4493].

The *Economist's* results show that a number of countries' currencies are also undervalued versus the US dollar, including Argentina's (49.79%), India's (53.22%), Indonesia's (57.42%) and Malaysia's (58.88%). Norway (5.32%) was the only country whose currency was found to be overvalued versus the dollar (The Economist, January 2020; https://www.economist.com/news/2020/01/15/the-big-mac-index). *The Economist* presents Big Mac price data using various base currencies. Data can be shown in "raw" form as above or can be adjusted for the country's standard of living.

The analysis does not necessarily mean that you should go to China or India (or that you should not go to Norway) to satisfy your yearning for a Big Mac. Remember that we made some simple assumptions about transportation costs and other costs of trade at the beginning of this section. Also, although the Big Mac analysis is interesting because of global familiarity with the product, we should remember that this is merely an exercise on the Law of One Price at a point in time. We cannot draw any general conclusions regarding the relationship between exchange rates and aggregate prices over time.

Special Papers in International Economics, No. 13, Princeton University, December 1979. Also, see Adler, M. and Lehmann, B. "Deviations from Purchasing Power Parity in the Long Run." *Journal of Finance*. 38, 1983, 1471–1487; and Abuaf, N. and P. Jorion, "Purchasing Parity in the Long Run." *Journal of Finance*, 45, 1990, 157–174 and Booth, G.G. and Koveos, P. "Purchasing Power Parity: A Reexamination of Prediction Errors." *Advances in Financial Planning and Forecasting*. Edited by C. F. Lee, Volume 3, 1989, 251–275. In addition, see Glick (1989), Voller (1981), Worthington (1991), Frankel and Johnson (1978), Friedrich (1974), and Jacque (1978).

Concept Questions

1. What does the Purchasing Power Parity Doctrine tell us about the relationship between exchange rates and prices?
2. What is the difference between the absolute and relative versions of the Purchasing Power Parity Doctrine?
3. What are some of the conceptual and empirical issues pertaining to PPP?
4. What is the Big Mac Index? How is it related to the concepts discussed in this section?

IV. Interest Rate Parity Theorem

The Interest Rate Parity Theorem (IRPT) features the relationship between exchange rates and interest rates. The IRPT posits that the differential between foreign and domestic nominal interest rates is equal in equilibrium to the ratio of the forward and spot exchange rates. This equality results when we assume that markets are efficient, capital is free to flow from one country to another, and securities of similar risk class available to the investor in perspective countries are perfect substitutes.

1. The IRPT Framework

To understand how exchange and interest rates are related within the IRPT framework, we can start by assuming that an investor is considering investing in two countries, the United States (US) and the United Kingdom (UK). Both investments involve purchasing a one-year risk-free security (or putting money in a one-year bank deposit). We also assume that the two investments have the same tax and marketability characteristics. The only difference between them is the currency of denomination: one is denominated in USD, the other in GBP. We can now analyze the two investment options in the following manner:

Investing an amount of X dollars in the US at the annual interest rate i_{us} yields a monetary outcome of A$:

$$X(1 + i_{us}) = A\$ \tag{3.9}$$

If, instead, the investor places X amount of dollars in the UK, she theoretically follows these steps:

Step 1. She first converts her X amount of dollars into the local currency, British pounds. If S is the spot exchange rate, expressed as the number of dollars per British pound, X/S pounds will be available for investment in the UK.

Step 2. She purchases the UK security.

Step 3. At maturity, she receives the principal amount of her investment plus interest in the local currency, pounds. The total amount will be:

$$[X/S]\ (1 + i_{uk}) \tag{3.10}$$

where i_{uk} is the UK interest rate and S is the exchange rate defined as the number of US dollars required to buy one British pound.

Step 4. She does not wish to bear the exchange risk involved in accepting pounds. To eliminate that risk, she sells the total amount of pounds in the forward market for the appropriate amount of dollars. The transaction can now be considered "covered"; it is not subject to changing outcome as a result of exchange rate fluctuations. Accordingly, the IRPT is also referred to as the Covered Interest Rate Parity Theorem.

When all these steps are completed, the investor receives the monetary outcome B$:

$$[X/S]\ (1 + i_{uk})\ [F] = B\$ \tag{3.11}$$

where F is the forward exchange rate expressed as number of dollars per pound and corresponding in maturity to that of the investment.

Next comes the investment choice: US or UK? To answer the question, she must compare the outcomes of the two options: A$ and B$. If

A$ > B$: she should invest in the US
B$ > A$: she should invest in the UK.
A$ = B$: she is indifferent between the two alternatives.

Assume that the investment amount (X above) is $1m and that there are no transactions costs. Also, assume that: S = $1.50 per £1; F = $1.75 per £1; i_{us} = 10%; and i_{uk} = 12%. Then:

$$A\$ = \$1m\ (1 + 0.10) = \$1.100m$$
$$\text{and } B\$ = [\$1m/1.50]\ (1 + .12)\ [1.75] = \$1.307m$$

Since B$ > A$, the investor should invest in the UK. In general, funds will flow into the UK. if

$$[X/S]\ (1 + i_{uk})\ [F] > X\ (1 + i_{us}) \tag{3.12}$$

or

$$[F/S]\ (1 + i_{uk}) > (1 + i_{us}) \tag{3.13}$$

or

$$[F/S] > (1 + i_{us})/(1 + i_{uk}) \tag{3.14}$$

The condition described by (3.14) points to an arbitrage opportunity. If every investor knew information about such an opportunity, they would all move their funds to the UK. As they engage in arbitrage between the two locations, interest rates and exchange rates adjust to the flow of funds. Thus, as funds leave the US, after the holders of US securities sell their holdings, prices of US securities fall, which implies that their interest rates go up.

The reverse occurs in the UK. The influx of funds raises prices of UK securities and therefore lowers their interest rates. The right hand-side of (3.14), then, increases in magnitude. The variables on the left-hand side may also change.

As US investors step up their purchases of UK securities, they convert their dollars into British pounds. If allowed to respond to this activity, the dollar will drop in value. In terms of the variables in (3.14), S, the spot exchange rate, will increase. These same US investors cover their foreign exchange risk by selling the foreign currency forward, resulting in the fall of the forward rate, F. The combined effect of the changes in S and F will be a decline in the magnitude of the left-hand side of relation (3.14).

If these adjustments take place, there should be a point beyond which transferring funds from one country to the other will not generate further advantage for our investor. This point is illustrated by

$$[F/S] = (1 + i_{us})/(1 + i_{uk}) \tag{3.15}$$

Relation (3.15) describes the markets at equilibrium. Equilibrium will be maintained until one or more of the variables changes in value as response to the influence of a variable outside those in (3.15). For example, easing of monetary policy in the US may decrease US interest rates, setting up a new arbitrage opportunity.

2. A Simplified Formulation of Equilibrium

We now want to simplify condition (3.15) and reformulate it to express equilibrium in terms of some familiar terms. In particular, by subtracting 1 from each side, the left-hand side becomes

$$[F/S] - 1 = F/S - S/S = (F - S)/S, \tag{3.16}$$

which is the forward premium (or discount), and the right-hand side is equivalent to

$$[(1 + i_{us})/(1 + i_{uk})] - 1 = [(1 + i_{us})/(1 + i_{uk})] - [(1 + i_{uk})/(1 + i_{uk})]$$

or

$$[(1 + i_{us})(1 + i_{uk})]/(1 + i_{uk})$$

or

$$(i_{us}\ i_{uk})/(1 + i_{uk}) \tag{3.17}$$

If i_{uk} is very small, expression (3.17) is approximately equal to

$$(i_{us} - i_{uk})/1$$

$$(i_{us} - i_{uk}) \tag{3.18}$$

which is the interest rate differential between the two countries.

Thus, equilibrium is reached when

$$(F - S/S) = (i_{us} - i_{uk}), \quad (3.19)$$

or when the forward premium (or discount) is (approximately) equal to the interest rate differential.

To examine these two related approaches, assume that the \$/£ spot rate is \$1.69/£ and the 12-month forward rate is \$1.66/£. The 12-month US risk-free rate is 8%. What is the respective UK rate necessary to attract investors to London?

Using the extended approach presented in (3.15), equilibrium can be shown as

$$\$1.66/\$1.69 = (1 + .08)/(1 + x)$$

Solving for x, we get 6.1% as the break-even point. An interest rate greater than 6.1% would entice investors to move their funds to London (transactions costs are assumed to be zero).

Using the second approach (shown in 3.19), we get

$$(1.66 - 1.69)/(1.69) = .08 - x$$

Solving again for x, we get x=6.2%. The difference between the results of the two approaches is a matter of rounding and of the assumption made about the size of the interest rate.

3. A Graphical Analysis of Equilibrium

Figure 3.1A illustrates condition (3.19). The vertical axis represents the interest rate differential, while the horizontal axis depicts the values of the forward premium. The 45^0 line is called the equilibrium, or parity, line. When the interest rate differential is greater than the forward premium, funds flow into the US. The relationship between the two magnitudes may be depicted by point N in Figure 3.1A, which is located above the parity line. When the interest rate differential is less than the forward premium, funds flow into the UK, shown in Figure 3.1A as point L.

When a point off the parity line illustrates the relationship between the two expressions, the transition to parity may be accomplished theoretically through changes in any or all of the variables: domestic interest rates, foreign interest rates, forward rates, and/or spot exchange rates. For example, if the relationship between interest rate differential and the forward premium is as depicted by point N of Figure 3.1A, funds will flow into the US. If the British government wishes to reverse the direction of funds, it will need to pursue policies that will change the value of any of the variables in (3.19). These may include raising the interest rate, devaluing the pound (spot), or a combination of the two measures. Ultimately, the system will go back to a point on the 45^0 line, reaching a new equilibrium.

4. Conceptual and Empirical Issues Regarding the IRPT

The general validity of the Interest Rate Parity Theorem has been debated on several fronts:

A. It does not hold when distortions exist in the markets for financial assets.

Lending and borrowing internationally does not always occur under the assumptions utilized to express IRPT. The existence of transactions costs and capital controls, for example, represent market imperfections and may have an impact on establishment of the parity condition. This is tantamount to stating that the parity line in Figure 3.1A, on which lie the combinations of interest rates and exchange rates that imply equilibrium, is surrounded by a band on either side. The size of the band depends on the extent of these imperfections. For example, the higher the transactions costs, the wider the band. This is illustrated in Figure 3.1B. Notice that if the relationship between the forward discount/premium and the interest rate differential is depicted by point L, which is inside the band, any possible gains from investing in London are more than offset by the existence of transactions costs. So, it would not make any sense for investors to move funds from New York to London. If the situation, however, is depicted by point N, we can conclude that the gains from investing in New York exceed any other costs incurred by the investor.

Our example was based on the impact of transactions costs. Deviations from interest rate parity may also occur as the result of factors such as political risk, or risk of government interference in general.

B. There is no consideration of risk.

In addition to the return of an asset, investors are concerned about its risk; changes in asset returns, then, may not be sufficient to bring about inflows or outflows of funds. Alternatively, fund movements may take place even when parity apparently holds. Thus, deviations from parity may be evident and even persistent if such deviations are compatible with portfolio adjustment decisions made by international investors.

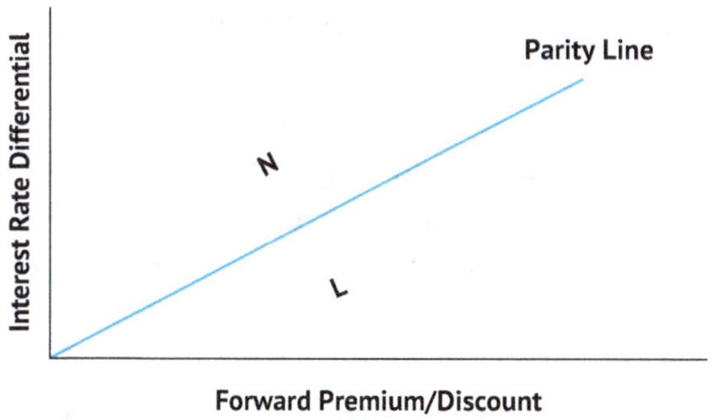

Figure 3.1A Interest Rate Parity Theorem.

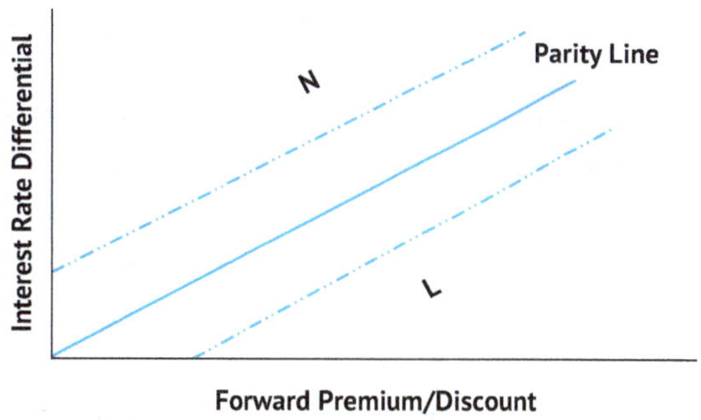

Figure 3.1B Interest Rate Theorem with Transactions Costs.

Incorporation of risk may also explain why funds flow in both directions. Indeed, the flow of funds into and out of a country needs to be explained if the Interest Rate Parity Theorem, or any other framework, is to be considered as explaining short-term or long-term capital flows.

C. Instruments sold in various countries may not be perfect substitutes.

Interest rate parity is achieved when the forward discount/premium is equal to the interest rate differential. For such a statement to be valid, these interest rates must be associated with comparable securities. In reality, however, many of the securities sold across countries are not directly comparable. Parity, then, may not hold or be directly observable. Still, as we previously noted regarding PPP, IRPT offers a useful framework of, at the least, initial analysis of inter-market relationships.

Concept Questions

1. What is the nature of the relationship between interest rates and exchange rates depicted by the interest rate parity theorem?
2. What is the interpretation of the parity line? What do points "above" the line indicate?
3. How is risk incorporated in the interest rate parity framework?

V. The Fisher and International Fisher Effects

1. The Fisher Effect

One of the most influential economists of all time, Irving Fisher (1896), described the relationship between interest rates and inflation as

$$\text{(Risk Free) Nominal Interest Rate} = \text{Real Interest Rate} + \text{Expected Inflation} \quad (3.20)$$

Equation (3.20), known as the Fisher Effect or Fisher Equation, implies that there is a direct relationship between the nominal interest rate and inflation. Assuming that the real interest rate is constant and independent of the inflation rate, an increase in the expected rate of inflation brings an equal increase in the nominal interest rate. For example, let us assume that the real rate of interest, which can be thought of as the rate of real economic growth, is 2% and that our investor expects that the rate of inflation over the following year will be 3%. She would then would not accept anything less that 5% as the rate of return on her investment. If, instead, she expects the rate of inflation to be 4%, she will require a minimum of 6% as return for her investment.

2. The International Fisher Effect

The Fisher Effect is applied to a domestic environment. What if our investor is considering investing outside her own country? She will then need to consider her domestic interest rate as well as the foreign interest rate in order to make an informed decision.

Let us assume that our investor does not use the forward market for purposes of eliminating the risk from foreign exchange rate fluctuations. Instead, she depends on her own expectations about the value of the two currencies at the end of the investment period. Let us analyze again the choices of placing funds in the US or the UK.

The outcome of investing at home remains as in (3.9):

$$X\,(1 + i_{us}) = A\$ \tag{3.21}$$

The outcome of investing abroad is B$':

$$[X/S_t]\,(1 + i_{uk})\,S_{t+n} = B\$' \tag{3.22}$$

where S_{t+n} is the exchange rate in effect at time t+n, with n being the number of periods that coincides with the time horizon of the investment. As the actual value of the future exchange rate is not known at present, the investor must evaluate the outcome of the foreign currency investment based on expected values of the currencies. This can be expressed as B$":

$$[X/S_t]\,(1 + i_{uk})E\,(S_{t+n}) = B\$'' \tag{3.23}$$

where $E(S_{t+n})$ refers to the expected value of the spot exchange rate at time t+n.

The investor is indifferent when A$=B$". Dealing with the two relations in a manner similar to the sequence followed in (3.9) through (3.19) results in the parity condition:

$$X(1 + i_{us}) = [X/S_t](1 + i_{uk})[E(S_{t+n})] \tag{3.24}$$

This condition, known as the International Fisher Effect, is expressed as

$$[E(S_{t+n})]/(S_t) = (1 + i_{us})/(1 + i_{uk}) \tag{3.25}$$

or

$$[E(S_{t+n}) - S_t]/S_t = i_{us} - i_{uk} \tag{3.26}$$

According to (3.26), the expected percentage change in the exchange rate is equal to the interest rate differential. In other words, the interest rate differential of 2% between the two countries reflects an expectation that the exchange rate will change by the same amount. If a US investor expects the yen to depreciate by 2% versus the dollar in the coming year, she will require that the Japanese investments she made in the beginning of the year will yield 2% more than her US investments. In equilibrium, then, the investor is indifferent with respect to the country in which she invests. Interest rates in the two countries are the same when adjusted for expected exchange rate movements.

Concept Questions

1. Explain the relationships included in the Fisher Effect.
2. What is the International Fisher Effect?
3. How does the International Fisher Effect differ from the Interest Rate Parity Theorem?

VI. Forward Market Theory of Exchange Rate Expectations

In addition to PPP, IRPT, and the International Fisher Effect, a fourth equilibrium condition revolves around the relationship between spot and forward exchange rates. Assuming (semi-strong) market efficiency, the forward rate applicable to a contract whose maturity is n periods away reflects all market conditions presently expected to prevail at maturity. If both parties to the contract have the same information, agreement would not be reached unless a forward dollar was exchanged right now for what a spot dollar is expected to be worth in the future. That is:

$$F_t^n = E(S_{t+n}) \tag{3.27}$$

According to (3.27), the forward rate applied at time t to contracts with n maturity is a proxy for the spot rate expected to hold at time t+n. Because we do not know the future spot rate right now, the forward rate can be viewed as its forecast. This is sometimes referred to as an "unbiased" forecast. That is, the forward rate neither systematically overestimates nor systematically underestimates the future spot rate.

1. Testing for the Validity of the Forward Market Theory

A number of approaches have been suggested to test for the efficiency of the forward market and the forecasts supplied by the forward rate. According to Levich (1979), they include

1.1. Testing a Form of the Regression

$$S_{t+n} = b_0 + b_1 F_t^n + e_t \tag{3.28}$$

where b_0 is the constant term, b_1 is the coefficient of the forward rate variable, and e_t is the regression-error term. Finding a constant term that is not statistically different from zero and a coefficient of F which is not statistically different from one represents evidence in favor of forward market efficiency.

If the variables in (3.28) are divided by S_t, then

$$S_{t+n}/S_t = b_0 + b_1F_t^n/S_t + e_t \tag{3.29}$$

When (S_t/S_t) is subtracted from both sides, the result is

$$(S_{t+n}S_t)/S_t = b_0 + b_1 [(F_t^n - S_t)/S_t] + e_t, \tag{3.30}$$

which expresses the percentage change in the spot rate (left-hand side) as a function of the forward discount/premium (right-hand side). An extension of (3.28) is represented by

$$S_{t+n} = b_0 + b_1F_t^n + b_2F_t^{n+1} + b_3F_t^{n+2} + e_t \tag{3.31}$$

If the market is efficient, then $b_0 = 0$, $b_1 = 1$, and the coefficients b_2, b_3 of the longer-maturity forward contract rates will be equal to zero. All information about the future spot rate, that is, is reflected in the pertinent forward contract. Inclusion of additional forward market information does not contribute to the forecast.

1.2. Analyzing the Behavior of the Forecast Error

Another method of testing if the forward rate is an unbiased predictor of future rates involves analysis of the following:

$$X_{t,n} = S_{t,n} - F_t^n \tag{3.32}$$

$X_{t,n}$ is the forecast error generated when using the framework provided by (3.28). Lack of bias is not rejected when these errors are small in size and random.

1.3. Comparative Forecasting

The forward market forecasting model may also be compared with other forecasting models. If the forward rate model is shown to be more accurate than alternative models, then market efficiency is verified.[6]

These tests could also be conducted using futures markets, instead of forward markets, measures. The development of both kinds of markets represents evidence of the ability of foreign exchange markets in general to adjust to the needs of market participants. At the least, their existence illustrates the degree of allocative efficiency that the foreign exchange markets unmistakably possess.

---

6 Levich, R.M. *The Efficiency of Markets for Foreign Exchange: A Review and Extension*, in Lessard, First Edition, 243–276.

Concept Questions

1. What is the importance of market efficiency in the relationship between forward and expected future spot rates?
2. What are some of the approaches used to test for the efficiency of the forward market?

VII. Integrating the Equilibrium Conditions

Giddy (in Lessard, 1985) and other scholars have shown that the four parity conditions described in this chapter are building blocks of an integrated framework. Within this framework, markets are interconnected at equilibrium. The four conditions may be summarized as follows[7]:

Condition I: Purchasing Power Parity

Percentage change in the spot exchange rate = change in the inflation rate differential

Condition II: Interest Rate Parity Theorem

Interest rate differential = forward discount/premium

Condition III: International Fisher Effect

Interest rate differential = expected percentage change in the spot exchange rate

Condition IV: Forward Market Theory of Exchange Rate Expectations

Forward premium = expected percentage change in the spot exchange rate

When all markets are at equilibrium, then

The expected percentage change in the spot rate is equal to the forward premium, which in turn is equal to the interest rate differential, which is equal to the expected inflation differential.

The equality between the last two terms has another interesting extension. Again, if the interest rate differential is expressed as $i_{us} - i_{uk}$, and the expected inflation differential is expressed as $E(I_{us}) - E(I_{uk})$, then,

$$i_{us} - i_{uk} = E(I_{us}) - E(i_{uk}), \text{ or}$$

$$i_{us} - E(I_{us}) = i_{uk} - E(I_{yk}), \text{ or}$$

$$T_{us} = T_{uk},$$

7 Giddy, I. H. 1979. *An Integrated Theory of Exchange Rate Determination*, in Lessard, First Edition, pp. 167–176.

where T_{us} and T_{uk} stand for the real interest rates in the two countries. This condition is referred to as the Fisher Effect.[8]

Under conditions of market efficiency, then, spot and forward foreign exchange markets, goods markets, and financial markets are related in indivisible ways.

This is illustrated in Figure 3.2. Let's start from quadrant I. Point A represents the equality between Interest Rate Differential and the Forward Premium/Discount at equilibrium,

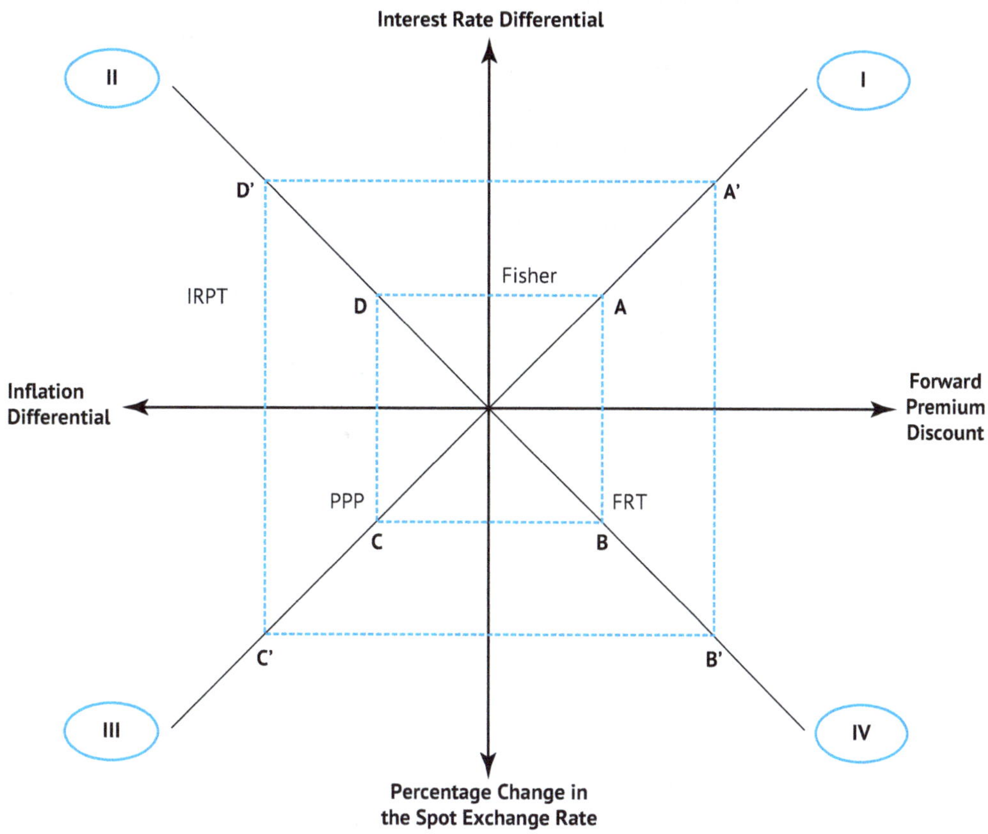

Figure 3.2 The Financial System in Equilibrium.

8 The Fisher Effect, attributed to Irving Fisher (Appreciation and Interest, *Publications of the American Economic Association*, XI, August, 1896, pp. 1–100) describes an equilibrium condition between goods and financial markets, stating that the nominal rate of interest is equal to the real rate, the inflation rate expected over the life of the instrument, and a cross product.

If N is the nominal rate of interest, R is the real rate, and I is the rate of inflation, then:

$$1 + N = (1 + R)(1 + I)$$

or

$$N = R + I + R*I$$

If the cross product is small, the nominal rate can be thought of as the sum of the real rate plus the rate of inflation. Alternatively, the real rate is equal to the nominal rate minus the rate of inflation. The equilibrium condition expressed, then, states that real rates are equal across countries.

in accordance with the Interest Rate Parity Theorem. Quadrant II, point B, would then be where the Forward Premium/Discount is equal to the Expected Percentage Change in the Exchange Rate (Forward Theory of Exchange Rate Expectations). For PPP to hold, point C in Quadrant III should show the equality between Inflation Differential and the Expected Percentage Change in the exchange rate. Finally, for the entire system to be in equilibrium, the Fisher Effect should produce the equality between Inflation and Interest Rate Differentials (Quadrant IV). If, on the other hand, the initial relationship between Interest Rate Differential and the Forward Discount/Premium is represented by point A', the system would be in equilibrium by generating points A', B', C', and D'.

The interrelationship among markets has important implications for all participants. Governments must consider the implications of interrelated decisions for the effectiveness of their policies. Can the spot rate be kept at a level favorable to the country's exports? Can interest rates be maintained at a level necessary to achieve domestic objectives? Firms need to understand the relationships among markets in order to formulate appropriate policies with respect to holdings of currencies, size, and composition of their working capital, borrowing, and dividend disbursement. Individual investors can use the information embodied in equilibrium conditions to forecast exchange rates and inflation differentials as well as to evaluate the outcome of their foreign investments.

Concept Questions

1. What do the four parity conditions reveal about the relationships among markets?
2. What are the implications of the relationships among the various markets for investors?

VIII. Summary

This chapter has explained some fundamental concepts and relationships in international finance. Within the framework of market efficiency, a number of theoretical models describe the relationships between spot and forward foreign exchange markets, markets for other financial assets, and commodities markets.

Market efficiency refers to the ability of the market to reflect all pertinent information. Weak form market efficiency incorporates only price and volume information. Semi-strong form efficiency considers all public information. Strong form efficiency includes all available information, private as well as public.

When markets are efficient and equilibrium is allowed to occur, the following relationships are observed: Purchasing Power Parity, Interest Rate Parity, the Interest Rate Theory of Exchange Rate Expectations, and the Forward Market Theory of Exchange Rate Expectations.

Equilibrium conditions imply that the expected change in the spot rate is equal to the forward premium (or discount), the interest rate differential between any two countries, and the expected inflation differential. Recognition of these conditions is essential for decisions to be made by individuals, firms, and governments.

Key Terms and Concepts

In the order in which they are presented in the text.

Market efficiency: The foreign exchange market is efficient if values of currencies fully reflect all information contained in the relevant set.

Weak form efficiency: The foreign exchange market is efficient in the weak form if current exchange rates reflect all available information contained in past exchange rates and volume traded of the same currency.

Semi-strong form efficiency: The foreign exchange market is semi-strong efficient if currency values reflect not just past market values but also every other related public information item.

Strong form efficiency: If the market is efficient in the strong form, there is no way to earn excess profits; rates reflect all available information, both public and private.

Implications of foreign exchange market efficiency: Markets have no memory; we should trust foreign exchange rates; we can rely on quotations; all currencies are alike; individual market participants can diversify their currency holdings through their own actions

The Law of One Price: The "international price" of goods is the same in all countries. The international price is simply the domestic price adjusted by the appropriate exchange rate.

Absolute Purchasing Power Parity: From the Law of One Price, we derive the Purchasing Power Parity (PPP) relation by aggregating across all commodities in each country. Absolute PPP states that the ratio of two countries' price indices is equal to the exchange rate of their respective currencies.

Real exchange rate: The real exchange rate is the ratio between the ratio of the two price indices and the exchange rate. When PPP holds, the real exchange rate is equal to one.

Relative PPP: The Relative version of PPP deals with price changes instead of levels; it states that, over a period of time, percentage changes in the exchange rate should be equal to the inflation differential between the two countries considered.

Classical version of PPP: According to the Classical version of the PPP, changes in the inflation differential between two countries are offset exactly by percentage changes in the exchange rate.

Efficient markets and PPP: If markets are efficient in the semi-strong sense, the exchange rate should reflect any changes in the inflation differential between the two countries. Today's spot rate, then, presumably includes all information available to forecast next period's spot rate, adjusted for any anticipated inflation.

Conceptual and empirical issues surrounding PPP: Some of the questions regarding PPP include: Is PPP a full theory? Is PPP a bilateral or multilateral framework? What is the appropriate price index? What about transportation costs and other obstacles to trade?

***The Economist's* Big Mac Index**: The Big Mac Index is an application of the Law of One Price to the Big Mac. The question asked: Is the price of the Big Mac the same around the world when we adjust for the exchange rate and the country's purchasing power? If not, currencies are classified as undervalued or overvalued.

Interest Rate Parity Theorem: The Interest Rate Parity Theorem (IRPT) states that the differential between foreign and domestic nominal interest rates is (approximately) equal in equilibrium to the forward premium (discount).

Conceptual and empirical issues regarding the IRPT: The IRPT framework has received numerous criticisms, including the following: It does not hold when distortions exist in financial markets; There is no consideration of risk; and, Instruments sold in various countries may not be perfect substitutes.

The Fisher Effect: The (risk-free) nominal interest rate is equal to the real interest rate plus the rate of expected inflation

The International Fisher Effect: According to the International Fisher Effect (IFE), the interest differential between the two countries is equal to the expected percentage change in the exchange rate.

Forward rate market theory of exchange rate expectations: The fourth equilibrium condition (PPP, IRPT, and IFE being the other three) states that today's forward rate, maturing N days ahead, is an unbiased predictor of the future (time N) spot exchange rate.

Integration of the parity conditions in equilibrium: When the financial system reaches equilibrium, the interest rate differential between two countries would be equal to the forward premium/discount, which would be equal to the percentage expected exchange rate change, which would be equal to the inflation differential.

Web Exercises

W1. Go to https://www.economist.com/news/2020/01/15/the-big-mac-index.

Comment on each of the following currencies' under/overvaluation versus the US dollar.

1. Argentina
2. Brazil
3. Euro area
4. India
5. Switzerland
6. United States

Questions and Problems

1. Define an efficient foreign exchange market. What are the characteristics of such a market? Explain the three forms of efficiency. How do efficient market characteristics and forms apply to the foreign exchange market?
2. In your opinion, does the concept of market efficiency apply to the following markets?

    a. The US dollar vs. Japanese yen market;
    b. The US dollar vs. Colombian peso market; and
    c. The US dollar vs. Chinese yuan rate

3. The text discusses a scenario where certain equilibrium conditions may be concurrently observed. What are the necessary assumptions for this simultaneous

occurrence to take place? Can you envision any factors or obstacles that would function to disrupt the equality between:

   a. The forward premium and the expected percentage change in the spot rate?
   b. The interest rate and expected inflation differentials? Explain your answers carefully.

4. Refer to the formulation of the absolute version of the real exchange rate. We noted that when the real exchange rate is equal to 1, PPP holds. What are the implications for the home currency's purchasing power when the real exchange rate is greater than 1? When it is less than 1? Explain carefully.
5. According to the text, relative PPP is expressed as the equality between the percentage change in the exchange rate and the inflation differential. Prove that this relation indeed holds. (Hint: Refer to the discussion of IRPT for the steps to be taken in your proof.)
6. Comment on the validity of this adage: "All currencies are alike. Owning one is just like owning any other." Do you agree with this statement? Explain your answer.
7. Use Figure 2.1A as the framework for your graph:

   a. Extend the parity line to the third quadrant and interpret your graph;
   b. Illustrate the relative version of PPP;
   c. Illustrate the International Fisher Effect;
   d. Illustrate the Forward Rate Theory of Exchange Rate Expectations; and
   e. Using a four quadrant framework, illustrate the (four) integrated equilibrium conditions.

8. Short-term funds are currently flowing out of the United States, raising concern among government and Federal Reserve officials. Describe your recommendation for dealing with the situation.
9. Assume that the three-month interest rate in the United States is 7%; the equivalent rate in Japan is 3%. The spot exchange rate is 110 yen per dollar.

   a. For interest rate parity to hold, what should the forward rate be?
   b. Assume that the forward rate is 130 yen per dollar instead of what you answered in part (a) above. What should the forward rate be now?

10. Now also assume that transactions are conducted at a cost of 1%. Are there any opportunities for arbitrage? Show graphically and describe the adjustments that would be observed as arbitrage takes place.
11. The GBP/USD rate was \$1.300 at the beginning of the year and \$1.500 at the end of the year. The inflation rates during the period were 10% for the US and 6% for the UK. Comment on the change in the real exchange rate.
12. Assume that the three-month rate of interest in Switzerland is 8% and in Germany 10%. The Swiss franc is at \$0.7081 and the US dollar is at €0.7451. What is the expected cross rate between the Swiss franc and the euro in three months? Explain.

13. Assume that the Japanese Yen is JPY102.58=USD1. The three-month forward is JPY102.50/USD. An investor decides to borrow in Japan for 2% and invest in the US for 5% over three months. Is this a sound decision?
14. "On August 4, 2014, the spot rate was JPY102.53=USD1. The three month forward was JPY102.5=USD1. On November 4, 2014, the spot is JPY108=USD1. Therefore, the forward rate is useless as a predictor of the future spot."
    Comment on the above statement made by the vice president of American National Bank.
15. The inflation rate is expected to be 2% next year in the United States and 5% in Canada. The US interest rate for the one year risk free security is 8%, while the current spot rate is Can$1.2=US$1.
    Assume that the system meets all the assumptions for the equilibrium conditions to hold. Find the Canadian interest rate, the forward premium, and the expected spot rate compatible with the above data.
16. According to *the Economist*, the average price of a Big Mac in the US in January 2020 was USD5.67; it was JPY390 in Japan. The exchange rate in January 2020 was 110.04 (yen per dollar). Is the yen overvalued or undervalued vis-à-vis the US dollar? By how much? Show your work.
17. JD Martinez, a foreign exchange trader at Back Bay Bank, is exploring interest arbitrage possibilities. JD wants to invest $5,000,000, or its yen equivalent at the current spot rate, in a covered interest arbitrage between US dollars and Japanese yen. He is facing the following exchange rate and interest rate quotes:

Assumptions	Value	Yen Equivalent
Funds available	$5,000,000	593,000,000
360-day forward (USD/JPY)	117.80	
360-day Japanese yen interest rate	3.400%	

    a. For the Interest Rate Parity Theorem to hold, what should the one-year US interest rate be?
    b. Now assume that the US interest rate is 4.80%. Is there an opportunity for JD to move funds from one market to the other in order to generate extra risk-free returns?
    c. Assuming that JD uncovers arbitrage opportunities, what adjustments are going to take place to eliminate their arbitrage opportunities (bring the system back to equilibrium)?
    d. Using a graph, show which investment (US or Japan) is preferred before arbitrage commences.

Selected References

Abuaf, N., and P. Jorion. 1990. Purchasing Parity in the Long Run. *Journal of Finance*. 45: 157–74.

Adler, M. and Lehmann, B. 1983. Deviations from Purchasing Power Parity in the Long Run. *Journal of Finance*. 38, 1471–1487.

Booth, G.G. and Koveos, P. 1989. Purchasing Power Parity: A Reexamination of Prediction Errors. *Advances in Financial Planning and Forecasting*. Edited by C. F. Lee, Volume 3. Bingley, UK: JAI Press/Emerald Press, 251–275.

Brealy, R., and S. Myers. 1984. *Principles of Corporate Finance*. New York: McGraw-Hill Book Company.

Economist. 2020. The Big Mac Index. Accessed at https://www.economist.com/news/2020/01/15/the-big-mac-index. Downloaded January 25, 2020.

Fisher, I. 1896. Appreciation and Interest. *Publications of the American Economic Association* XI (August): 1–100.

Francis, J. C. 1986. *Investments*. New York: McGraw-Hill Book Company.

Frankel, Jacob A., and Harry G. Johnson. 1978. *The Economics of Exchange Rates: Selected Studies*. Reading, Massachusetts: Addison-Wesley Publishing Company.

Friedrich, K. 1974. *International Economics*. New York: McGraw-Hill Company.

Giddy, I. H. 1979. An Integrated Theory of Exchange Rate Equilibrium. In *International Financial Management: Theory and Application,* edited by D. R. Lessard. Boston: Warren Gorham and Lamont. 167–78.

Glick, R. 1989. How Good is PPP? *Weekly Letter*. Federal Reserve Bank of San Francisco, June 9, 1989.

Humphrey, T. M., and R. E. Keleher. 1982. *The Monetary Approach to the Balance of Payments, Exchange Rates, and World Inflation*. New York: Praeger Publishers.

Jacque, L. 1978. *Management of Foreign Exchange Risk*. Lexington, MA: Lexington Books.

Katseli-Papaefstratiou, L. T. 1979. The Reemergence of the Purchasing Power Parity Doctrine in the 1970s. *Special Papers in International Economics*, No. 13, Princeton University.

Koveos, P., and B. Seifert. 1985. Purchasing Power Parity and Black Markets. *Financial Management* (Autumn): 40–46.

Lessard, D. R., ed. 1979. *International Financial Management. Theory and Application*. Boston: Warren Gorham and Lamont.

Levich, R. M. 1979. The Efficiency of Markets for Foreign Exchange: A Review and Extension. In *International Financial Management: Theory and Application,* edited by D. R. Lessard. Boston: Warren Gorham and Lamont. 243–76.

Officer, L. H. 1982. *Purchasing Power Parity and Exchange Rates*. Greenwich, CT: JAI Press, Inc.

Roll, R. 1979. Violations of Purchasing Power Parity and their Implications for Efficient International Commodity Markets. In *International Finance and Trade,* by M. Sarnat, M and G. Szego, editors. Vol. I. Cambridge, MA: Ballinger. 133–76.

Voeller, J. 1981. *Purchasing Power Parities in International Comparisons. Mathematical Systems in Economics*. 72. Cambridge, Massachusetts: Oelgeschlager, Gunn & Hain Publishers.

Worthington, P. R. 1991. Investment, GNP, and Real Exchange Rates. *Economic Perspectives*. Chicago: Federal Reserve Bank of Chicago (July/August): 2–10.

Chapter 4

The International Monetary System

Overview of Chapter Material

We now turn our attention to the overall environment in which exchange rates are determined: the international monetary system (IMS). The IMS is an important component of the global business environment in general. The smoothness with which countries carry out their financial relationships is a barometer of the quality of the international system. Chapter 4 examines the various forms that the IMS has taken over the years and the distinguishing elements of each form. It also describes the principle agencies and agreements supporting international trade and finance. Finally, it discusses important developments of the system and their implications.

After Studying This Chapter, You Will Be Able To

- Understand the importance and evolution of the international monetary system
- Identify the types and objectives of government intervention
- Discuss the nature and functions of agencies and agreements supporting international monetary and trade relations
- Analyze recent developments in regional monetary integration

Chapter Outline

I. Introduction to the International Monetary System
II. Types of Exchange Rate Systems
III. Exchange Rate Intervention
IV. Institutions Supporting International Trade and Finance
V. A Historical Overview of the International Monetary System
VI. From Finance to Trade: GATT and WTO
VII. Regional Arrangements
VIII. Managerial Implications
IX. Summary

I. Introduction to the International Monetary System

1. Definition of the International Monetary System

According to Cooper (1987), the international monetary system refers to the set of "rules and conventions that govern the financial relations between countries." Selection of the appropriate system has been the root of conflicting positions for as long as countries have had trade and financial relations with each other. The debate still fuels disagreement among nations and intense arguments inside national boundaries. As the world enters a stage of increasing interdependence and cooperation, the issue remains of considerable significance to policy makers as well as all other participants and elements of the global financial architecture.

The international monetary system contains various components. The two critical components we will be discussing in this text are the international exchange rate system, which includes the rules pertaining to currencies, and the international financial system, which includes the cross-border flow of financial instruments (bonds, stocks, etc.). Cooper distinguishes among systems in terms of the following:

1. The role of exchange rates. The variety of exchange rate systems observed by a single country or a country group has included:
    a. Fixed-rate.
    b. Free float.
    c. Managed float.
    d. Adjustable peg.
2. The reserve asset used. Countries have used one or more assets for reserve purposes. These assets have included:
    a. Gold.
    b. Silver.
    c. Special Drawing Rights.
    d. Individual (or multiple) national currencies.
3. The extent of control of international capital movements. Capital flows in a particular system may be:
    a. Free.
    b. Controlled by the government.
    c. Conducted through alternative markets.

There are other relevant characteristics:

4. The key currency utilized by the system. For example, the British pound served as the key currency during the first part of the twentieth century. The US dollar replaced the British pound after the 1944 Bretton Woods Conference.

5. The extent of coverage of the international monetary system. Is the system global in coverage, super-regional (covering more than one region), or regional? For example, the European Monetary System may be viewed as regional (European) within the global monetary system.

2. Why the International Monetary System Matters

As we already indicated, the international monetary system (IMS) establishes the set of rules governing a country's international relations. A well-functioning international monetary system facilitates exchange of goods, services, and capital. The IMS has a large impact on how business is conducted across national borders. All participants of the global business system need to know the specifics of the system in order to function effectively. For example, individuals who travel to, invest in, or have a business relationship with someone in another country must possess a good understanding of the rules of the country's economic relations with the rest of the world. Is the country's currency convertible? What approach is the country following in setting the value of its currency? Can foreign citizens bring capital into the country? Businesses, governments, international organizations, and any entity doing business with another country must also have understanding of these issues.

The importance of the international monetary system will become evident as we discuss the various topics included in this book: exchange rate determination, exchange rate forecasting, foreign exchange risk management, and bond and equity markets.

We now turn our attention to a more detailed description of the nature of the international monetary system in general and the international exchange rate system specifically.

Concept Questions

1. What is the international monetary system?
2. What are the distinguishing characteristics of international monetary systems according to Cooper?

II. Types of Exchange Rate Systems

One of the most important characteristics distinguishing among monetary systems is the type of exchange rate system used. The fixed-versus-flexible-rates debate has been especially noteworthy and prevalent through the history of the international monetary system. In this section, we examine the major characteristics of selected exchange rate systems. It should be noted that different organizations and scholars might use slightly different exchange rate system designations from those used in this text. For an alternative list, you could consult the International Monetary Fund's *Annual Report on Exchange Arrangements and Exchange Restrictions* (2014).

1. Fixed Exchange Rate Systems

Fixed exchange rate systems provide for the exchange rate between two currencies to have a fixed value as specified by governments. There are many examples of such systems, with some interesting ones found in the several versions of the international gold standard.

1.1. The Classical Gold Standard

The classic gold standard commits a government to exchange gold at specified prices in terms of its own currency. It is a fixed-rate system that uses gold as the reserve currency. All participating countries make a similar commitment, so the values of all currencies are expressed in terms of a certain quantity of gold and, therefore, in terms of each other. Changes in the exchange rate between currencies occur as one country alters the rate of exchange between its currency and gold.

Figure 4.1 shows the implications of the classical gold standard when two governments have committed to buy and sell gold at specific rates in terms of their own currencies. The most familiar example is between the US dollar and the pound sterling in terms of gold. If these rates stood at \$35 and £14 per fine ounce of gold, the \$/£ rate would be \$2.50 = £1, which is called the "mint parity rate." The actual price paid for gold is adjusted by an amount reflecting the costs involved in buying and selling gold, such as insurance or shipping. If these costs (denoted as X in Figure 4.1) amount to \$.05 per conversion, then the upper bound would be \$2.55 and the lower bound \$2.45. A trader interested in buying British pound sterling would use the foreign exchange market if the exchange rate were below \$2.55. If it were higher than \$2.55, the trader would buy gold with dollars in the United States, ship the gold to Britain, and exchange it for sterling there. The higher level, then, is not sustainable. Arbitrage also ensures that a level below \$2.45 is not sustainable.

1.2. The Gold Exchange Standard

The classical gold standard, in effect in the 1870s, ended with the advent of World War I in 1914. After the War, the world financial system remained in flux. England, followed by the

Figure 4.1 The Classic Gold Standard.

Netherlands, established a gold bullion standard in 1925, and the US returned to the gold standard by 1919. The dollar began to replace the pound sterling as the primary international currency. Stability remained elusive, however, as the world endured the effects of the Great Depression and World War II.

The gold exchange standard established after World War II also offered a fixed exchange rate framework. Currency values were defined in terms of a certain weight of gold, although they were not convertible into gold, with the sole exception of the reserve currency. The post-WWII gold exchange standard established the U.S. dollar as the reserve currency. Participating governments agreed to keep exchange rates within indicated ranges, which required them to buy and sell foreign exchange as pressures on the currencies drove them away from the agreed-upon level.

2. Free Float Exchange Rate System

In a free float system, unfettered interplay between foreign exchange market supply and demand forces determines exchange rates. Any shift in these forces will cause equilibrium to change. As participants receive information about new developments, they react by buying and selling currencies and thus establishing a new equilibrium position.

The strict condition of "free interplay" between supply and demand makes the free float system a rarity in the evolution of the international monetary system. The period of the early 1920s, when the British pound, the French franc, the Italian lira, and other currencies were floating, probably comes as close as any other to exemplifying free float. Political and economic realities more often force countries to stray from the "free market" rule and, instead, manage the path of their currencies.

3. Managed Float Exchange Rate System

When authorities interfere with supply and demand forces to generate a more desirable exchange rate, the system is characterized as managed float. The managed float is a hybrid between flexible and fixed systems. The flexible nature of the system is the central component of the system, but government decisions still play a role in setting currency values. The dollar, for example, reached a high in February 1985; it subsequently started falling in a manner that caused concern for the countries known at the time as the Group of Seven (G7): Britain, Canada, France, Germany, Italy, Japan, and the United States. The G7 (today's G8 after inclusion of Russia) representatives met in the Louvre and agreed to stabilize currency values through appropriate macroeconomic policies and foreign exchange market intervention.

Following the Louvre Agreement, central banks did indeed intervene by purchasing dollars in the foreign exchange market. During 1987, for example, dollars held by (West) Germany as international reserves increased from $52 billion to almost $80 billion; Japan's dollar reserves increased from about $42 billion to $81 billion. Italy, the United Kingdom, and Canada also increased their foreign currency reserves, while the United States and France experienced a slight decrease.

4. Adjustable Peg

An adjustable peg exchange rate system establishes limits around an official exchange rate, with temporary deviations from the official rate financed by a country's central banking authority. When these deviations reach a level considered excessive by participating countries, the system is said to have entered a phase of "fundamental disequilibrium." The authorities abandon temporary financing of the country's external position and revalue or devalue the country's currency.

Proponents of an adjustable peg system claim it combines most of the advantages of fixed and floating exchange rate systems. Opponents call the system both rigid and unstable, subject to the disadvantages of the extreme systems.

5. Additional Arrangements

5.1. Selective Peg

A smaller country may fix (peg) the value of its currency to that of a larger country, usually a major trading partner. This practice mitigates undue fluctuations in a country's economy. For example, some Caribbean and Central American countries peg their currency to the US dollar. Similarly, many Gulf States peg their currencies to the dollar since payments for their main export, oil, are in US dollars.

In addition to traditional pegging, there are two variations of pegging practices: currency boards and dollarization.

5.2. Currency Boards

In a currency board arrangement, the country maintains a fixed exchange rate and commits to exchanging its own currency for a fixed quantity of a "hard" currency, such as the dollar or the euro. To meet its obligations, the country must amass sufficient quantities of foreign exchange reserves. Countries such as Indonesia have adopted currency boards in order to improve their international credibility, lower their inflation, and keep interest rates low. Adoption of a currency board, however, implies holding adequate international reserves whose opportunity cost may be significant; it also hinders the central bank's ability to pursue independent monetary policy, or even provide liquidity to the economy when domestic economic conditions so dictate (Spiegel, 1998).

5.3. Dollarization and Cocirculation

The concept of dollarization is similar to that of a currency board in terms of the country's reliance on a foreign currency in order to attain international credibility and monetary stability. Specifically, dollarization means that a foreign currency is used for transactions, investment, or reserve purposes by private and public sectors in a country. Dollarization is usually measured by the ratio of foreign currency deposits to total bank deposits. Latin American countries and former Soviet Union countries have traditionally been highly dollarized, with the ratio being between 30% and 70%. The degree of dollarization may vary from country to country. How "dollarized" a country is depends on a number of factors, such as the strength of national institutions (the legal system, for example), interest rate differentials between instruments denominated in terms of the home versus those denominated in terms of the foreign currency, inflation, or the general level of confidence of the public in the government and the national currency. Dollarization can be "official" or "unofficial." The former implies that the country has officially made a foreign currency as the preferred legal tender. The latter implies that citizens of a country prefer to keep their savings in terms of a foreign currency even though the foreign currency is not legal tender. Ecuador, for example, has a 100% dollarized economy. In Latin American countries, dollarization (foreign currency deposits to total deposits) has in general decreased since the 1990s but still remains significant (Uruguay: 88%; Bolivia: 87%; Peru: 68%). On the other hand, Argentina's dollarization degree has declined from 74% in 2001 to 4% in 2004 (Alvarez-Plata and Garcia-Herrero, September 2007; for expanded discussion on dollarization, see Berg and Borensztein, 2000).

In smaller countries, Bermuda being one example, the US dollar performs the same functions as the national currency, the Bermudian dollar. This system is referred to as cocirculation (Cartas, March 2010).

5.4. Dual or Multiple Markets

When countries put controls on the holdings of their currencies and on capital flows, multiple markets may develop in an effort to circumvent these controls. In addition to government restrictions, multiple markets may develop as developing countries are experiencing high inflation or other weakening of their economies; such markets may also develop when there is a lack of confidence in government policies or even when countries have failed to adjust their peg towards a major currency. Although these markets are illegal in some countries, the authorities usually tolerate them. They are sometimes referred to as "black" markets. The difference between the black market and official exchange rate is termed the black market premium; the premium can vary even within the country. A traveler taking a cab from the airport to the hotel might be given 100 pesos to the dollar. In the hotel, the rate may be 110 pesos. It may be 90 pesos at the beach. Although unsettling to the traveler, this variation reveals the ability of markets to reflect their environment.

The prevalence of black markets has diminished since the advent of the recent globalization experience. However, black markets have not disappeared completely. A *Wall Street Journal* article, for example, reported that Argentina's black market peso weakened prior to election, with the black market premium increasing by 20 centavos and bringing the value of the dollar to ARS10.10 (www.wsj.com; October 22, 2013/ Argentina's Black-Market Peso Weakens ahead of election. Downloaded 10/13/13). Black markets are also today found in Egypt, Iran, and Venezuela.

Concept Questions

1. What is a fixed exchange rate system?
2. Distinguish between the classical gold standard and the gold exchange standard.

3. State the differences between free and managed float.
4. What is a currency board? What are its implications?

III. Exchange Rate Intervention

Following the 2014 Ukraine Crisis, the sanctions western countries imposed on Russia, and sliding oil prices, the ruble weakened to the point that the Russian government considered it necessary to spend $1.75 billion over a three-day period in early October to support the currency. Up to that point, the Russian Central Bank had allowed the ruble to fluctuate within a range considered acceptable. Pressure on the currency, however, forced the government to both intervene in the foreign exchange market and widen the ruble range (Ostroukh, 2014).

The above is not an isolated example of central bank intervention in the foreign exchange market. Governments, through their monetary authorities, intervene in the market to accomplish a number of objectives. They may want to achieve certain values for their currencies, or they may be interested in minimizing currency variability. The period of an intervention may vary from brief to long term. Depending on its objective, intervention may be characterized as neutral, leaning against the wind, or unofficial pegging. According to the approach used, intervention also may be monetary, or "non-sterilized," or non-monetary, or "sterilized."

1. Zero Intervention/Free Float

When a currency is allowed to float freely, the country does not need to use its international reserves to support the value of its currency. As the currency fluctuates, international reserves remain stable.

2. Neutral Intervention

The objective of neutral intervention is to mitigate very short-term (such as daily) fluctuations in a country's currency. Since the government is not concerned with long-term trends, this type of intervention by itself should have no significant effect on a country's holdings of international reserves.

3. Leaning Against the Wind

At times, a currency may face pressure to change its value. The authorities may then intervene in order to avert or at least delay the inevitable adjustment. International reserves in this case will decline while the currency is being supported. After some point, however, the government discontinues its support program and reserves start stabilizing, although lower than their initial level.

4. Unofficial Pegging

Unofficial pegging in an environment of generalized floating refers to a single country following a policy of support of its currency. At least as long as its international reserves allow, the country maintains its currency's value at or around a target value.

5. Alternative Approaches to Intervention: Monetary, or Non-Sterilized, Intervention Versus Non-monetary, or Sterilized

To maintain the relationship between the US dollar and the British pound, the Bank of England (the country's central bank) might buy dollars from a British bank and credit the bank's reserve position in British sterling pounds. This increases the excess reserves of the English banking system and expands its lending capacity. Interest rates in England thereby decline, leading to a capital flow out of the country. US securities become more attractive to international investors, thereby leading to an increase in the demand for US securities and for US dollars. The dollar, then, appreciates. This approach is also called monetary, or "non-sterilized."

The effect of intervention on the US dollar will be much smaller if the British government decides to "sterilize" its operations. The government, that is, may engage in sales of domestic securities through open-market operations. A shift in the composition of bank portfolios toward domestic securities bolsters bank reserves. This eventuality (more domestic and fewer foreign securities than before) signals adjustments and possible exchange rate changes. These changes should be smaller than the exchange rate changes under monetary intervention.

6. Intervention and Exchange Rates: Channels of Influence

Under a managed float system, countries intervene in the foreign exchange market to accomplish their various objectives. According to the International Monetary Fund's (IMF) 1974 Annual Report, a country that is a member of the Fund with a floating exchange rate should intervene on the foreign exchange market as necessary to prevent or moderate sharp and disruptive fluctuations from day to day and from week to week in the exchange value of its currency (IMF. *Annual Report, Guideline 1*, p. 113; http://www.imf.org/external/pubs/ft/ar/archive/pdf/ar1974.pdf; downloaded 7/31/2014).

Central bank intervention may affect the value of the currency through one or more channels, including

- Shifting of the demand or supply curve for the currency as a result of direct buying or selling by the monetary authority.
- Changing the expectations of other market participants as they realize the central bank's involvement. Central bank intervention in the dollar market, for example, may be interpreted as a sign of lower future variability of the currency.
- Increasing the flow of information about the market.
- Changing the currency portfolios of market participants.
- Signaling international monetary coordination to the market.

The effectiveness of central bank intervention in maintaining exchange rates at a certain level is difficult to assess, especially because the formal intervention of the sort that we described is at times interwoven with informal intervention. There also exist complicated relationships between exchange rate policy and monetary policy that are hard to disentangle. The concern of monetary authorities for currency values has at times influenced domestic policy decisions made by the US Federal Reserve, the Bank of England, and the Bank of Japan.

Foreign exchange market intervention is a complex activity, which, as we already indicated in our discussion of Currency Wars, shows no sign of abating in the future.

The differences between the two intervention approaches are illustrated through Table 4.1. Assuming that the monetary authority's net worth is zero, then:

$$\text{Net Foreign Assets (NFA)} + \text{Domestic Assets (DA)} = \text{Monetary Base (MB)} \quad (4.1)$$

When the government intervenes to support the foreign currency, it buys foreign assets with its own currency. The balance sheet effect will be an increase in net foreign assets offset by an increase in monetary base:

$$\Delta NFA = \Delta MB \quad (4.2)$$

Under non-sterilized intervention, the country's monetary base changes by the amount of the change in foreign assets. This initial change will set off a multiple expansion on the money supply.

Under sterilized intervention, the government elects to offset the effect on the monetary base by changing the amounts of other domestic assets. Then:

$$\Delta MB = -\Delta DA \quad (4.3)$$

In the US, the Treasury, in consultation with the Fed, is responsible for foreign exchange market intervention. The New York Fed executes US intervention policy. To buy foreign exchange, the US uses Federal Reserve holdings and the Exchange Stabilization Fund of the Treasury. The stated purpose of US intervention is to counter disorderly market conditions by slowing drastic exchange rate changes and signaling the view of the US government about the relationship between actual and equilibrium exchange rates (www.newyorkfed.org/aboutthefed). In recent years, however, the US has intervened infrequently. For example, the

Assets	Liabilities
• Net Foreign Assets (NFA) ◦ Gold ◦ Foreign exchange ◦ SDR ◦ Net position in IMF • Domestic Assets (DA) ◦ Government securities ◦ Loans to depository institutions ◦ Other	• Monetary Base (MB) ◦ Currency ◦ Reserves

Table 4.1 Monetary Authority Balance Sheet

Adapted from Humpage, O.F., 1991

US intervened eight different days in the first eight months of 1995; from the last part of 1995 until the end of 2006, however, the US intervened only twice.

Concept Questions

1. Distinguish between neutral and leaning against the wind intervention.
2. Differentiate between monetary and non-monetary intervention.
3. Explain how intervention can influence foreign exchange rates.

IV. Institutions Supporting International Trade and Finance

The foundations of the current international monetary system were put in place in Bretton Woods, New Hampshire toward the end of World War II (July 1944). Participants in the Bretton Woods Conference and signatories to the synonymous agreement sought to avert such disruptive developments as those of the period after World War I by designing more cooperative exchange rate policies. They agreed that these policies had to be backed by a workable framework that would promote exchange rate stability and the reserves necessary to maintain that stability.

The conference culminated in a series of related agreements that were to be implemented through establishment of the International Monetary Fund (IMF) and the World Bank.

1. The International Monetary Fund (IMF)

1.1. The IMF's Structure and Mission

At the time of its formation at the 1944 conference, the IMF had 44 nation members. By 1990, the IMF had 152 members; the number was up to 189 by 2019. The original objectives of the IMF included

1. Promoting exchange rate stability;
2. Providing members with resources necessary to meet difficulties associated with external payments, thus shortening the magnitude and duration of balance of payments disequilibrium;
3. Helping members secure balance of payments financing from other sources by promoting measures that make countries more attractive risks to potential lenders;
4. Serving as a repository for the reserves of its members;
5. Providing a forum for international monetary cooperation;
6. Offering members consultation on matters of economic policy; and
7. Conducting research and generating analysis of global, international, and national economic developments (http://www.imf.org/external/np/exr/facts/glance.htm).

To amass reserves for lending to members, the Fund follows a quota system. Member countries receive a quota commensurate with their contributions to the Fund. Quotas for individual members are determined based on factors such as their relative ability to contribute and the importance of international trade in these countries. As originally established, the formula specifically considered variables such as national income, gold and dollar balances, average imports, variability of exports, and ratio of exports to national income. Among members, the US has the single highest quota share and voting rights (17–18% of the total). Quotas are reviewed periodically and adjusted as appropriate.

The IMF can also borrow to increase its resource base. It provides financial assistance to members by purchasing currencies. Members use their currencies to buy other currencies and then repurchase their currencies at the time of repayment.

Members using the resources of the Fund are expected to follow certain types of policies, a practice referred to as conditionality. The term means simply that the use of IMF resources will be compatible with the nature of the imbalances the member faces. Conditionality guidelines promote consistency and efficiency in the use of resources by the members. One guideline encourages the establishment of appropriate policies by a member country as soon as possible following recognition of a balance of payments problem. Another guideline states that countries must meet certain conditions before an arrangement with the IMF can be approved.

1.2. Financial Assistance to Members

The terms and availability of IMF financing have been liberalized over the years. Since 1980, the Fund has been able to enlarge its scope of financing activities through appropriate private market borrowings. Depending on the nature of the problem encountered, a country may take advantage of a number of policies and facilities available. For example, in 2012–2013, the IMF assisted some European countries (Cyprus, Greece, Ireland, and Portugal) to receive financial assistance through

- Stand-by arrangements (SBA). Arrangements put in place in 1952 make it possible for a member nation to receive appropriation of funds in advance of the actual time of use.
- Extended Fund Facility (EFF). This fund facility offers countries assistance in dealing with difficulties arising from structural factors, such as production deficiencies or from a weakness in the country's external debt that impedes a country's efforts to establish appropriate policies.
- Flexible Credit Line (FCL). This credit line is used to assist countries for the purpose of crisis prevention and resolution.
- Precautionary and Liquidity Line (PLL). The PLL is used for crisis intervention and resolution for countries with strong implementation record.

Countries can also get financing from other IMF sources, including

- Structural Adjustment Facility (SAF). The facility provides funds to low income developing member nations encountering long-term balance of payments problems. Funding allows members to formulate medium-term macroeconomic and structural adjustment programs.

- Enhanced Structural Adjustment Facility (ESAF). The ESAF has objectives and structure that are similar to those of the SAF. The differences between the two facilities pertain to provisions for access, monitoring, and funding.
- Compensatory Financing Facility. Established in 1963, compensatory financing is designed primarily to assist exporters of primary products or other exporters facing balance of payments.

The IMF's efforts to assist economies in trouble have not always been well received. Restrictive terms included in rescue packages have required politically unpopular tight budgets and resulted in high unemployment rates. The Fund, however, became a critical player in the global fight against crises and an indispensable guardian of the stability of the international monetary system.

1.3. Special Drawing Rights, 1970

Ongoing balance of payments problems facing various countries generated the need for extra reserves. To provide some relief, the General Agreement to Borrow (GAB) was reached in October of 1962. Under the GAB, the Group of Ten (Belgium, Britain, Canada, France, Germany, Italy, Japan, the Netherlands, Sweden, and the United States) committed $6 billion to help countries deal with international financial problems.

However, the need for international reserves persisted. To satisfy this need the IMF allocated additional reserves, called Special Drawing Rights (SDRs). SDRs are book entries credited to the accounts of the IMF members. Allocation takes place by quota, with the first allocation on January 1, 1970, for SDR 3.5 billion. Exactly one year later, a second allocation of over SDR 2.9 billion was made. As of 1991, six different allocations had been made totaling SDR 21.4 billion. By April 30, 1991, SDR holdings amounted to 3.6% of the total non-gold reserves of the IMF member countries.

Creation of SDRs was but one indication that the stock of international reserves at the time was just not sufficient to provide for smooth functioning of the system. In addition, speculative capital flows that were facilitated by the fixed-rates regime were pressuring the system. The SDR allocations since 1970 represent permanent additions to international liquidity. SDRs can be used to acquire foreign exchange, to settle financial obligations, and to lend or donate. They also may be used for spot, forward, or swap transactions. SDRs must be used in certain operations and transactions with the IMF, such as paying for the use of Fund resources. Despite some restrictions (SDRs cannot be used to acquire gold in swap or forward transactions), use is not subject to conditionality provisions. SDRs, then, offer a flexible means of enhancing the international reserves of IMF membership. Holdings of SDRs can be income generators, as the IMF pays interest to members on their holdings. It also charges against allocations at an interest rate changing weekly.

When the SDR was first introduced, value was set at SDR 35 per one ounce of gold. From 1974 until the end of 1980, the value of the SDR was determined as the weighted average of the daily value of a basket of sixteen currencies. Each currency, with the exception of the US dollar, entered the valuation formula at a weight corresponding to the country's relative share in world exports during the 1972–1976 period. The dollar was given a weight of

33% in recognition of the special position of the US in the international financial and trade scene. On January 1, 1981, the basket used for valuation was reduced to five currencies: the Deutsche Mark with a weight of 19%; the French franc, Japanese yen, and pound sterling, each with a weight of 13%; and the US dollar with a weight of 42%. The weights changed after the introduction of the euro. In December 2010, the SDRs weights were as follows: the euro 37.4%, the yen 9.4%, the British pound 11.3%, and the US dollar 41.9%. On December 10, 2013, the SDR's price stood at $0.65, €0.89, and £1.07 (www.imf.org).

On October 1, 2016, the IMF's executive board recognized the Chinese renminbi as a freely usable currency. This determination, as well as China's rising role in the global economy, led to the inclusion of the renminbi in the SDR as the fifth currency. The weights of the currencies included in the new SDR are as follows: US dollar, 41.73%; euro, 30.93%; Chinese renminbi, 10.92%; Japanese yen, 8.33%; and, pound sterling, 8.09%. The weighted average of representative interest rates in the money markets of these five currencies is used to calculate the SDR interest rate. The SDR interest rate is the interest rate that the IMF charges to its members when they borrow from the Fund. (http://www.imf.org/external/np/fin/data/rms_mth.aspx?SelectDate=2017-08-31&reportType=CVSDR).

2. The World Bank Group

The World Bank Group (www.wb.org; also, see World Bank, 2015) comprises five agencies providing assistance to developing countries in order to

- End extreme poverty by decreasing the percentage of people living on $1.25 per day to 3% at maximum.
- Foster income growth and increase the overall quality of life of the bottom 40% for each country, thus bringing shared prosperity.

Membership in the World Bank is contingent upon membership in the IMF. The focus of the Bank, however, is emerging economies and economies in transition; the IMF, on the other hand, works with countries at any stage of their development. In 1944, twenty-eight countries committed to participation in the World Bank. As indicated below, membership has expanded considerably in the Bank's major components.

The World Bank Group is composed of the following:

1. The International Bank for Reconstruction and Development (IBRD). The IBRD came into existence with the IMF and started operations in 1946. It provides financing for long-term productive projects undertaken by developing countries. Membership in 2014 included 188 countries.
2. The International Development Association (IDA). The IDA began operations in 1961. Its objective is compatible with the World Bank's. The IDA, however, finances loans to the neediest of the members and does not charge them interest. As countries advance on the development ladder, they start dealing with the IRBD. Membership in 2014 included 184 countries.

   The IRBD and IDA comprise what we have traditionally referred to as the World Bank.

3. The International Finance Corporation (IFC). The IFC acts as a lender or investor in industrial projects, along with private investor groups that it helps bring together. Since its establishment in 1956, it has participated in many developments in international financing methods in developing countries. The IRBD and the IFC have also been active on the environmental front; they are globally the largest issuers of green bonds. Membership in 2014 included 180 countries.
4. The International Centre for Settlement of Investment Disputes (ICSID). This institution provides the framework for the settlement of legal disputes pertaining to transnational investments. It has operated since 1966, offering conciliation and arbitration facilities as well as data on foreign investment law. 2014 membership: 173 countries.
5. The Multilateral Investment Guarantee Agency (MIGA). The most recent institution of the World Bank Group was established in 1988 to promote the flow of capital to developing member nations. MIGA provides guarantees against non-commercial risks facing companies undertaking large capital-intensive foreign investments, especially in infrastructure. Membership in 2014 included 150 countries (World Bank, 2014).

3. The Newcomer: The Asian Infrastructure Investment Bank (AIIB) and the New Development Bank

Many emerging market (EM) countries have criticized the workings and effectiveness of the IMF and the World Bank, the twin organizations that came out of the Bretton Woods Agreement. China was one of the countries most vocal in their criticism of the USA's domination of the World Bank and Japan's domination of the Asian Development Bank. In October 2013, China initiated the establishment of the AIIB. Headquartered in Beijing, the new bank's mission is to finance infrastructure projects, such as railways and ports, in Asia. The AIIB has been well received, with fifty-seven countries becoming the Bank's founding members. To the dismay of the US, even traditional allies such as the UK, France, Germany, and the Philippines joined in.

China also initiated the establishment of the New Development Bank (NDB) in July 2014. Also called the BRICS Bank because of its BRICS country membership (Brazil, Russia, India, China, and South Africa), the Shanghai-headquartered financial institution will also be financing infrastructure projects.

The two new institutions are parts of China's "One Road, One Belt" strategy, aiming to recreate the historic Silk Road that connected China to the Mediterranean, Central Asia, the Middle East, and Europe.

4. The Bank for International Settlements (BIS)

BIS (www.bis.org) is described as a bank for central banks. Established in 1930 in Basel, Switzerland, BIS is the oldest of currently existing international financial bodies. Central banks are the primary owners/shareholders of BIS, holding about 85% of all shares, with the private sector holding the rest. In addition to paying dividends, BIS provides very similar banking services to those that commercial banks provide to their own clients. It conducts research on policy issues. BIS also promotes central bank cooperation in order to strengthen the soundness and stability of the international monetary system by setting standards for capital requirements. The primary force behind these changes has been the Basel Committee on Banking Supervision (BCBS), which was established in 1974.

In 1988, BCBS designed the Basel Accord (or Basel I), setting minimum capital standards for international banks. The Accord targeted minimization of credit risk. Standards were applied to banks in over one hundred countries, bringing about significant improvements in bank capital positions by requiring that banks with riskier assets hold more capital. Each bank's required capital, then, was calculated by breaking down its asset portfolio according to risk. Less capital was required for safer assets (with weights all the way to zero) and more for riskier assets (with weights up to 100).

A new capital adequacy measure, Basel II, was proposed in 1999 and implemented in the mid-2000s. It consisted of three "pillars:"

Pillar 1: *Minimum capital requirements.*

Pillar 1 entails consideration and calculation of minimum capital requirements based on

1. On- and off-balance sheet credit risk
2. Market risk
3. Operational risk

Pillar 2: *Supervisory review.*

To ensure compliance with capital requirements as defined in Pillar 1.

Pillar 3: *Market discipline.*

To increase transparency and information flow, financial institutions are required to disclose their capital.

The global financial crisis revealed that Basel I and Basel II were inadequate in preventing future crises. It therefore provided further impetus for regulation and risk management of the financial sector. Basel III adds to the previous accords by focusing on crisis aversion. The new 2013 Accord requires banks to hold more high-quality capital while being more stringent in the treatment of risk-weighted assets, protects shareholders against excessive leverage, and promotes asset liquidity. The regulatory structure designed to put Basel III into effect will vary from country to country, which will add to implementation time and complication. Thus, as illustrated in Table 4.2, Basel III will go into effect in 2022 and be phased in over five years at minimum (https://www.bis.org/bcbs/basel3.htm).

Given the magnitude and scope as well as the contagion effects of the global financial crisis, it is still too early to conclude whether the Basel Accords as a whole have succeeded. They have, however, brought about a new sense of accountability and risk-averse behavior that will hopefully contribute to a relatively stable international monetary system.

	Phases	2013	2014	2015	2016	2017	2018	2019
Capital	Leverage Ratio		Parallel run Jan 1 2013-Jan 1 2017 Disclosure starts Jan 1 2015				Migration to Pillar 1	
	Minimum Common Equity Capital Ratio	3.50%	4.00%		4.50%			**4.50%**
	Capital Conservation Buffer				0.63%	1.25%	1.88%	**2.50%**
	Minimum common equity plus capital conservation buffer	3.50%	4.00%	4.50%	5.13%	5.75%	6.38%	**7.00%**
	Phase-in of deductions from CET1*		20%	40%	60%	80%	100%	**100%**
	Minimum Tier 1 Capital	4.50%	5.50%		6.00%			**6.00%**
	Minimum Total Capital							
	Minimum Total Capital plus conservation buffer		8.00%		8.63%	9.25%	9.88%	**10.50%**
	Capital instruments that no longer qualify as non-core Tier 1 or Tier 2 capital		Phased out over a ten-year period beginning 2013					
Liquidity	Liquidity coverage ratio-minimum requirement			60%	70%	80%	90%	**100%**
	Net stable funding ratio						Introduce minimum standard	

Table 4.2 Basel III Phase-In Arrangements.

**Including amounts exceeding the limit for deferred tax assets (DTAs), mortgage servicing rights and financials.*

-- transition periods

Source: http://www.bis.org/bcbs/basel3/basel3_phase_in_arrangements.pdf Accessed on 6/4/19.

Concept Questions

1. What is the IMF? What does it do?
2. What is the World Bank? What are its functions?
3. What is the BIS? What are its main functions?
4. What are Basel I, Basel II, and Basel III? What is their significance?

V. Historical Overview: The Shaping of the International Monetary System

The 1944 Bretton Woods Agreement remains a significant development not only with respect to the direction that the international monetary system was to follow in the post-War economy, but also with respect to its structure. Bretton Woods gave its seal of approval to a system of many members and only one leader: the United States. Recognition of the United States as the system leader and of the US dollar as the principal instrument of international trade and finance was neither a surprising development nor an impulsive reaction at the time. It was the logical outcome of the political, military, and economic position occupied by the United States following WWII.

1. Bretton Woods

Bretton Woods established the key position of the U.S. dollar by allowing that currency alone the privilege of free convertibility into gold. This privilege, of course, necessitated that the United States hold reserves of gold, while the other signatories held dollar reserves. The parities of other currencies were fixed in terms of the dollar.

According to the 1944 system, each currency was allowed to fluctuate within a band of plus or minus 1% from the stated value. Pressure to change the exchange rate outside the band would be countered by central bank intervention. If a country's balance of payments situation were to dictate a change greater than 10% in its currency in relation to the dollar, the country was said to have reached a state of "fundamental disequilibrium," requiring its currency to be devalued or revalued. In September of 1949, for example, many of the European countries devalued their currencies; the Belgian franc was devalued by 12.3% while the British pound was devalued by 30.5%.

Devaluation of these currencies at a time when European currencies were not mutually convertible contributed to the global stature of the dollar. To facilitate the clearing of claims generated by European countries, the European Payments Union was formed in 1950. The European Economic Community (EEC) came into existence on January 1, 1958, and the Union ceased to function when convertibility was restored.

Critics challenging the status enjoyed by the dollar maintained that, since dollars were primarily held rather than readily exchanged by countries in need of reserves, the world was in fact financing the creation of a US balance of payments deficit and facilitating expansion of US interests. Apart from these distributional implications, the system was precarious for other reasons. The dollar was a reserve currency as well as an international medium of exchange. With the growing volume of international payments, more and more dollars were required. Yet, if the volume of dollars in circulation got out of hand, the reserve system would collapse—no one would want to accumulate a worthless or potentially worthless currency.

The relationship between gold and the dollar was an interesting and important linkage within the system. Maintenance of the $35 parity with gold was predicated on the assumption that sales of gold would be conducted only through official channels. To ensure that parity would be maintained, a group of seven countries (Belgium, Britain, Germany, Italy, the Netherlands, Switzerland, and the United States) formed the London Gold Pool in 1960. Other countries, such as France, were apprehensive to the point of buying large quantities of gold (Friedrich, 1974).

Meanwhile, the continuing US deficits were draining the country's gold reserves, culminating in abandonment of the gold pool by 1968. In its place, a two-tier, private, and official system was created, with the private market free to arrive at its dollar price of gold. The official rate remained at $35 until August 1971.

2. The Smithsonian Agreement: 1971

While the financing assistance afforded by introduction of the SDR was timely, it was not enough to relieve strains exerted on the system. Exchange rate adjustments had then been relatively infrequent, but in November 1967, Britain had to devalue its pound sterling by 14.3% in terms of the dollar (from $2.80 to $2.40) in response to payments deficits and losses of reserves. Pressures on the French franc and the Deutsche Mark became cause of sufficient concern to call a meeting of the Group of Ten in November of 1968 in Bonn. No action was taken at that time, but recurring German payments surpluses and speculative actions required that the mark be allowed to float. The floating of the mark lasted only for about a month in late 1969, ending by revaluation of the mark by 9.4% against the dollar (from $.25 to $.2732).

Experiments with floating rates in this period proved to be far from over. On May 31, 1970, the Canadian dollar was allowed to float to mitigate the impact of heavy capital flows to the United States. In May of 1971, Germany and the Netherlands floated their currencies, and Austria revalued. The United States was facing large payments deficits and losing its gold reserves, while other countries were accumulating huge dollar reserves. On August 15, 1971, as part of his New Economic Policy, President Nixon announced that the United States would no longer freely buy and sell gold for the settlement of international transactions. With the suspension of dollar convertibility and the flight from par values, the Bretton Woods Agreement lost two of its underpinnings.

A substantial reform of the international monetary system was underway. Fund members negotiated intensely as the major players supported alternative solutions. The United States, for example, had already placed a 10% surcharge on imports in order to protect its international position. The US also supported a substantial revaluation of the major European currencies and the Japanese yen. The Europeans and the Japanese, on the other hand, wanted the United States to withstand the worst of the adjustment by devaluing its own currency. To the United States, dollar devaluation opened the possibility of nullification by retaliatory devaluations among trading partners (Friedrich, 1974).

Negotiations lasted about four months. On December 18, 1971, the Group of Ten produced the Smithsonian Agreement, which provided for a realignment of the major currencies as the price of gold increased from $35 to $38. The bands around currency par values also were raised to plus or minus 2.25%, and the controversial US import surcharge was eliminated.

3. The "Snake in the Tunnel" and the "Worm": 1972

On April 24, 1972, a joint agreement was signed among members of the European Economic Community (Belgium, France, Italy, Luxembourg, the Netherlands, and West Germany) plus Britain, Denmark, Ireland, and Norway. It became known as the "snake in the tunnel" because it created a band within a band. Participating members agreed to limit the margin of fluctuation within their currency group to 2.25%, half the plus or minus 2.25% margin permitted under the Smithsonian. As a group, currencies could still float at 4.5% maximum margin with respect to other currencies. An even narrower margin of 1% was to be maintained between Belgium, Luxemburg, and the Netherlands; this agreement became known as "the worm in the snake in the tunnel."

4. Generalized Floating: Post-1973

The snake did not crawl long in its original form. On June 23, 1972, Britain left the group and allowed the pound to float freely. Italy and Switzerland also abandoned the Smithsonian Agreement. The former pursued a free market for its capital transactions, while the latter floated the franc in 1973. Meanwhile, the dollar was still facing downward pressures. In its support, foreign central banks, especially the Bundesbank, bought dollars at record-setting pace. On February 14, 1973, the inevitable occurred. The dollar was devalued by 10% with respect to gold, going from $38 to $42. About one month later, a period of generalized floating began as the European Community countries announced that their currencies would float jointly against the dollar.

The arrival of generalized floating came at a fortuitous time for the troubled world economy. In October of 1973, the price for Saudi Arabian crude oil was raised from about $3 per barrel to over $5 per barrel; further price increases took place in December. Because the United States was relatively less dependent on imported oil than Europe or Japan, in the short run this provided the United States with a competitive advantage. This advantage, in conjunction with the practice of paying for country oil bills in dollars, kept the dollar strong. The improving balance of payments situation and the ability of the US to recycle petrodollars, as the dollar balances held by the oil-exporting countries were termed, allowed elimination of the controls the US had placed on capital flows, such as the interest equalization tax, the foreign direct investment program, and the Fed's Foreign Credit Restraint Program. The official end of the fixed exchange rates period came in January 1976; the Jamaica Agreement demonetized gold as a reserve asset and signaled the beginning of the system whose major characteristics are still present today.

The Generalized Float was in essence a managed float system. As we saw from the discussion of currency wars, the demise of Bretton Woods did not imply the end of government intervention. Flexibility in currency values also brought about greater volatility. The period 1980–1985 witnessed an unprecedented rise in the value of the dollar. The major industrialized countries convened in the Plaza Hotel in September 1985 in New York City to produce the Plaza Agreement. Through multilateral intervention, the dollar lost considerable value. The dollar depreciated by 20% against the yen and 15% against the French franc and the German Deutsche Mark. The situation generated the need for more significant international cooperation, however, as the US was experiencing significant trade deficits. To stop or even slow down the dollar's downward spiral, the six major industrialized countries (Canada, France, Great Britain, Japan, the United States, and West Germany) convened in France in February 1987 to sign the Louvre Accord. The Louvre Accord included currency realignments as well as policy coordination among the signatory nations. The result was positive, as moderate stability was brought into the markets.

The advent of float went into effect primarily in major industrialized countries. Many smaller countries were reluctant to deviate from alternative systems, including currency boards and dollarization.

5. The 1976 Jamaica Agreement

The post-Bretton-Woods exchange rate system was formalized by the 1976 Jamaica Agreement. The agreement declared floating exchange rates acceptable but also allowed member

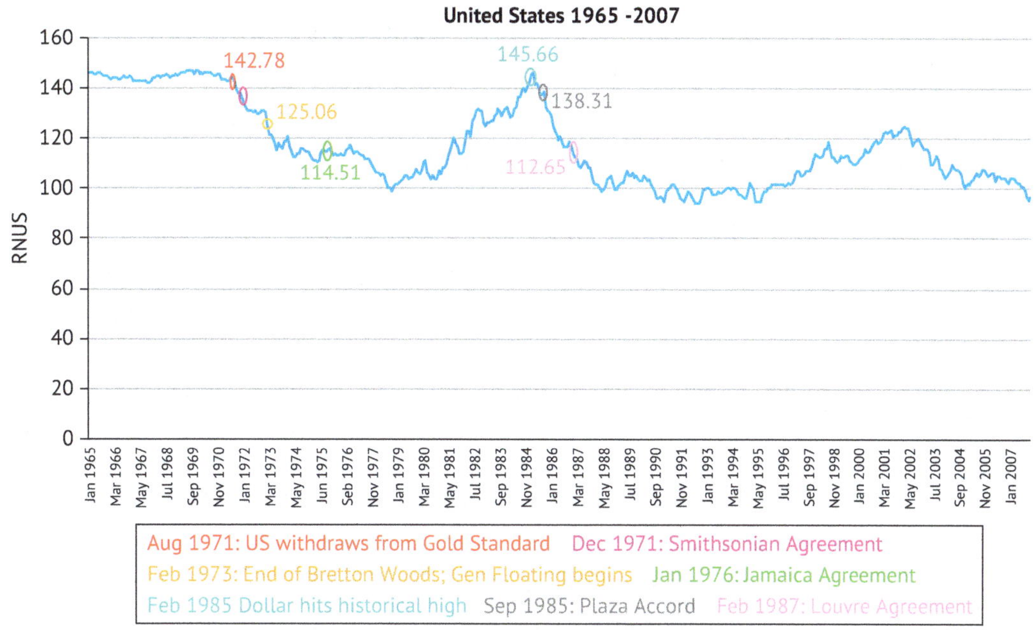

Figure 4.2 US Dollar Index, 1965–2007. Data from imf.org.

nations to protect their currencies against speculative attacks. The agreement also "demonetized" gold and increased member quotas to the IMF. The period of managed float had thus officially begun. In other words, the Jamaica Agreement confirmed the current exchange rate system (for more on the Jamaica Agreement, see De Vries, 1976, and Haberler, 1977).

The behavior of the US dollar index since 1965 and until the Global Financial Crisis is shown above (Figure 4.2). The position of the dollar versus other currencies prior to the various critical dates illustrates the rationale for the agreements signed among participating currencies.

6. Fixed Rates versus Flexible Rates

International monetary or exchange rate arrangements have indeed been a topic of interest, importance, and disagreement through the years and across and within national boundaries. The question: Is one system better than the other? The answer probably depends on the criteria used to assess each system. Some of these criteria include

1. Economic efficiency: How does the exchange rate system affects the allocation of resources?
2. Contribution to the entire spectrum of international relations: Does the system promote cooperation?
3. National independence: Does the system accommodate independence in national economic policy? And
4. Distribution of the gains arising from the regime: Do all participating countries benefit from the system?

Some of these criteria are often employed in the "fixed versus flexible rates" debate. Arguments in favor of fixed rates include

1. Fixing exchange rates mitigates uncertainty associated with international transactions.
2. Fixed rates protect against speculative runs.

Arguments in favor of flexible rates include

1. Flexible exchange rates are associated with currency changes (that is, depreciations or appreciations) that are not as large as those associated with devaluations or revaluations under fixed rates.
2. Exchange rate flexibility reduces the need for a large international reserve base.
3. Flexible rates improve market efficiency in that there is a quick reaction to any information. The rate setting is out of the inefficient hands of the government and instead in the efficient and objective invisible hands of the market.

7. Another Look at Exchange Rate Systems

Based on what we have covered in this chapter, we can classify the two dominant exchange rate systems according to some of the characteristics presented by Cooper at the beginning of the chapter. Table 4.3 illustrates the characteristics of the Bretton Woods system and the current system.

System Characteristic	Bretton Woods	Current
Monetary Anchor	Externally determined: Gold	Internally determined: Price Stability
Exchange Rates	Fixed (but adjustable)	Hybrid (floating for major currencies)
Key Currency	US Dollar (de facto)	US Dollar (less exclusive dominance)
Capital Mobility	Restricted	Hybrid (unrestricted for developed countries)

Table 4.3 Characteristics of the Monetary and Financial System

Source: Bank for International Settlements: 85th Annual Report, 2014–2015. June, 2015, p. 84.

Accessed at http://www.bis.org/publ/arpdf/ar2015_ec.pdf on 10/21/2016.

It is easy to see the differences between the two systems as well as their complicated nature. Their differences in characteristics are also shown through differences in behavior. As Figure 4.2 shows, the period up to 1971 shows very little volatility in the US dollar, in contrast to the volatility of the system following the collapse of Bretton Woods. The Bretton Woods system, however, was able to survive for less than three decades, while the current system is in its fifth decade and is operating in what admittedly is a much more challenging global financial environment.

8. The Impossible Trinity

So, what is a country to do? In international macro-finance, the usual answer is: it depends! Countries, that is, should prioritize their goals and strive to achieve what is most important to them. As many scholars point out (Obstfeld, Shamaugh, and Taylor, 2004; Mankiw, 2010), policymakers face what is called The Impossible Trinity, or The Trilemma or Triad. That is, there are three possible policy objectives:

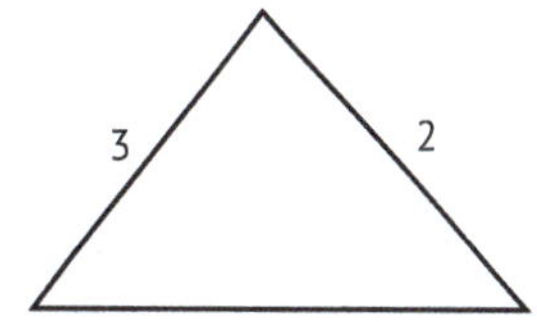

Figure 4.3 The Trilemma

1. Fixed (stable) exchange rate;
2. Free capital mobility; and
3. Independent monetary policy.

Unfortunately, all three of them cannot be accomplished at the same time (Figure 4.3).

Let's say that a country wishes to achieve Objective 1 (Fixed exchange rates and free capital mobility) but cannot also pursue independent monetary policy. Similarly, achieving Objective 2 implies giving up on fixed exchange rates; achieving Objective 3 implies imposition of capital controls. The explanation for The Trilemma goes back to what we learned in Chapter 2 about the relationship between interest rates and exchange rates and on the power of arbitrage. Therefore, if policymakers want to maintain fixed exchange rates and allow capital to move freely in and out of the country, interest rates will be affected; monetary policy is not independent anymore.

A definitive resolution to the fixed vs. flexible exchange rates issue will probably never be given. The stance taken by either side is to some extent based on the underlying assumptions about the ability of each system to withstand the shocks of the world economy. Would a fixed-rate system have been catastrophic during the global financial crisis of 2008–2010? The arguments also reflect the extent to which proponents trust either the government or the market. The only sure thing is that the international monetary system will continue to evolve and remain a controversial topic in international finance.

Concept Questions

1. What is the Bretton Woods Agreement? What is its significance?
2. Why do countries need international reserves?
3. What are SDRs? What comprises an SDR?
4. What is the Smithsonian Agreement? The Jamaica Agreement?
5. How would you characterize the current exchange rate system? How does the current system compare to the Bretton Woods system?
6. What is The Impossible Trinity?

VI. From Finance to Trade: The General Agreement on Tariffs and Trade (GATT) and the World Trade Organization (WTO)

1. The GATT

The GATT came into existence soon after the establishment of the IMF and the World Bank Group. GATT was the outcome of a meeting convened in Geneva in 1947 to consider the functioning of a new multilateral trade body, the International Trade Organization (ITO). Even though the United States was one of the twenty countries attending the meeting, the US Congress did not ratify the ITO. A new blueprint for international trade policy was therefore sought.

The GATT is structured in accordance with three fundamental principles:

- Reciprocity. When one country lowers a tariff imposed on the products it imports from another country, the other country should reciprocate.
- Non-discrimination or Most-Favored-Nation (MFN). According to this clause, no one of the agreement signatories may receive preferential treatment over the other signatories. All members, then, are to receive equal treatment.
- Transparency. The agreement prohibited the use of quantitative restrictions, such as quotas. These restrictions were to be replaced by tariffs, which are more transparent and whose level was not to increase.

The GATT functioned effectively as the general level of tariffs decreased substantially during the post-War period. Participating countries have met during successive rounds, listed in Table 4.4, to deal with particular issues and reaffirm their cooperative spirit. The list indicates where each round began; most of the negotiating, however, took place in subsequent Ministerial Conferences associated with each round. As the global economy became more complicated, though, trade issues became more contentious. The transition of economies from manufacturing to service and knowledge also necessitated a new perspective on economic cooperation. GATT's last round, the Uruguay, dealt with the treatment of intellectual property, trade-related investment measures, services, agriculture, textiles, and dispute resolution. The talks expired before full agreement was reached. The Uruguay Round culminated into the creation of the WTO.

Location	Year(s)
Geneva	1947
Annecy	1948
Torquay	1950
Geneva II	1956
Dillon	1960–61

Table 4.4 GATT/WTO Rounds

For more on the GATT and WTO, see http://www.wto.org/english/thewto_e/whatis_e/tif_e/fact4_e.htm.

Location	Year(s)
Kennedy	1964–72
Tokyo	1973–79
Uruguay	1986–1994: Establishment of the WTO
Doha	2001–2015

Table 4.4 *(Continued)*

2. The WTO

The existing GATT framework proved to be inadequate in dealing with these issues. So, after forty-seven years of precarious existence, GATT was replaced by the WTO. The WTO represented a organizational arrangement with greater standing than the GATT, since the GATT's status as an "agreement" often caused the US Congress to disregard its directives. The WTO also offered the promise of quicker resolution than the previous system and coverage of a wider range of international trade deals, including services, trade-related investment, and intellectual property. The WTO has multiple objectives (www.wto.org), including to

- Settle disputes and reduce trade tensions.
- Support health and the environment.
- Cut the cost of doing business internationally.
- Give the weak a stronger voice.
- Cut living costs and raise living standards.

Despite its lofty goals, the WTO has not fully succeeded in securing the cooperation of its 159 members. The latest round, the Doha, was stalled for many years. The 2013 meeting in Bali, aimed at "trade facilitation," focusing on cutting the costs, time, and procedures required to move goods across borders, bringing in about $1tr to the global economy and aiding the development of some of the poorer countries (Donnan, 2013). The meeting ended successfully, bringing about the first global deal in WTO's short history. It was then hailed as quite an accomplishment. However, the euphoria emanating from Bali's successful conclusion was short-lived. Not long after Bali, national interests resurfaced. The next stop in the negotiations was Nairobi, in December 2015. The differences between developed countries and their developing counterparts, especially China and India, were too severe to overcome. Developed countries asked that developing countries begin to tear down their barriers to imported products. China and India refused, so negotiations ended without a resolution. The Doha Round had just found its place in history.

Concept Questions

1. What role does the IMF play within the international monetary system?
2. Identify the three agencies comprising the World Bank Group and explain the ways in which each provides assistance to developing countries.

3. Explain the significance of the three fundamental principles of the GATT.
4. What are the objectives of the WTO?
5. What was the WTO's most recent Round?

VII. Regional Arrangements

In addition to participating in the WTO and other global trade and finance arrangements or in trying to compete on their own, some countries also found arrangements that included a smaller number of participants to be more pragmatic and manageable. Such arrangements have been known as regional integration arrangements and are usually classified as one of the following:

- Free Trade Area (FTA). An FTA means elimination of intra-area tariffs. Goods can flow freely from one participant to another. Individual participants, however, maintain their own tariff structure towards their other trading partners.
- Customs Union (CU). In addition to the provisions contained in the FTA, CU participants adopt a common tariff structure towards countries outside the Union.
- Common Market (CM). The CM extends the CU to incorporate free movement of labor and capital in addition to goods.
- Economic (exchange rate, monetary and fiscal policies) and Political Union (EPU). This is a far more advanced form of integration, for all practical reasons eliminating national borders. The U.S. and the former Soviet Union are examples of this ambitious structure, although the two achieved integration though different means.

Regional arrangements can be as contentious as their global counterparts can. Not all of them have succeeded in generating the anticipated benefits. Still, they are considered an indispensable part of the global economy.

FTAs represent the primary medium of formal international economic cooperation for the US. Participation in FTAs aims at opening up international markets for US companies and protects the interests and legal rights of US companies abroad. By 2014, the US had fourteen FTAs in effect, involving twenty countries: Canada and Mexico (NAFTA); Australia, Bahrain, Chile, Colombia, Costa Rica, Dominican Republic, El Salvador, Guatemala, Honduras, and Nicaragua (CAFTA); Israel, Jordan, Korea (KORUS), Morocco, Oman, Panama, Peru, and Singapore. NAFTA is the most familiar one, but the others are also considered important for US businesses. In 2019, NAFTA was replaced by the US-Mexico-Canada Agreement, USMCA (http://www.ustr.gov/trade-agreements/free-trade-agreements).

1. The European Union

European countries became concerned about the instability of the international monetary system and its effects on their economies. To achieve stability, the European Monetary System (EMS) was established and began functioning in March 1979 (for more information on the EU, see http://europa.eu/index_en.htm, official website of EU). Ten of the European Community, or EC countries as they were then called, had become members by 1991. Britain joined on October 5, 1990, and became a member of the Exchange Rate Mechanism (ERM) at a central rate of Deutsche Mark (DM) 2.95. The ERM is the framework through which participants maintain the appropriate exchange rate parities. Even though Britain was not a member of the system or an ERM participant at the system's inception, the pound sterling was part of the basket of currencies making up the European Currency Unit (ECU). The Greek drachma was also included in the ECU when Greece joined the EC, but the country did not participate in the ERM. Both Greece and Britain contributed 20% of their gold and gross dollar assets in exchange for ECUs, a practice in which the other nine System participants also engaged. ECU composition was reviewed every five years.

The principal characteristic of the EMS was a fixed but adjustable exchange rate system. A band of 2.25% (6% for the Italian lira) was established around the bilateral exchange rate. The band set the intervention points for each currency compared to the others. Another characteristic of the EMS was its use of a "divergence indicator," which showed the movements of an individual member's exchange rate against the weighted average movement of the other participants. Behavior of the indicator is intended to signal any need for corrective action on behalf of the authorities.

Creation of the EMS had both short-term and long-term implications. According to its advocates, the system had indeed succeeded in promoting a "zone of currency stability." Convergence of economic objectives among members of the ERM and greater cooperation among the monetary authorities of these countries contributed to increased stability. The system also faced a number of problems, including differences of opinion among members regarding currency realignment and membership. However, it did provide the impetus for even greater cooperation among European nations, culminating in what we today know as the European Union.

The European Monetary System was an important development in the rich history of the foreign exchange market. Furthermore, it represented a necessary step to the success of the European Monetary Union (EMU), which brought about a broad degree of economic integration culminating in a common currency and the European Central Bank.

The European Community took a step toward realization of the Monetary Union during a meeting in December 1991 in the Dutch city of Maastricht. The meeting produced a treaty that set up a timetable for the union as well as conditions that members had to meet. The road to monetary union would follow three stages.

1. During stage one (1990), members were to increase the level of coordination of their economic and monetary policies within the existing institutional framework. In particular, stage one included the following:

    - full participation of all member nations in the ERM;
    - greater central bank coordination on inflation, interest rate, and exchange rate policies; and
    - revision of the Rome Treaty to allow for economic and monetary union.

The beginning date for stage one, July 1, 1990, coincided with the withdrawal of all barriers to capital flows.

2. Stage two (1994) included

    - narrowing the margin of currency fluctuation to 2.5% for all participants;
    - establishing the institutional framework necessary for monetary union. Patterned after the US Federal Reserve System, the European System of Central Banks (ESCB) was established. The central unit of the ECSB was the European Central Bank (ECB). Until complete union was to be achieved, the ECB was responsible for the coordination of national monetary policies;
    - setting national budget targets for members; and
    - promoting the ECU as a viable European currency.

3. The final stage (1997) encompassed

    - full operation of the central bank as the Community's monetary authority; and
    - adoption of the final set of intra-Community exchange rates and of the ECU as the Community's currency.

The attainment of monetary union was seen as generating both benefits and costs for firms considering doing business within the Union. For example,

- a single capital market will allow firms to manage their working capital and long-term funding requirements in a more efficient manner;
- a single currency will eliminate foreign exchange risks generated by doing business across national borders.

These benefits were seen as being especially pronounced for smaller firms, presumably the ones that can least afford the transactions and other costs imposed by the present system. The Union also imposed costs on some firms as they experienced erosion in their relative bargaining power when they operate in a monetary and banking environment controlled by a single authority.

Establishment of the European Monetary Union and the European Union in general has been both challenging and time consuming. As the EU Timeline (Appendix 4.1) indicates, the true beginning of the movement dates back quite a few decades. Although not perfect, the EU has brought new hope for the continent. It has also faced some deep economic challenges, the epitome of which is represented by the European debt crisis.

The European economy as a whole was performing well in 2007. The global financial crisis of 2007–2008, however, hit the continent hard. The subprime crisis and the burst of the housing bubble affected the portfolios of most European banks; the global market slowdown affected European firms and their markets, contributing to the continent's recession (see Appendix 4.2 for a chronology of the crisis). The Union's problems were magnified by the sovereign debt crisis that particularly affected Greece, Spain, Italy, Portugal, and Ireland. Although the problems faced by each country were different, they all complicated Europe's recovery from the global downturn. Appendix 4.2 illustrates how events unfolded as the global crisis became more pronounced. In June 2012, Europe took another step towards enhancing the scope of the Union. The ECB announced it was working to establish a framework of centralization of bank supervision activities across the member countries. The step was deemed necessary because of the poor health of many of the European banks and the asymmetry of bank regulatory enforcement from country to country. Towards that end, ECB is to conduct an Asset Quality Review (AQR) of financial institutions on a regular basis. In an effort to stimulate the European economy, in March 2015, the ECB undertook an ambitious bond-buying program, similar to the quantitative easing program of the Federal Reserve. The ECB committed to buying about €60B a month until September 2016 for a total of about €1.1tr.

The benefits of the European Banking Union and the ECB are expected to include regaining trust in Europe's maligned banking system, reestablishing the all-important interbank market, and eventually rebuilding the sovereign debt market. However, EU's crisis is still not resolved. New developments (Brexit, immigration crisis, political instability) have put additional strain to the functioning of the Union. At this point, the full implications of these developments are not known (see *The Economist*, 2012, on the relationship between the IMF and the EU).

2. The EU Crisis and the IMF

The role of the IMF in the post-2008 European crisis has been both significant and controversial. As of September 12, 2013, the Fund has had arrangements with seven countries in Europe, for a total of €103bn. The IMF has used stand-by arrangements (Bosnia, Kosovo); extended fund facility (Cyprus, Greece, Ireland, Portugal); and flexible credit line (Poland). In addition, the IMF has provided technical assistance in such areas as macroeconomic policy, tax policy and revenue administration, financial sector stability, and others.

As a member of the "Troika" (IMF, the European Commission, or EC, and the European Central Bank, or ECB), the IMF had a voice in determining the path towards crisis resolution. On many occasions, however, the IMF view contradicted that of EC and/or the ECB. In particular, the IMF eventually concluded that the austerity measures supported by the EC and ECB, which primarily reflected Germany's position, were misconceived; austerity seemed to make the situation worse rather than better. Since the EC/ECB view has dominated, some IMF observers concluded that the Fund's credibility had therefore been damaged because of its inability to exert its influence over the process. Whether the IMF or the EC/ECB/German view is the correct one still remains to be seen. The fact remains that Europe is still under the spell of the crisis, and Greece, Portugal, Spain, and other countries remain in state of deep economic recession. Yet, the deep north–south divisions function as a severe obstacle in the region's ever becoming a true union.

3. Brexit

In January 2013, British Prime Minister Cameron announced that a referendum would be held to decide whether Britain would remain a member of the EU. On June 23, 2016, the referendum was indeed held, with the majority of the votes casted in favor of Britain's exit from the EU. Prime Minister Cameron, who had campaigned in favor of Britain's remaining in the EU, stepped down and was succeeded by Theresa May. On March 29, 2017, Prime Minister May invoked Article 50 of the Lisbon Treaty. Article 50 gives Britain and the EU two years to agree on the terms of the separation. Following successive rejections of her Brexit plan in the Parliament, Theresa May also announced her resignation in May 2019. Boris Johnson, one of the architects of the Brexit movement, succeeded her.

Britain's departure from the EU will potentially have significant impact on the country's economy and its financial sector. It will also affect the EU, since Britain is such an important part of the Union. The exact impact, of course, will not be known until details of the agreement between the two parties have been finalized. December 31, 2020, is the new critical deadline for the terms of Britain's departure.

VIII. Managerial Implications of the International Monetary System

The workings of the international monetary system are of great interest to all foreign exchange market participants, both private and public. Investors and managers must understand the "rules of the game" with respect to the currency environments. Is a given country's currency convertible to other currencies? Is it pegged to another currency? To what degree is there government intervention in the system? How critical are these considerations to the formulation of forecasts of the foreign exchange rate?

The study of the international monetary system offers a rich and ever-changing account of economic, financial, and political pressures exerted on markets and governments. As the world enters the twenty-first century, new chapters are being written. The new Europe has some potentially interesting developments in store. China's rise as a global economic power has placed the yuan in a new light. Will it eventually replace the dollar as a key currency? Will the Pacific become a new common market? Will fixed exchange rates make a comeback? Are governments to continue their intervention in the foreign exchange market?

While these are problematical issues and open-ended questions, familiarity with the IMS is a prerequisite to understanding the issues and their implications. For firms operating internationally, understanding the structure of the international monetary system is a necessary even though not sufficient condition for survival. The system evolves continually, and developments in one part of the world have impacts on financial markets and international transactions in other parts.

As the world enters into a new political environment, the importance of global cooperation has become even more obvious. No international system (political, monetary, or trade) can be successful without the cooperation of the world's governments. Systems may be wonderful in their design, but may prove unworkable if countries view their actions as zero-sum games and pursue nationalistic policies.

IX. Summary

The chapter dealt with an important component of the world business environment, the international monetary system (IMS). Various classifications of the IMS were offered, with particular attention directed toward the role of exchange rates. Exchange rate systems identified included fixed rates, free float, managed float, and adjustable peg. The impact of government intervention in the foreign exchange market was also analyzed.

The nature of the IMS is also shaped by the various international agencies and agreements that have been formulated following the end of WWII. The IMF, the World Bank, and the GATT were discussed. A historical overview of the IMS was also offered.

We must keep in mind that the IMS is not a static construct. The events surrounding the European unification efforts certainly illustrated how changes can come about, either in the entire system or its components. World business system participants, then, must be familiar with the current environment and anticipate changes.

Key Terms and Concepts

In the order in which they are presented in the text.

International monetary system: The set of "rules and conventions that govern the financial relations between countries."

Fixed exchange rate systems: In fixed exchange rate systems, governments set exchange rates between two currencies.

The classical gold standard: The classical gold standard commits governments to exchange gold at specified prices in terms of its own currency. It is a fixed rate system that uses gold as the reserve currency. All participating countries make a similar commitment, so all currencies are expressed in terms of gold and therefore in terms of each other. Changes in the exchange rate between currencies occur as one country alters the rate of exchange between its currency and gold.

The gold exchange standard: Under the gold exchange standard, currency values were defined in terms of a certain quantity of gold, although they were not convertible into gold, with the sole exception of the United States dollar. Keeping exchange rates within indicated ranges was agreed upon by the participating governments, requiring them to buy and sell foreign exchange as pressures on the currencies drove them away from the agreed-upon level.

Free float exchange rate system: In a free float system, unfettered interplay between foreign exchange market supply and demand forces determine exchange rates. Any shift in these forces will cause equilibrium to change. As participants receive information about new developments, they react by buying and selling currencies and thus establishing a new equilibrium position.

Managed float exchange rate system: The exchange rate system is classified as managed or "dirty" float when authorities interfere with supply and demand forces to generate a more desirable exchange rate. It is a hybrid between flexible and fixed systems, with the flexible component being central to the system.

The Plaza Accord (1985): The ascent of the US dollar to its historical high in February 1985 prompted the five major industrialized western countries (France, Japan, the United Kingdom, the United States, and West Germany) to meet in September 1985 and agree to coordinate their policies in order to devalue the dollar.

The Louvre Agreement (1987): The dollar fell drastically after the Plaza Accord, and started falling in a manner that caused concern to the countries known at the time as the Group of Seven (G-7): Britain, Canada, France, Germany, Italy, Japan, and the United States. The G-7 (today's G-8 after inclusion of Russia) representatives met in Louvre and agreed to stabilize currency values through appropriate macroeconomic policies and foreign exchange market intervention (February 1987).

Adjustable peg: An adjustable peg exchange rate system is a fixed exchange rate system, but it also establishes limits around the official exchange rate. When the actual exchange rate deviates temporarily from the official rate, the authorities intervene to bring the exchange rate back in line with the official rate. When these deviations reach a level considered excessive by participating countries, the system is said to have entered a phase of "fundamental disequilibrium." The authorities then resort to revaluing or devaluing the currency as appropriate.

Selective peg: A smaller country adopts this system by pegging its currency to that of its largest trading partner in order to limit fluctuations in its economy.

Currency boards: In a currency board arrangement, the country adopts a fixed exchange rate and commits to exchanging its own currency for a fixed quantity of another hard currency, such as the dollar.

Dollarization: Under dollarization, private and public sectors in a country use a foreign currency for transactions, investment, or reserve purposes.

Cocirculation: In smaller countries, a major currency, such as the US dollar circulates in conjunction with and performs the same functions as the national currency.

Dual or multiple markets: A currency may be sold in multiple markets, official and unofficial, when countries put controls on the holdings of their currencies and on trade or capital flows, multiple markets may develop in an effort to circumvent these controls. Multiple markets may also develop as developing countries are experiencing economic or political turbulence. These markets, also sometimes referred to as black markets, may be illegal but are usually tolerated by the authorities.

Zero intervention/free float: When a currency is allowed to float freely, the country does not intervene in the foreign exchange market in order to support the value of its currency.

Neutral intervention: The objective of neutral intervention is to mitigate very short-term (such as daily) fluctuations in a country's currency.

Leaning against the wind: A leaning-against-the-wind approach involves intervention by the authorities in the foreign exchange market in order to avert or at least delay devaluation or revaluation of the currency.

Unofficial pegging: Unofficial pegging refers to a country supporting its currency in order to maintain its currency's value at or around a target value.

Non-sterilized (monetary) intervention: Non-sterilized (monetary) intervention in the foreign exchange market by a country's central bank influences the money supply without any mitigating action.

Sterilized (non-monetary) intervention: Sterilized, or non-monetary, intervention in the foreign exchange market takes place in conjunction with action to mitigate the impact on the money supply.

The International Monetary Fund (IMF): The IMF is an international membership organization established in 1944 by the Bretton Woods Conference with the purpose of providing stability to the international monetary system. The Fund's original objectives included (1) Promoting exchange rate stability; (2) Providing members with resources necessary to meet balance of payments imbalances; (3) Helping members secure balance of payments financing; and, (4) Serving as a repository for the reserves of its members.

Special Drawing Rights (SDRs): SDRs are international reserve assets distributed by the IMF in 1970 in order to enlarge member countries' reserves. SDRs have been termed "paper gold" because they can be used as a form of international payment just as gold can.

The World Bank Group: The World Bank Group is comprised of five agencies (The International Bank for Reconstruction and Development, The International Development Association, The International Finance Corporation, The International Centre for Settlement of Investment Disputes, and The Multilateral Investment Guarantee Agency. The World Bank's purpose is to provide assistance to developing countries in order to end poverty and improve economic development and the overall standard of living.

Asian Infrastructure Investment Bank (AIIB): In 2013, China initiated the establishment of the AIIB, whose mission is to provide for the financing of infrastructure investment projects, such as railways and ports, in Asia.

Bank for International Settlements (BIS): BIS is the "Central Bankers' Bank." Established in 1930 in Basel, Switzerland, BIS is the oldest of currently existing international financial bodies. BIS provides very similar banking services to those that commercial banks provide to their own clients. It conducts research on policy issues. BIS also promotes central bank cooperation in order to strengthen the soundness and stability of the international monetary system by setting standards for capital requirements. The primary force behind these changes has been the Basel Committee on Banking Supervision (BCBS), which was established in 1974. Its shareholders own the bank; central banks are the primary owners, holding about 85% of all shares.

Basel Accords: The Basel Accords (Basel I, II, and III as of 2017) establish capital adequacy, leverage, and liquidity measures designed by the Basel Committee on Banking Supervision to promote the safety and soundness of the international banking system.

Bretton Woods: The Bretton Woods Conference was held in New Hampshire in 1944 to establish the post-World War II international monetary system. The conference established the key position of the United States dollar by allowing that currency alone the privilege of free convertibility into gold. This necessitated that the United States hold reserves of gold, while the other signatories held dollar reserves. The parities of other currencies were fixed in terms of the dollar.

The Smithsonian Agreement: Following the US withdrawal from the Gold Standard in August 1971, the major industrialized countries met in December of that same year and agreed to a devaluation of the dollar.

The snake in the tunnel: On April 24, 1972, a joint agreement signed among members of the European Economic Community (Belgium,

France, Italy, Luxembourg, the Netherlands, and West Germany) plus Britain, Denmark, Ireland, and Norway on April 24, 1972. It created a band within a band. Participating members agreed to limit the margin of fluctuation within their currency group to 2.25%, half of the plus-or-minus 2.25% margin permitted under the Smithsonian. As a group, currencies could still float at 4.5% maximum margin with respect to other currencies.

The worm in the snake in the tunnel: The worm refers to an extension to the snake in the tunnel agreement further narrowing the margin to 1% between Belgium, Luxemburg, and the Netherlands.

The 1976 Jamaica Agreement: This agreement (January 1976) formalized the post-Bretton Woods exchange rate system by declaring floating exchange rates acceptable, demonetizing gold, and increasing IMF member quotas. The agreement also allowed members to defend their currencies against speculative attacks, thus ushering the current managed float system.

The Impossible Trinity (or Triad or The Trilemma): The Impossible Trinity (or Triad or The Trilemma) refers to the choice monetary authorities must make to achieve only two of the three possible policy objectives: fixed exchange rates, capital mobility, and policy independence.

The General Agreement on Tariffs and Trade (GATT): The GATT was a multilateral trade agreement formed to promote international trade after WWII. The Agreement provided for members to receive equal tariff treatment (a provision known as the Most Favored Nation), lowering of tariffs, and removal of non-tariff trade barriers. It also provided for special tariff treatment for poorer nations. GATT went into effect in 1948 and was succeeded by the WTO in 1995.

The World Trade Organization (WTO): The WTO replaced and continued the mission of the GATT. The WTO expanded the scope of the GATT by including coverage on services, trade-related investment, and intellectual property rights. The purpose of the WTO also included dispute settlement, support of the environment, giving the poorer countries a stronger voice, and raising living standards.

Free trade area (FTA): An FTA is an agreement between two or more countries to eliminate tariffs in trade between them, but to keep their individual tariff structure towards their other trading partners.

Customs union (CU): Under a CU, participating countries adopt a common tariff structure in addition to an FTA.

Common market (CM): The CM includes free movement of labor and capital among member countries, in addition to free movement of goods and a common tariff structure.

Economic (exchange rate, monetary and fiscal policies) and political union (EPU): This is a very advanced form of integration, for all practical reasons eliminating national borders.

The European Union (EU): The EU is comprised of twenty-seven countries (following the United Kingdom's exit) that have formed a monetary and political union. To achieve its present state, the EU went through several stages, including free trade area, customs union, common market, currency, and monetary and political union.

Brexit: UK's withdrawal from the European Union.

Questions and Problems

1. State the arguments in favor of and against government intervention in the foreign exchange market. What is the impact of intervention on the market in the short run and in the long run?
2. State the arguments for and against the gold standard. In your opinion, should the US go back to the gold standard? Why? Explain your answer.
3. How would you characterize the current international monetary system? What are its major components?
4. Your firm has been exporting to the country of Krakowia. You hear that the country is going to be admitted to the European Union. What would this mean to your firm?
5. A small US exporter made the following statement: "Fixed rates, floating rates. What do I care? Foreign exchange is foreign exchange! I will eventually convert it to my own currency anyway!" Comment on the statement.
6. A US trade official was recently quoted as saying, "The notion of European integration is contrary to the spirit of multilateralism espoused by GATT." Do you agree? Explain your answer.
7. An Italian exporter to Venezuela says, "I will never do business in a country that has exchange controls. It's just too risky." Do you agree? Explain your answer.
8. "As long as the whole world cannot agree on a single set of international arrangements, groups of regional arrangements in currency, trade, and resource mobility would be satisfactory."

   Comment on this statement in relation to recent developments.
9. Bob Jones works for agricultural products company in upstate New York. When his supervisor expressed concern about an upcoming international agreement on agricultural products trade, Jim reassured her that the outcome of these negotiations would have absolutely no impact on the firm because all sales are domestic. What do you think of his future prospects with the firm? Why?
10. "The rise of regional trade blocs will mean the demise of the WTO." Do you agree with this statement from a distinguished US trade official?
11. What do you think the international monetary system will be like in the year 2020? In 2050? Give reasons for your answers.
12. In your opinion, what is the future of the European Union after Brexit? What is the future of the euro? What are the prerequisites for the Union's success?

Web Exercises

W1. Go to imf.org. Give a brief overview of the system and its history. What does the IMF do?

W2. Go to wb.org. Give a brief overview of the World Bank and its history. What are the World Bank's current projects?

W3. Go to the website of the European Union (http://europa.eu/about-eu/institutions-bodies/index_en.htm). What are the major EU institutions? How many countries are members of the EU? How many others are close to achieving membership to the EU?

Selected References

Alvarez-Plata, P., and A. Garcia-Herrero. 2007. *To Dollarize or De-Dollarize: Consequences for Monetary Policy*. Prepared for Asian Development Bank. September. www.bis.org/repofficepubl/apresearchpapagh071227. Downloaded 12/15/2013.

Bank for International Settlements. 2015. *85th Annual Report, 2014–2015*. Basle: Bank for International Settlements, June, p. 84. Also accessed at http://www.bis.org/publ/arpdf/ar2015_ec.pdf. Downloaded on 10/21/2016.

Bank for International Settlements. 2020. *Basel Committee on Banking Supervision Reforms-Basel III*. Accessed at https://www.bis.org/bcbs/basel3.htm. Accessed 5/29/20.

Berg, A. and E. Borensztein. 2000. Full Dollarization: The Pros and Cons. *Economic Issues*. Number 24. Washington: International Monetary Fund, December. Accessed at https://www.imf.org/external/pubs/ft/issues/issues24. Downloaded may 21, 2019.

Cooper, R. N. 1987. *The International Monetary System: Essays in World Economics*. Cambridge, Massachusetts: The MIT Press.

De Vries, T. 1976. Jamaica, or the Non-Reform of the International Monetary System. *Foreign Affairs*. April. ww.foreignaffairs.com/articles/25591/tom-de-vries/jamaica-or-the-non-reform-of-the-international-monetary-system. Downloaded 7/31/14.

Donnan, S. 2013. WTO: Up in the Air. *Financial Times*. December 2. www.ft.com. Downloaded 1/2/13.

Economist. 2012. The IMF and the Euro Crisis. Less Cash, More Impact. October 6. www.economist.com/notes. Downloaded 12/13/13.

European Union. http://europa.eu/index_en.htm (official website of EU)

Friedrich, K. 1974. *International Economics: Concepts and Issues*. New York: McGraw-Hill.

Haberler, G. 1977. The International Monetary System after Jamaica and Manila. *Weltwirtschaftilches Archive* 113 (1): 1–30.

Humpage, O. F. 1991. Central-Bank Intervention: Recent Literature, Continuing Controversy. *Economic Review*. Federal Reserve Bank of Cleveland 27 (2): 12–26.

International Monetary Fund. *Annual Report*, various years.

International Monetary Fund. *The Role and Functions of the International Monetary Fund*. Washington, D.C., various years.

International Monetary Fund. 1991. SDRs: Evolution of IMF-Created Instrument is Linked to Role As Principal Reserve Asset. *IMF Survey*. September.

International Monetary Fund. 2013. *The IMF and Europe*. September 30. www.imf.org/external/np/exr/facts/europe.htm

International Monetary Fund. 2014. *Annual Report on Exchange Arrangements and Exchange Restrictions, 2014*. Washington, DC: International Monetary Fund.

Mankiw, G. N. 2010. The Trilemma of International Finance. *New York Times*, July 10, 2010. http://www.nytimes.com/2010/07/11/business/economy/11view.html?_r=0; downloaded 7/31/14.

Obstfeld, M., J C. Shambaugh and A. M. Taylor. 2004. The Trilemma in History: Tradeoffs among Exchange Rates, Monetary Policies, and Capital Mobility. Working Paper 10396.

National Bureau of Economic Research, Cambridge, MA, March. http://www.nber.org/papers/w10396

Ostroukh. A. 2014. Russian Central Bank Props Up Ruble. *Wall Street Journal*, October 7, 2014. Downloaded October 12, 2014 http://online.wsj.com/articles/russian-central-bank-props-up-ruble-1412667867.)

Rosenberg, M. R. 1983. Foreign Exchange Controls: An International Comparison. In *International Finance Handbook, Volume 1,* edited by A. M. George and I.H. Giddy. New York: John Wiley & Sons, 358-374.

Spiegel, M. 1998. A Currency Board for Indonesia? *Economic Letter.* Federal Reserve Bank of San Francisco, March 20, 1998.

Wall Street Journal. 2013. Argentina's Black-Market Peso Weakens ahead of election. October 22. Accessed at *wsj.com*. Downloaded 10/13/13)

World Bank. 2015. *The World Bank Group: A to Z.* International Bank for Reconstruction and Development. Washington, D.C: The World Bank.

Credits

Table 4.1: Source: Owen F. Humpage.

Table 4.2: Source: http://www.bis.org/bcbs/basel3/basel3_phase_in_arrangements.pdf.

Fig. 4.2: Source: imf.org.

Table 4.3: Source: http://www.bis.org/publ/arpdf/ar2015_ec.pdf.

Table 4.4: Source: http://www.wto.org/english/thewto_e/whatis_e/tif_e/fact4_e.htm.

Chapter 5

Exchange Rate Determination Theories

Chapter Overview

The previous chapter described the characteristics of the various exchange rate systems. We noted that, under fixed exchange rates, exchange rates change as a result of decisions and actions taken by the government. Under floating rates, however, exchange rates move from one equilibrium to another when influenced by variables other than government. These variables provide the foundations for the formulation of various theoretical frameworks. In Chapter 5, we examine the various exchange rate determination theories. We also examine the dynamic relationships between exchange rates and macroeconomic variables.

After Studying This Chapter, You Will Be Able To

- Evaluate the various theories explaining the determination of foreign exchange rates
- Understand the intricacies of option valuation
- Recognize the impact exchange rates have on the global economy

Chapter Outline

I. Exchange Rate Determination Theories and Models
II. Macroeconomic Models
III. Asset Pricing Models
IV. Market Microstructure and the Foreign Exchange Market
V. Short Run and Behavioral Approaches
VI. Currency Options Valuation
VII. Summary

I. Exchange Rate Determination Theories and Models

The determination of exchange rates is a complicated process, involving both economic and non-economic considerations. The question "What drives exchange rates?" has been answered in multiple ways, the answer usually depending upon the assumptions posited. For example, are we interested in answering the question in the short term or long term? The answer may be different under each time horizon. In this chapter, we will discuss some of the explanations behind exchange rate movements that have been offered during the long history of the literature of international finance.

We may classify the forces that affect exchange rate movements as belonging in one or more of the following groups:

1. Those associated with a single government, a group of governments, or an international institution. They include:

    a. The international monetary system. As we learned in the previous chapter, the exchange rate determination issue depends a great deal on whether the system is primarily based on currency values fixed at a certain amount and changing through government action or is allowed to move freely subject to market forces.
    b. Government Intervention. Buying and selling of a currency by the government may also affect its value. We covered this topic in the previous chapter.

2. Forces associated with macroeconomic variables. A number of exchange rate determination theories have been constructed using these variables. Such theories include

    a. The Traditional Flow Model;
    b. The Monetary Model; and
    c. The Portfolio Balance (Asset) Model

In addition to these three models, macroeconomic variables were also used in the construction of the well-known parity or equilibrium conditions. As we noted, however, these conditions do not represent full-fledged theoretical arguments.

3. Explanations about exchange rate determination have also been generated using the tools of modern finance in general and asset pricing in particular. Such explanations may come from

    a. The International Asset Pricing Model; and
    b. The International Arbitrage Pricing Theorem

4. The literature of conventional finance also provides the background for the Microstructure Theory of Exchange Rate Determination.
5. Additional explanations, mostly emphasizing short time horizons, come from non-economic factors, such as those associated with market psychology. Behavioral Finance, for example, has become a fertile ground for raising such explanations.

This chapter presents the principal arguments behind exchange rate movements. Although some of the theories and models presented may appear contradictory to each other, we should remember that theory construction depends largely on the assumptions upon which the theory is built. We should also keep in mind that the theories and models presented in this chapter do not exhaust the entire set of exchange rate determination theories formulated by scholars. In addition, some of the theories may include multiple versions. We should therefore view each theoretical framework not as offering the unchallenged explanation behind exchange rate movements, but as a way of acquiring some general insights into the determination of exchange rates (see Bergstrand, 1983, and Pearce, 1983).

II. Macroeconomic Models

1. The Traditional Flow Model

According to the traditional model, alternatively termed the balance of payments model, the exchange rate is determined by the variables behind flow, supply of, and demand for a currency. To understand the nature of these variables, we can examine a country's balance of payments accounts. The balance of payments is the record of international transactions of one country versus the rest of the world during a period of time, usually a year or a quarter. US balance of payments data are collected and published by the Bureau of Economic Analysis under the heading of International Transactions (Table 5.1).

[Millions of dollars]		
Line		2019P
	Current Account	
1	**Exports of goods and services and income receipts (credits)**	**3,763,944**
2	**Exports of goods and services**	**2,498,034**
3	**Goods**	**1,652,806**
4	General merchandise	1,633,066
5	Foods, feeds, and beverages	131,133
6	Industrial supplies and materials	525,705
7	Capital goods except automotive	547,363
8	Automotive vehicles, parts, and engines	161,848
9	Consumer goods except food and automotive	205,689
10	Other general merchandise	61,327
11	Net exports of goods under merchanting	430
12	Non-monetary gold	19,310
13	**Services**	**845,228**

Table 5.1 US International Transactions

14	Maintenance and repair services n.i.e.	32,525
15	Transport	91,356
16	Travel (for all purposes including education)[1]	213,482
17	Insurance services	18,281
18	Financial services	111,275
19	Charges for the use of intellectual property n.i.e.	128,932
20	Telecommunications, computer, and information services	47,813
21	Other business services	180,071
22	Government goods and services n.i.e.	21,492
23	**Primary income receipts**	**1,123,101**
24	Investment income	1,116,266
25	Direct investment income	579,988
26	Portfolio investment income	427,643
27	Other investment income	107,760
28	Reserve asset income	873
29	Compensation of employees	6,835
30	**Secondary income (current transfer) receipts**[2]	**142,809**
31	**Imports of goods and services and income payments (debits)**	**4,262,295**
32	**Imports of goods and services**	**3,114,459**
33	**Goods**	**2,519,049**
34	General merchandise	2,508,429
35	Foods, feeds, and beverages	151,597
36	Industrial supplies and materials	528,974
37	Capital goods except automotive	681,551
38	Automotive vehicles, parts, and engines	376,956
39	Consumer goods except food and automotive	656,165
40	Other general merchandise	113,186
41	Non-monetary gold	10,620
42	**Services**	**595,409**
43	Maintenance and repair services n.i.e.	8,823
44	Transport	110,116
45	Travel (for all purposes including education)[1]	152,321
46	Insurance services	48,581
47	Financial services	33,670
48	Charges for the use of intellectual property n.i.e.	57,073
49	Telecommunications, computer, and information services	43,156
50	Other business services	117,566

Table 5.1 *(Continued)*

51	Government goods and services n.i.e.	24,105
52	**Primary income payments**	**866,105**
53	Investment income	845,785
54	Direct investment income	245,770
55	Portfolio investment income	485,233
56	Other investment income	114,782
57	Compensation of employees	20,320
58	**Secondary income (current transfer) payments**[2]	**281,732**
	Capital account	
59	**Capital transfer receipts and other credits**	**0**
60	**Capital transfer payments and other debits**	**10**
	Financial account	
61	**Net US acquisition of financial assets excluding financial derivatives (net increase in assets / financial outflow (+))**	**426,912**
62	**Direct investment assets**	**197,670**
63	Equity	207,046
64	Debt instruments	-9,376
65	**Portfolio investment assets**	**35,875**
66	Equity and investment fund shares	-250,967
67	Debt securities	286,842
68	Short term	167,502
69	Long term	119,339
70	**Other investment assets**	**188,709**
71	Currency and deposits	106,199
72	Loans	81,427
73	Insurance technical reserves	n.a.
74	Trade credit and advances	1,083
75	**Reserve assets**	**4,659**
76	Monetary gold	0
77	Special Drawing Rights	237
78	Reserve position in the International Monetary Fund	4,271
79	Other reserve assets	150
80	Currency and deposits	-12
81	Securities	162
82	Financial derivatives	0
83	Other claims	0

Table 5.1 *(Continued)*

84	**Net US incurrence of liabilities excluding financial derivatives (net increase in liabilities / financial inflow (+))**	**784,440**
85	**Direct investment liabilities**	**310,811**
86	Equity	282,418
87	Debt instruments	28,393
88	**Portfolio investment liabilities**	**231,617**
89	Equity and investment fund shares	-226,801
90	Debt securities	458,418
91	Short term	-44,792
92	Long term	503,210
93	**Other investment liabilities**	**242,012**
94	Currency and deposits	196,357
95	Loans	35,687
96	Insurance technical reserves	n.a.
97	Trade credit and advances	9,967
98	Special Drawing Rights allocations	0
99	**Financial derivatives other than reserves, net transactions[3]**	**-38,378**
	Statistical discrepancy	
100	**Statistical discrepancy[4]**	**102,456**
	Balances	
101	**Balance on current account (line 1 less line 31)[5]**	**-498,351**
102	Balance on goods and services (line 2 less line 32)	-616,425
103	Balance on goods (line 3 less line 33)	-866,244
104	Balance on services (line 13 less line 42)	249,819
105	Balance on primary income (line 23 less line 52)	256,997
106	Balance on secondary income (line 30 less line 58)	-138,923
107	**Balance on capital account (line 59 less line 60)[5]**	**-10**
108	**Net lending (+) or net borrowing (–) from current- and capital-account transactions (line 101 plus line 107)[6]**	**-498,361**
109	**Net lending (+) or net borrowing (–) from financial-account transactions (line 61 less line 84 plus line 99)[6]**	**-395,906**

Table 5.1 *(Continued)*

p Preliminary r Revised n.a. Not available (*)Transactions are between zero and +/- $500,000

1. All travel purposes include 1) business travel, including expenditures by border, seasonal, and other short-term workers and 2) personal travel, including health-related and education-related travel.

2. Secondary income (current transfer) receipts and payments include US government and private transfers, such as US government grants and pensions, fines and penalties, withholding taxes, personal transfers (remittances), insurance-related transfers, and other current transfers.

3. Transactions for financial derivatives are only available as a net value equal to transactions for assets less transactions for liabilities. A positive value represents net US cash payments arising from derivatives contracts, and a negative value represents net US cash receipts.

4. The statistical discrepancy, which can be calculated as line 109 less line 108, is the difference between total debits and total credits recorded in the current, capital, and financial accounts. In the current and capital accounts, credits and debits are labeled in the table. In the financial account, an acquisition of an asset or a repayment of a liability is a debit, and an incurrence of a liability or a disposal of an asset is a credit.

5. Current- and capital-account statistics in the international transactions accounts differ slightly from statistics in the national income and product accounts (NIPAs) because of adjustments made to convert the international transactions statistics to national economic accounting concepts. A reconciliation between annual statistics in the two sets of accounts appears in NIPA table 4.3B.

6. Net lending means that US residents are net suppliers of funds to foreign residents, and net borrowing means the opposite. Net lending or net borrowing can be computed from current- and capital-account transactions or from financial-account transactions. The two amounts differ by the statistical discrepancy.

Notes: Details may not add to totals because of rounding. See international transactions accounts table 1.3 at apps.bea.gov/iTable/index_ita.cfm for geographic detail.
Source: U.S. Bureau of Economic Analysis

Source: Bureau of Economic Analysis. Accessed at https://www.bea.gov/data/intl-trade-investment/international-transactions.

Downloaded; March 21, 2020

United States international transactions are comprised of two major components: the current account and the financial account. The current account includes exports of goods and services and income receipts (from investment income and employee compensation) and imports of goods and services and income payments. The US, for example, exports and imports consumer goods, automobiles, industrial supplies, and other goods; in addition, it exports and imports services, such as insurance and financial services. Finally, it receives income from investment abroad, as well as pays income to foreign investors in the US. The financial account reflects the various assets that the US owns abroad and the US assets owned by international investors. If we can identify the factors behind changes in these accounts, then we can identify the factors behind changes in the exchange rate. This is due to the compensating entry that accompanies each export and import transaction. As goods and services are transferred across borders, they are associated with respective receipts and payments from one country to the other. These receipts and payments involve exchanges of one currency for another, thus affecting demand and supply of currencies in the foreign exchange market and, ultimately, leading to changing currency values.

1.1. The Current Account

As we noted, items included in the current account are goods and services exchanged between countries. At the individual product or service level, the quantity demanded is a function of the price of the good, the prices of substitutes and complements, consumer income, number of consumers and consumer preferences, among other factors. These factors are also important at the aggregate level, so national price levels and incomes can be viewed as determinants of total demand for goods and services and, therefore, the current account. We now examine the impact of each variable on the exchange rate as suggested by the traditional model.

1.1.1. Prices

As the general level of prices in our country increases, our goods become relatively less attractive in the international marketplace. Assuming that prices of our trading partners remain unchanged, foreign spending on our goods will decrease, and the amount of foreign currency converted to the domestic currency will decrease. The increase in domestic prices, then, leads to reduced demand for our currency and to its eventual depreciation. Another way of analyzing this scenario is to view it from the point of view of the other country's currency. Since its goods are now relatively more attractive, the increase in our prices also means that our consumers want to buy more foreign goods. To buy those goods, they have to buy the foreign currency, thus increasing the demand and ultimately the price of that currency. Thus, if

$$S = f([P_d/P_f]), \tag{5.1}$$

Then, according to the theory, we hypothesize that

$$S' > 0 \tag{5.1'}$$

where S is the exchange rate defined as the number of units of the domestic currency needed to buy one unit of the foreign currency, and P_d and P_f stand for the levels of domestic and foreign prices respectively. The hypothesis is expressed in terms of S', the first derivative of the exchange rate function with respect to the ratio of the two prices. The first derivative is expected to be greater than zero since the increase in domestic prices relative to foreign prices is expected to be associated with increases in the exchange rate. For example, if S represents the US dollar to British pound exchange rate, an increase in US prices, other things equal, leads to the depreciation of the dollar according to the traditional flow model.

Figure 5.1 shows the effect of a change in relative prices on the exchange rate. Let us assume that we live in a world of flexible exchange rates and that the foreign exchange market is initially at equilibrium. Equilibrium occurs at point E, where the supply of pounds is equal to the demand for pounds. Supply of pounds is generated by British purchases of foreign goods and services. Demand for pounds in the foreign exchange market arises when foreign residents, in this case US residents, wish to buy British goods. Notice that since supply of pounds implies payment to US residents and demand for pounds implies payment to British residents, equilibrium in the foreign exchange market is tantamount to equilibrium in the balance of payments.

If prices of US goods now increase while British prices remain the same, US residents will want to buy more British goods. To do so, they convert their dollars into pounds. The demand curve for pounds shifts to the right, resulting in a new equilibrium at E' and a new exchange rate S'. The pound thus appreciates versus the dollar; conversely, the dollar depreciates versus the pound.

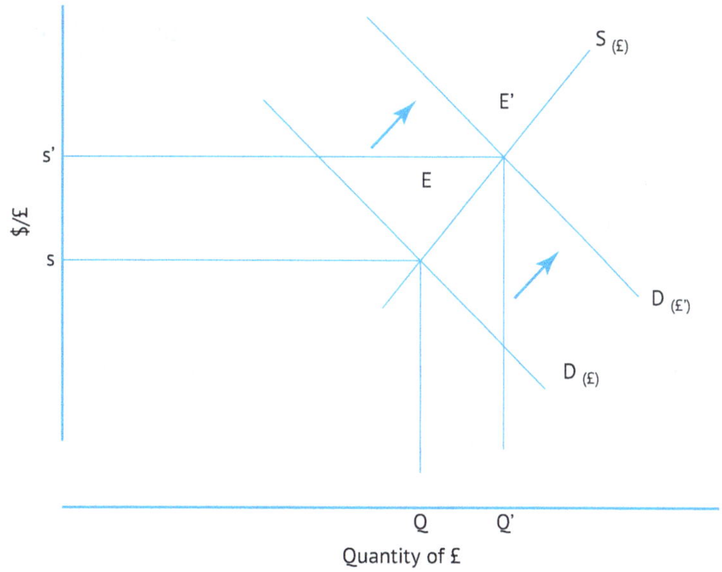

Figure 5.1 The Impact of Changing Relative Prices on the Foreign Exchange Rate.

1.1.2. Incomes

Consumer incomes affect demand for goods and services. An increase in real income increases demand for all goods, including imports. An increase in purchases of imports necessitates increased purchase of foreign currency.

Thus,

$$S = f\,(Y_d/Y_f) \tag{5.2}$$

where Y_d and Y_f represent domestic and foreign real income, respectively; according to this theory, the hypothesis is stated as:

$$S' > 0 \tag{5.2'}$$

The relationship indicates that an increase in domestic real income relative to foreign real income leads to a depreciation of the domestic currency (that is, the exchange rate as defined increases). Thus, if real income in the US increases, while real income in Britain stays the same, US residents will increase their consumption of imports from Britain. The exact degree of the increase will depend on the real income elasticity of the demand for British exports in the US. Therefore, when US spending on British goods increases, the demand for British pounds increases and the British pound appreciates versus the dollar.

1.2. The Financial Account

Imbalances in a country's current account can be offset by developments in the financial account, which describes returns on assets. Differentials in asset returns come about through differentials in interest rates prevailing in each country.

Increases in the foreign interest rate encourage both domestic and foreign investors to invest in foreign assets. Thus,

$$S = f((i_d - i_f) \tag{5.3}$$

where i_d and i_f represent domestic and foreign interest rates. The hypothesis pertaining to the relationship between interest rate differential and the exchange rate can be expressed as:

$$S' < 0 \tag{5.3'}$$

This relationship indicates that an increase in the domestic interest rate, holding the foreign interest rate constant, will be expected to lead to an appreciation of the domestic currency. An inflow of funds into the home country increases the demand for the domestic currency, and the number of units of foreign currency required to buy one unit of domestic currency increases.

1.3. The Combined Model

We now incorporate all these exchange rate determinants in one equation to develop the testable relation

$$S = a + b(P_d/P_f) + c(Y_d/Y_f) - d(i_d i_f) + U \tag{5.4}$$

where a is the constant parameter; b, c, and d are the estimated coefficients for the independent variables; and U is the error term. The signs preceding the coefficients denote the expected direction of influence from independent to dependent variable.

Concept Questions

1. What variables determine exchange rates according to the traditional flow model?
2. Graphically illustrate the impact of a decline in domestic prices on the exchange rate.

2. The Monetary Model

The monetary model offers an alternative way of examining the factors behind exchange rate changes. The fundamental element of the model is the importance of the money market, through which all necessary adjustments take place. There are various versions of the monetary model. The version used here is built on several assumptions, including

Assumption 1. Purchasing Power Parity holds.

Commodity arbitrage between two countries results in (exchange-rate-adjusted) price level equality. Thus,

$$S = P_d/P_f \tag{5.5}$$

Assumption 2. Domestic and foreign assets are perfect substitutes.

For a given class of assets, financial arbitrage results in equal real interest rates (adjusted for exchange rate expectations or, in accordance with the first assumption, adjusted for expectations in the inflation rate).

Assumption 3. The demand-for-money function includes interest rates and real incomes.

Specifically, an increase in interest rates brings a decrease in the quantity of money demanded. An increase in real income, on the other hand, increases the demand for money (shifts the demand for money curve to the right). This is shown as

$$Md = f\ (i,Y) \tag{5.6}$$

where Md is the quantity of real money balances demanded, i is the interest rate, and Y is real income.

Assumption 4. Movement toward equilibrium is achieved through adjustments in the money market.

In case of excess supply or demand in a market, prices will react to bring the money market back to equilibrium.

To develop the monetary model, we start with the equilibrium condition for the money market:

$$Md = Ms/P \tag{5.7}$$

where Ms is the domestic nominal stock of money. We may restate (5.7) to show the level of prices commensurate with equilibrium:

$$P = Ms/Md \tag{5.8}$$

Substituting equation (5.8) in the purchasing power relationship between price and exchange rate (equation 5.5), we derive a relationship between the exchange rate and the money variables:

$$S = (Ms/Md)_f/(Ms/Md) \tag{5.9}$$

or

$$S = (Ms_f/Ms)/(Md_f/Md) \tag{5.10}$$

where the subscript $_f$ indicates the foreign country variable.

We can expand equation 5.10 further by replacing Md with its functional determinants, the interest rate (i) and real income (Y), from equation (5.6). This yields one version of the monetary model:

$$S = (Ms_f /Ms)/[f(i,Y)_f/f(i,Y))] \quad (5.11)$$

The testable form of this equation is

$$S = a + b(Ms_f/Ms) - c(Y_f/Y) + d(i - i_f) + u \quad (5.12)$$

The monetary model, then, includes the real income and interest rate variables that appear in the traditional flow model, although the nature of the relationship is different. According to the traditional flow model, an increase in domestic real income leads to depreciation of the domestic currency. In the monetary model, an increase in domestic real income leads to an increase in money demand. Assuming that the money stock remains unchanged, prices will fall; the domestic currency then appreciates.

Changes in domestic and foreign interest rates also interact with the exchange rate. According to the monetary model, an increase in the domestic interest rate is a signal of more inflation to come. As a result, the demand for money decreases, bringing about higher prices, which in turn causes the domestic currency to depreciate. Finally, an increase in domestic money raises prices and depreciates the home currency.

Concept Questions

1. State the assumptions of the monetary model.
2. What are the variables influencing exchange rates according to the monetary model?
3. Contrast the impact of an increase in US real income on the dollar/mark rate under the traditional flow model with the impact under the monetary model.

3. The Portfolio Balance Model

Portfolio balance (asset) models are generally described as general equilibrium models (see Bergstrand, 1983; Frankel, 1983, International Monetary Fund, 2008). They describe a state of equilibrium that incorporates all asset markets, not just the money market. Equilibrium in these models is reached because of continual interaction between money and other markets, such as the bond market. The financial asset markets equate stock demand and supply, while the goods market equates flow demand and supply. The portfolio balance framework assumes that financial assets reach their prices as their owners adjust their portfolio holdings in accordance with their respective yields (as well as those of related assets).

Assume there are two countries: Japan and the United States. The portfolio balance model considers the following assets: Japanese government bonds, net US bonds issued in dollars, and the Japanese monetary base. Interest rates and exchange rates change as stocks of financial assets change. Thus

(a) If the Japanese government finances its deficits through bonds, the public holdings of that asset increase. This increase in bond holdings is considered an increase in wealth, which leads to an increase in the demand for foreign assets and a consequent increase in the demand for and price of the foreign currency. In this case, the exchange rate, S, which is defined as number of JPY per USD, increases:

$$S = f(Bd) \tag{5.13}$$

where Bd represents the value of Japanese bonds. According to the portfolio balance model, the relationship between domestic bond holdings and the exchange rate forms the following hypothesis:

$$S' > 0 \tag{5.13'}$$

According to (5.13'), the Japanese yen depreciates as the Japanese government issues its bonds. The direction of the impact of the increase in bond holdings on the exchange rate, however, is not always clear. As the Japanese government goes into debt, interest rates at home rise, making Japanese securities more attractive and US securities relatively less so. Japan's residents, then, may decide to decrease their holdings of foreign securities. This process implies an increase in the demand for Japanese yen and leads to an appreciation of the yen. It is depicted as:

$$S = f(Bd) \tag{5.14}$$

The hypothesis here is:

$$S' < 0 \tag{5.14'}$$

Under this scenario, then, the yen appreciates versus the dollar. The net impact on the exchange rate depends on the relative magnitude of the two effects described by relations (5.13) and (5.14).

(b) At least a portion of the country's current account surplus may be settled through US bonds. As the net holdings of US bonds eventually increase, asset holders find themselves with more foreign bonds in their portfolios than the desired level. They then adjust by shifting their holdings toward Japanese assets, which leads to a stronger yen.

$$S = f(Bf) \tag{5.15}$$

where Bf is the amount of foreign bonds, in this case from the US, generating the hypothesis:

$$S'<0 \quad (5.15')$$

According to (5.15'), an increase in net US claims held by Japanese residents will ultimately lead to portfolio adjustments, which will lead to an appreciation of the yen.

(c) An increase in the monetary base resulting from money-financed deficits leads to further portfolio shifts. Asset holders adjust to new positions by increasing their holdings of foreign bonds, thereby making the foreign currency stronger. This is illustrated in relation (5.16):

$$S = f(MB) \quad (5.16)$$

where MB is the country's monetary base. The hypothesis is:

$$S'>0 \quad (5.16')$$

(d) The final component of the model is the interest rate. An increase in the US interest rate makes US securities more attractive and leads to a portfolio shift away from Japanese towards US bonds. The yen, then, depreciates. Thus,

$$S = f(i_{us}) \quad (5.17)$$

The hypothesis, then, is:

$$S'>0 \quad (5.17')$$

We now combine relations (5.13) through (5.17) to test a complete version of the Portfolio Balance Model:

$$S = a + b(Bd) - c(Bf) + d(MB) + g(i_{us}) + U \quad (5.18)$$

According to (5.18), the Japanese yen/US dollar rate increases (or decreases) when Japanese government debt that is held by Japanese residents (Bd) increases; it decreases when the net US claims held by Japanese residents (Bf) increase; increases when the Japanese monetary base (MB) increases; and increases when the US interest rate increases. The yen appreciates when net US claims held by Japanese residents increase and depreciates when either the Japanese monetary base or the US interest rate increases. When Japanese government debt held by Japanese residents increases, however, the yen may appreciate or depreciate.

Concept Questions

1. Explain the nature of general equilibrium models.
2. What are the variables affecting exchange rates within the framework of the portfolio balance model?

III. Asset Pricing Models

This section explains two asset pricing models used in finance: the International Capital Asset Pricing Model (ICAPM) and the International Asset Pricing Theorem (IAPT).

1. The International Capital Asset Pricing Model (ICAPM)

Another approach to the valuation of currencies follows the models used for valuing other financial assets. One such model is the Capital Asset Pricing Model (CAPM). The CAPM expresses the required rate of return on a security in terms of the degree of its systematic risk. Thus,

$$E(Rj) = Rf + [E(Rm) - Rf]\ bj \qquad (5.19)$$

where E(Rj) is the expected return on security j, Rf is the risk-free rate, E(Rm) is the expected return on the market index, and bj is the security's index of systematic risk. This relation can now be used to formulate a valuation approach for a particular asset. That is, if the price of a security, Pj, is

$$Pj = (\text{expected cash flow})/(1 + \text{required return}) \qquad (5.20)$$

then

$$Pj0 = E(P1)/\{1 + [Rf + (Rm - Rf)\ b]\} \qquad (5.21)$$

where E(P1) is the expected price at time 1.

The CAPM has been criticized on several grounds. Application of the CAPM and the market model to an international valuation scheme, such as that presented by exchange rate determination, raises certain important questions, in particular: What is the appropriate risk-free rate? What is the relevant market index? How should inflation differentials be treated?

There are no firm answers to these questions. In formulating the ICAPM for currencies, the US Treasury bill rate is often used as the risk-free rate, although the London Interbank Offered Rate (LIBOR) has also been used. The S&P 500 or a weighted average of major indices of the countries incorporated in the analysis can be used as a proxy of the market rate. Another possibility is the use of a currency-based index, such as the Special Drawing Rights composite. The ICAPM for the U.S dollar/Swiss franc exchange rate, then, may take the form:

$$E(R_{SF,USD}) = Rf + [E(Rm) - Rf]b \qquad (5.22)$$

where $E(R_{SF,USD})$ is the expected (or required) rate of return on holding francs to exchange them for dollars at the end of the period. The current exchange rate, S_0, would then be:

$$S_0 = E(S_1)/\{1 + [Rf + (Rm - Rf)\ b\} \qquad (5.23)$$

where $E(S_1)$ is the expected exchange rate at time 1.

2. The International Arbitrage Pricing Theorem (IAPT)

The International Arbitrage Pricing Theorem, or IAPT, is also used to price financial assets. While the CAPM can be faulted on its use of only one explanatory factor or index, the APT allows for the working of many factors (Roll and Ross, 1980; Roll, 1977). Furthermore, the theoretical framework surrounding the APT is much simpler than that used to derive the CAPM. For example, instead of requiring the construction of efficient portfolios, APT concentrates on expressing the return on each security as dependent on the influence of several factors.

The general version of the theorem can be stated as:

$$ERj = a + b\,(\text{factor }1) + c\,(\text{factor }2) + \ldots + z(\text{factor }n) \tag{5.24}$$

where ERj is the expected return on security i. The relation (5.24) can also be expressed in terms of risk premia. The risk premium on security j, then, is expressed as a function of risk premia allotted to the determining factors

$$pj = b(pf1) + c(pf2) + \ldots + z(pfn) \tag{5.25}$$

where pj is the risk premium, or excess return over the risk-free rate, of security j, and pf1,2,..n are the risk premia on the other factors. The question we may want to ask here is what are the relevant factors? In a study pertaining to the stock market, Burmeister and Wall (1986) offer a linkage between the stock market and macroeconomic activity within a domestic APT framework. The factors they identify are the unexpected change in risk premia, the unexpected change in the term structure, the unexpected inflation, and the unanticipated change in the growth rate of real final sales. Currency theorists can rely on the traditional flow, monetary, and portfolio balance models to provide them with relevant factors. Further developments in IAPT for exchange rates, then, could come from the use of these theories within an arbitrage pricing model context.

Concept Questions

1. What is the ICAPM? How can it be used in determining the value of a certain currency?
2. How does the formulation of the IAPT differ from that of the ICAPM?

IV. Market Microstructure and the Foreign Exchange Rate

Although the models above are elegant and generated from accepted theories in monetary international economics and international finance, they rely solely on macroeconomic variables. Yet, empirical studies have shown that these variables explain a relatively small portion of the variation in exchange rates. An alternative model is based, instead, on microeconomic variables (Lyons, 2001). Microstructure models consider a different set of institutional concerns:

price information, order flow, matching of buyers and sellers, and dealer pricing policies. The models relax some of the assumptions of macro-based models, most of which have been borrowed from theories applicable to perfectly competitive markets. For example:

I. Information: Microstructure models do not assume that all information is available to all participants, as is assumed in macro-models. Furthermore, not all information is absorbed quickly by the market. Induced effects of news will have to be considered in the more distant future as well.
II. Participants: In a macro-based approach, each participant has the same influence on price and quantity traded. Microstructure models, on the other hand, acknowledge the asymmetry in market information by different groups of participants.
III. Market mechanisms: Microstructure models do not necessarily assume that all trading mechanisms affect prices to the same extent.

The defining characteristics of the foreign exchange market make it an appropriate candidate for a microstructure-based explanation. Foreign exchange market microstructure models are motivated by three characteristics of the market (IMF, 1990):

- Its size. As we have already pointed out, the foreign exchange market is the largest of all financial markets.
- The lack of transparency (for many participants) of the market order flow. The market does not have information on customer-dealer and interbank trades; dealers, therefore, look at order flow for price discovery signals.
- The market's dependence on interbank trading.

The dimensions of market order flow form the foundation of the microstructure approach. Foreign exchange dealers have information about market orders that their customers do not have. Orders arrive at a random fashion. Risk-averse dealers balance their positions by adjusting prices. If they have more long positions than anticipated, they will lower their price to attract buyers. The impact of order flow on exchange rates can then be channeled either through asymmetric risk sharing (dealers versus customers) or through the private information that orders carry and upon which trades are made and price changes occur.

V. Short Run and Behavioral Approaches

In the short run, exchange rates may be affected by various non-economic factors. Thus, currency movements may be influenced by global and/or national developments. At times of global economic or political unrest, investors will "fly to safety." In general, that means preference towards the US dollar. When a country or a region is facing economic or political instability, their currency feels the pressure. Market participants dump the currency in favor of a stronger one. For example, in December 2013, allegations of corruption within Turkey's government increased the country's political-risk perception, thus battering the Turkish lira.

Another set of explanations comes from behavioral economics and finance. Market participants are influenced by their emotions, which are assumed away by traditional finance models.

Emotions include excessive optimism or pessimism. Some investors may be over-optimistic about the future value of the euro versus the US dollar, while others may be pessimistic. Since there is no guarantee that the actions of one group will offset those of the other, currency values will change. Biases or failure to incorporate all available information may also influence investor behavior.

VI. Currency Options Valuation

As we noted in Chapter 2, the price of an option is reflected in its premium. The size of that premium may be shaped by a variety of factors, including the expected volatility of the underlying currency, the time to maturity, and the strike price.

Several option-pricing models have been constructed, including those provided by Black and Scholes (1973). Valuation of foreign exchange options is more complicated than stock option valuation. As Garman and Kohlhagen (1983) state, the Black-Scholes model assumes a single interest rate. In the foreign currency market, however, both foreign and domestic interest rates must be considered. When parity is achieved, the differential between these rates must equal the forward premium or discount. The relationship between domestic and foreign interest rates on one hand and forward rates on the other can be extended to options.

The model offered by Garman and Kohlhagen (1983) pertains to European options; that is, to options that can be exercised at expiration time only. The price of a call option, then, is expressed as

$$C(S,T) = e^{-rT} SN(x + \sigma\sqrt{T}) - e^{-rDT} KN(x) \qquad (5.26)$$

where

$x = [\ln(S/K) + \{r_D - r_F - (\sigma^2/2\}T]/\sigma\sqrt{}\,T$

and S = spot currency price expressed as domestic units per foreign unit

T = time remaining until the maturity of the option

C(S, T) = price of a foreign exchange call option expressed as number of domestic units per foreign unit

r_D = domestic risk-free interest rate

r_F = foreign risk-free interest rate

K = exercise price of option expressed as domestic units per foreign unit

T = time remaining until the maturity of the option = spot currency price variability

N(.) = cumulative normal distribution function

Giddy (1983) extends the Garman-Kohlhagen model to find the price for a put currency-options contract through the forward market. Since the difference between the price of a call and that of a put is equal to the difference between the forward rate and the exercise price, K (call-put forward parity), can be extended to the valuation of put options by referring to the parity relationship between puts and calls. Giddy's basic relationship is

$$C(k) - P(k) = (F - k)/(1 + k)^t \quad (5.27)$$

where C(k) is the call option price, P(k) is the put-option price, F is the forward currency at option maturity, and k is the interest rate for time t (the period of the contract). Giddy calls this relationship the "put-call-forward exchange parity (PCFP) theory."

Concept Questions

1. What are the variables entering the currency-options valuation expression?
2. Explain the meaning of put-call parity and its importance to options valuation.

VII. Summary

This chapter has discussed the market determinants of foreign exchange rates. The theories covered provide explanations about currency movements based on one or more of three groups of factors: The goods sector (traditional and monetary models); financial assets (monetary, portfolio, ICAPM, and IAPT); and market microstructure.

The importance of knowing what affects the value of currencies cannot be overstated. Governments want to know what factors influence their currencies so that they can formulate appropriate policies. For example, if the monetary model is viewed as credible by the authorities, they can achieve depreciation of the domestic currency through an increase in the domestic money supply. An expansionary policy resulting in increases in real income will have different effects within a monetary framework from those associated with the traditional flow framework. Other market participants also need to know what is behind exchange rate movements in order to formulate their own market strategies.

Despite the great need to understand what determines foreign exchange rates, no theoretical model has provided the complete and unequivocal explanation. Some of the models differ in the explanatory factors they propose. Even when the factors are the same, the direction of influence exerted may differ. Does this imply that these models are not reliable?

Before we discard the models described in this chapter, we should consider that models or theories are simplified representations of reality. Their ability to describe reality depends as much on their structure as it does on their assumptions and their time horizon. It depends on the way they view how markets interact with each other and how they portray the decision making by market participants in formulating expectations and making decisions. Usually these expectations are considered more important in the short run than in the long run. Monetary factors may also be considered more important in the short run than in the long run. On the other hand, changes in the current account may be more significant over the long run. These questions and explanations may at least partially account for the differences in the structure and performance of these models.

Finally, government intervention and the nature of the international monetary system are major considerations in the determination of currency values by whatever theory one chooses to adopt.

Key Terms and Concepts

In the order in which they are presented in the text

The traditional flow model: The traditional model, also called the balance of payments model, views the exchange rate as being determined by the variables behind flow, supply of and demand for a currency. According to this model, exchange rates are determined by relative incomes, relative prices, and the interest rate differential between the relevant countries.

The monetary model: In the monetary model, the adjustments necessary to determine the exchange rate take place through the money market. The model makes the following assumptions: Purchasing Power Parity holds; domestic and foreign assets are perfect substitutes; the demand for money function includes interest rates and real incomes; and, movement toward equilibrium is achieved through adjustments in the money market. The exchange rate, then, is determined by relative money supplies, relative incomes, and the interest rate differential between the two countries.

The portfolio balance models: Portfolio balance (asset) models are general equilibrium models. Equilibrium incorporates all asset markets, and is reached as a result of continual interaction between money and other markets, such as the bond market. The financial asset markets equate stock demand and supply, while the goods market equates flow demand and supply. The model assumes that financial assets reach their prices as their owners adjust their portfolio holdings in accordance with their respective yields (as well as those of related assets). At equilibrium, the exchange rate is a function of domestic and foreign bonds, the monetary base, and interest rates.

The International Capital Asset Pricing Model (ICAPM): The exchange rate determination version of the ICAPM states that the exchange rate is a function of the expected exchange rate, the risk-free rate, and the market rate of return.

International Asset Pricing Theorem (IAPT): The IAPT expresses the exchange rate as a function of the risk premia associated with the relevant factors.

Market microstructure theories: Microstructure theories relax some of the assumptions of macroeconomic-based models. Instead, these models consider a set of institutional concerns, such as price information, order flow, matching of buyers and sellers, and dealer pricing policies.

Short run theories: In the short run, exchange rates may be influenced by various economic and non-economic factors, such as national and global political and economic developments.

Behavioral theories: When buying or selling currencies, foreign exchange market participants may be influenced by their emotions, including optimism and pessimism, biases, or failure to incorporate all available information.

Currency options pricing: According to currency pricing models, the size of the premium is shaped by the expected volatility of the underlying currency, the time to maturity, the strike price, and the interest rates of the two countries.

Marshall-Lerner condition: The Marshall Lerner condition states that devaluation of the currency will affect a country's imports and exports. If the absolute sum of the elasticity of demand for exports and the elasticity of demand for imports is greater than one, the devaluation will improve the country's balance of trade.

Currency substitution: Substitutions between domestic and foreign currency facilitate the transmission of monetary shocks between countries.

The fundamental equilibrium exchange rate (FEER): The FEER is the exchange rate that is consistent with both internal and external balance simultaneously.

Web Exercises

W1. Using annual data from the International Monetary Fund's *International Financial Statistics* for the JPY/USD exchange rate between 1975 and 2018, conduct an empirical test on

a. The traditional model (equation 5.4), and
b. The monetary model (equation 5.12)

What do your results reveal about the validity of each of the models?

Note: Examine the statistical properties of your regressions, and suggest alternative formulations.

Questions and Problems

1. Discuss the assumptions of the monetary model. Assess the importance of each of these assumptions to the conclusions of the model.
2. According to the traditional flow model, an increase in domestic prices relative to foreign prices leads to a depreciation of the domestic currency. Figure 5.1 shows what happens to the exchange rate during a period of flexible exchange rates. Redraw Figure 5.1 assuming that the increase in domestic prices takes place during a period of fixed rates. Comment on the differences in the impact on the exchange rate during the two periods.
3. "The US dollar experienced wide fluctuations during the last five years." Explain this phenomenon using what you know about foreign exchange rate determination.
4. Critically evaluate the ICAPM as it applies to currencies. How would you formulate the model? How would you express the variable representing the expected return on the currency? What would you use as the risk-free rate? Why? What is the nature

of the market index you would include? What are the implications of the model? What are its shortcomings?

5. Formulate the IAPT for the yen/dollar rate. How many factors would you include? Why?
6. What is the impact of an increase in US interest rates on the dollar? Why? (Hint: Start by referring to the theories of exchange rate determination discussed in this chapter.)
7. What are the differences between exchange rate determination and other models of asset price determination? Explain. (Suggestion: Select a specific financial market, such as the stock market or the bond market. Then contrast that market with the foreign exchange market in terms of price determination.)
8. The director of FX trading of your firm feels exuberant about the British pound and directs you to buy. How would you classify the exchange rate determination that she adheres to?
9. Your company does a great deal of business in Switzerland. Your supervisor wants to know how the value of the Swiss franc is determined in the foreign exchange market. She also has a particular interest in learning about the factors behind changes in the Swiss franc in response to changes in the value of the euro.
10. You are hired by the South-Korean government to assist in determining whether the won is currently undervalued or overvalued. Could you use the theories presented in this chapter as the foundation of your report? Explain.

Selected References

Batten, D.S., and R. W. Hafer. 1984. Currency Substitution; a Test of its Importance. *Review* 66. Federal Reserve of St. Louis (August/September): 5–11.

Bergstrand, J.H. 1983. Selected Views of Exchange Rate Determination After a Decade of Floating. *New England Economic Review.* Federal Reserve Bank of Boston (May/June): 14–29.

Black, F. and M. Scholes. 1973. The Pricing of Options and Corporate Liabilities. *Journal of Political Economy* (May–June): 637–54.

Branson, W.H., H. Halttunen, and P. Masson. 1979. "Exchange Rates in the Short Run." *European Economic Review* 12 (4): 395–402. https://doi.org/10.1016/0014-2921(79)90029-1.

Burmeister, E. and K.D. Wall. 1986. The Arbitrage Pricing Theory and Macroeconomic Factor Measures. *The Financial Review* 21, no. 1 (February): 1–20. https://doi.org/10.1111/j.1540-6288.1986.tb01103.x.

Canto, V. A., and G. Nickelsburg. 1987. *Currency Substitution: Theory and Evidence from Latin America.* Boston: Kluwer Academic Publishers.

Cline, W. 2014. Estimates of Fundamental Equilibrium Exchange Rates, November 2014. *Policy Brief,* Number PB14-25. Washington, DC: Peterson Institute for International Economics.

Curley, A. J., and R. M. Bear. 1979. *Investment Analysis and Management.* New York: Harper & Row Publishers.

Evans, M.D. D., and R.K. Lyons. 2002. Informational Integration and FX Trading. *Journal of International Money and Finance* 21(6): 807–31.

Evans, M.D. D., and Richard K. Lyons. 2005. Do Currency Markets Absorb News Quickly? *Journal of International Money and Finance* 24(2): 197–217.

Evans, M. D. D., and R.K. Lyons. 2008. "How is Macro News Transmitted to Exchange Rates?" *Journal of Financial Economics* 88(1): 26–50.

Flood, M. D. 1991. Microstructure Theory and the Foreign Exchange Market. *Federal Reserve Bank of St. Louis Review* (November/December): 52–70.

Frankel, J. A. 1983. Monetary and Portfolio-Balance Models of Exchange Rate Determination. In *Economic Interdependence and Flexible Exchange Rates*, edited by J. S. Bhandari and B. H. Putnam, 84–115. Cambridge, Massachusetts: The MIT Press.

Frankel, J. A., G. Galli, and A. Giovannini. 1996. *The Microstructure of Foreign Exchange Markets*. University of Chicago Press/NBER.

Garman, M., and S. Kohlhagen. 1983. Foreign Currency Option Values. *Journal of International Money and Finance*. (December): 231–37.

Giddy, I. H. 1983. Foreign Exchange Options. *The Journal of Futures Markets* (Summer): 143–66.

International Monetary Fund. 1990. *International Capital Markets*. Washington, DC: International Monetary Fund Publications, 125–28.

International Monetary Fund. 2008. The Equilibrium Exchange Rate: Alternative Concepts and Their Applications in IMF Surveillance. 2008. *Background Document 3*. Washington DC: International Monetary Fund Publications.

Jacque, L. 1968. *Measurement of Foreign Exchange Risk*. Lexington, MA: Lexington Books, D.C. Heath and Company.

King, M. R., C. Osler, and D. Rime. 2013. The Market Microstructure Approach To Foreign Exchange: Looking Back and Looking Forward. *Working Paper*. Norges Bank Research, February 2013.

Lindert, P. H., and C. P. Kindleberger. 1982. *International Economics*. Seventh Edition. Homewood, Illinois: Richard D. Irwin, Chapter 15.

Lyons, R. K. 2008. *The Microstructure Approach to Exchange Rates*. Boston, MA: The MIT Press.

Pearce, D. K. 1983. Alternative Views of Exchange-Rate Determination. *Economic Review*. Federal Reserve Bank of Kansas City, (February): 23–30.

Reynolds-Allen, P., and P. Kenen. 1980. *Asset Markets, Exchange Rates, and Economic Integration*. Cambridge: Cambridge University Press.

Roll, R. 1977. "A Critique of the Asset Pricing Theory's Tests." *Journal of Financial Economics*, (March): 129–76.

Roll, R. and S.A. Ross. 1980. An Empirical Investigation of Arbitrage Pricing Theory. *The Journal of Finance*. 35(5), December, 1073-1103.

Root, F. R. 1984. *International Trade and Investment*. Fifth Edition. Cincinnati: South-Western Publishing Co..

Rose, A. K. 1991. "The role of exchange rates in a popular model of international trade: Does the Marshall-Lerner' condition hold?" *Journal of International Economics*, 30, 301–16.

Rosenberg, M. R. 2003. *Exchange Rate Determination: Models and Strategies for Exchange Rate Forecasting*. New York, NY: McGraw-Hill.

Williamson, J. 1994. Estimates of FEERs. In *Estimating Equilibrium Exchange Rates*, edited by J. Williamson. Washington, DC: Institute for International Economics.

Credit

Table 5.1: Source: https://apps.bea.gov/iTable/iTable.cfm?ReqID=62&step=1#reqid=62&-step=6&isuri=1&6210=1&6200=1.

Chapter 6

Exchange Rate Forecasting

Overview of Chapter Material

Forecasting is one of the most challenging aspects of the study of financial assets in general and exchange rates in particular. Since the advent of floating rates in 1973 and the ensuing increasing volatility in currency values, reliable and accurate currency forecasts have been in great demand. This chapter discusses various forecasting approaches available and shows how they can be applied to alternative exchange rate systems. It explains several measures for evaluating forecasts and notes some managerial implications of forecasting. The ability to understand and practice the science and art of forecasting will be enhanced by combining what you will learn from this chapter with as many applications as possible. Students are strongly encouraged to refer to some of the classic works in forecasting noted in the Reference section of this chapter.

After Studying This Chapter, You Will Be Able To

- Explain the rationale behind formulating exchange rate forecasts
- Understand the various approaches to forecasting exchange rates under alternative exchange rate systems
- Evaluate exchange rate forecasts
- Assess the implications of forecasting for management

Chapter Outline

I. Forecasting Considerations
II. Forecasting Approaches
III. Why Do We Forecast Foreign Exchange Rates?
IV. Forecasting Exchange Rates Under Alternative Exchange Rate Systems
V. Forecasting Under Floating Rates

VI. Forecasting Real Exchange Rates
VII. Forecasting in a Fixed Exchange Rate System
VIII. Evaluating Forecasts
IX. Managerial Implications of Forecasting
X. Summary

I. Forecasting Considerations

The market fundamentals covered up to this point are essential background for understanding what goes on in the foreign exchange market. The fundamentals include the structure of the foreign exchange market, the different types of international monetary systems, and the theories of foreign exchange rate determination.

Understanding the theories that explain past and present circumstances is a necessary but in most cases not sufficient ingredient for successful decision making. By its nature, decision making requires forward looking. Forecasting, then, is essential in decision making. It entails costs and challenges, and it is risky because the future entails risk. Forecasting processes, then, lead to uncertain outcomes. The forecaster must know both the uses and limitation of the forecast(s) generated.

To achieve the best possible forecast, the forecaster must first consider certain important aspects of each forecast employed (Granger, 1980). These considerations include

1. The objective and time horizon of the forecast. What is the purpose of the forecast? A forecast formulated for the purpose of working capital management will be different in form and emphasis from a forecast intended as an input to a long-term investment decision.
2. The information available to the forecaster. One of the basic rules of forecasting is know your data! The forecaster must understand the characteristics of the available data series, such as incomes and interest rates, and the relationships among them. The length and form of each series must be evaluated and any distinguishing characteristic such as trend, seasonality, or outliers identified. If the information has been used in the past, its record of forecasting effectiveness should be investigated. Finally, the cost of acquisition of additional information needs to be examined.
3. The forecasting approach used. As we discuss in the next section, there are various approaches available to the forecaster, each of them with advantages and shortcomings. If various approaches generate different results, the forecaster must examine ways results can be reconciled.
4. Evaluation and revision of the forecast. After providing the forecast, the forecaster must evaluate the extent to which it deviates from the realized value. If possible, the forecast approach should then be revised appropriately. In selecting a forecast, then, the forecaster must consider the manner in which it lends itself to evaluation and revision. Is the forecast to be evaluated using in-sample or out-of-sample

information? Is the forecast going to be evaluated on its own or in relation to other forecasts?

5. Management of the forecast. The ultimate test of the value of a forecast lies in its use. This requires that the forecast must be effectively communicated to the decision makers and its full implications made clear. In short, forecasts for management must be manageable in themselves.

II. Forecasting Approaches

Taxonomies of forecasting approaches have been offered by many scholars and practitioners (Nelson, 1973). Indeed, the forecaster's tool kit includes a variety of approaches, including:

1. Subjective.

   Subjective forecasting relies on the particular knowledge of the forecaster, who may generate a forecast based on some unique knowledge or intuition. Sometimes the subjective approach is preferred because of the speed with which the forecast becomes available. More often, it is adopted because of dissatisfaction with other approaches, reluctance to bear the costs of other approaches, or even inability to comprehend them.

2. Structural and Econometric.

   Structural and econometric modeling involves the formal examination of the economic environment within which the forecasting problem arises. This environment may be depicted in the form of equations representing the relevant relationships. These equations become part of a structural model. If the model is based on economic theories, it is called an econometric model. Models dealing with finance or accounting relationships may also be termed econometric for our purposes. Certain logical steps are followed in putting together a structural model:

   - First, the model must be appropriately specified. That is, the model builder needs to correctly and completely define the variables that should be included in the model.
   - Second, values of the coefficients of the appropriate variables must be estimated.
   - Finally, model results must be evaluated and, if necessary, the model must be revised.

   Although structural models enable us to gain an understanding of the comprehensive nature of the market, they can be very complicated. In their place, then, forecasters may use a reduced equation form of the structural model; the reduced-form equation represents the solution of the structural model. A simple example would be the quantity demanded and quantity supplied equations, forming the structural model, and the resulting price-determination equation (reduced form equation).

3. Deterministic.
   Deterministic models feature the relationship between the variable to be forecasted and time. The forecast, then, is an expression of that relationship. As the dependent variable, time can be represented in a linear (T) or non-linear (T^2) fashion, where T refers to the unit of time appropriate to the particular forecast.

4. Ad-Hoc.
   Ad-hoc methods use the history of the variable to be forecasted. The forecast is then derived by formulating a relationship among the past and present and the future. Some of the weighted moving-average models that are used to eliminate randomness from a series are examples of ad-hoc forecasting.

5. Time Series Analysis.
   Time series analysis also incorporates the history of the variable. Instead of relying on ad-hoc formulations, however, time series models are representations of stochastic processes, since "the sequence of observations evolves through time according to a probability law" (Nelson, 1973; Granger, 1980, Tsay, 2012).

Forecasting is both an art and a science. Forecasters must be both knowledgeable of statistical techniques and economic theory and sufficiently innovative in generating alternative forecasting approaches.

Concept Questions

1. What aspects of a forecast must be considering before deciding on the forecasting method to be used?
2. State and explain each of the available forecasting approaches.

III. Why Do We Forecast Foreign Exchange Rates?

Each and every foreign exchange market participant has a reason for forecasting foreign exchange rates. For example:

Travelers want to know how much their own currency can buy in a foreign country. Forecasting gives them an idea of the expected costs of the trip.

Central banks use forecasts to establish and evaluate possible courses of action they might take regarding their currency or the future value of their international reserves.

Exporters and importers need accurate forecasts to estimate the home currency value of receipts or payments due sometime in the future.

Individual investors want to know the return and risk associated with their investments. If consumption takes place within the home country, the investor will want to know the future value of the exchange rate between the home currency and that of the currency in which the investment has occurred.

Multinational firms have needs for foreign exchange rate forecasting in just about every aspect of their operations. Working capital management decisions, capital budgeting decisions, financing decisions, intercompany funds transfer decisions, and dividend decisions all incorporate to some extent the value of the future exchange rate.

As we indicated already, all market participants need to generate appropriate forecasts in order to make sound decisions in the foreign exchange market.

IV. Forecasting Exchange Rates Under Alternative Exchange Rate Systems

Forecasting foreign exchange rates may require different methodologies depending on the exchange rate system in effect. An analogy is forecasting the price of a commodity when the market is free from intervention versus when it is subject to price control or intervention programs. As long as the prospect of controls or intervention looms on the horizon, it is not enough to assess the pressures exerted on prices by purely economic factors; the forecaster must also gauge the extent to which controls will affect prices if they are effective. The forecasting discussion must therefore distinguish between forecasting under floating and under fixed exchange rates. We should keep in mind that this distinction is not always clear-cut in practice, since observed exchange rate systems do not look or behave exactly like their theoretical counterpart.

Concept Questions

1. Why would General Motors be interested in forecasts of the US dollar/British pound rate? Why would the Bank of China be interested in the US dollar/British pound forecast?
2. To what extent is the exchange rate system an important consideration in formulating exchange rate forecasts?

V. Forecasting Under Floating Rates

We start with forecasting under a system of floating exchange rates. Forecasting methods applied under floating rates are similar to those used to forecast prices of other financial assets, such as stocks and bonds. Some of the methods used, then, are

1. Equilibrium models
2. Fundamental approach
3. Technical approach
4. Market-efficiency approach
5. Mixed approach

Each approach has its own assumptions, advantages, and disadvantages. These approaches may also be used in combination with each other or as a forecast consistency check.

1. Equilibrium Models

The market equilibrium conditions discussed in Chapter 3 can be used to generate simple and quick forecasts.

1.1. Purchasing Power Parity

According to PPP, changes in the foreign exchange rate will follow changes in the rates of inflation in the two countries. For example, if the US inflation rate is expected to be 5% this coming year and Japan's inflation rate is expected to be 2%, then the US dollar is expected to depreciate by 3% versus the Japanese yen (Booth, Duggan, and Koveos, 1985).

1.2. International Fisher Effect

If interest rates reflect inflationary expectations, then relative changes in interest rates between two countries imply changes in relative inflation rates which, in turn, will change the exchange rate. So, if the US risk-free interest rate is 4% and the UK rate with similar maturity is 2%, the dollar is expected to depreciate by 2% versus the pound.

2. Fundamental Approach

The fundamental approach emphasizes fundamental factors in forecasting exchange rates. Fundamental factors include macroeconomic factors such as money supply, inflation rates, trade flows, capital flows, and interest rates. The Traditional Flow and Monetary models of exchange rate determination, as well as combinations of the two, offer frameworks upon which forecasting models can be built. The requirements of the forecast must be clarified in order to specifying the variables to be included in the analysis. That is, the values of the independent variables must be known to the forecaster. One way to assure that is to use independent variables that lag the variable to be forecasted by one or more periods. Using the Traditional Model, then, we can formulate the forecasting equation as

$$S_{t+1} = a + b(P_f/P_d)_t + c\,(Y_f/Y_d)_t + d\,(i_f - i_d)_t + e_t \qquad (5.1)$$

Because fundamental factors reflect basic economic trends, the fundamental approach is intermediate or long term in nature. The use of economic variables with quantifiable magnitudes enables forecasters to build econometric models that can potentially be of considerable complexity. For the most part, fundamental models use monthly or quarterly data and allow a forecast of several quarters ahead (mostly six to eight quarters, but sometimes as many as ten).

Forecasters must at all times be familiar with the characteristics of the data included on both sides of the forecasting equation. Issues regarding data availability and reliability must be addressed early in the analysis. Forecasters must know when each country publishes the appropriate data and how reliable a country's agencies are with respect to data collection and dissemination. Many countries issue preliminary data first and then revise them later on. Forecasters must clearly justify the use a particular data set. Should published data prove unreliable or of limited use, the forecasting approach may need to be reevaluated and/or alternative data sources must be sought.

3. Technical Approach

According to technical analysts, exchange rates are simply the result of interaction between the demand for and the supply of the currencies represented. Technical analysts may accept the fundamental approach as sound enough logically but regard it as impractical and unnecessary. The technical approach instead presupposes certain modes of behavior by market participants, which in turn generate predicted patterns in the exchange rate (Rosenberg, 2003; Edwards and Magee, 1958; Neely, 1997; Neely and Weller, 2011; Luca, 1997). The assumptions of technical forecasting are stated as:

1. The interaction of supply and demand is the sole determinant of market value.
2. Numerous factors, both rational and irrational, are behind supply and demand.
3. Disregarding minor fluctuations in the market, exchange rates tend to move in trends which persist for an appreciable length of time; they thus reveal a pattern. Changes in trends are brought about by shifts in supply and demand.
4. Shifts in supply and demand, whatever their origin, can be detected by the analyst. Some of these detected patterns tend to repeat themselves.

The technical analyst believes that the market can be "beaten" by identifying trend patterns that repeat themselves. The patterns become the basis of primarily short-term forecasts, which in turn dictate the appropriate buy/sell strategy. Technical analysis has its roots in the beginning of the twentieth century, when Charles Dow wrote a series of editorials that appeared in the *Wall Street Journal* in the two-year period of 1900–1902. His views on stock price behavior have withstood the test of time and have become the basis of numerous writings on the subject as well as of the practice of many forecasters. The tools of the foreign exchange technical analyst include technical indicators (such as trend and volume indicators) and chart patterns. Chart patterns may be of the trend continuation of trend reversal variety (www.ifcmarkets.com). Continuation patterns include such formations as triangles, rectangles, flags, pennants, and wedges. Trend reversal patterns, showing the end of one trend and the beginning of another, include head and shoulders, double and triple top and bottom, diamonds, and other formations. Different analysts use different tools and look for different sets of patterns depending on the data used and the emphasis placed on certain market movements. Even though the advent of the computer has made the technical approach quite expeditious, the continuing variety of technical methods seems to indicate that the approach has been evolving for more than a century. Since it has become much easier for everybody, analysts face much tougher competition in promoting their services and face ever greater pressure to produce accurate forecasts.

4. Market Efficiency Approach

The notion of market efficiency, which we discussed in Chapter 3, has special implications for forecasting. The most frequently discussed cases involve the weak and semi-strong forms of efficiency (Giddy and Dufey, 1975, Goodman 1979, Jacque, 1978).

4.1. Weak Form Efficiency

The issue of weak form efficiency is implicit in our discussion of technical analysis. If technical approach can indeed produce profits on a consistent basis, the foreign exchange market is not efficient in the weak form sense. In fact, technical analysis and weak form market efficiency can be viewed as inverse of each other. If the market is weak form efficient, exchange rate changes are random. Past changes can provide no useful information regarding future changes. The foreign exchange market has no memory, so patterns cannot be expected to repeat themselves.

4.2. Semi-strong Form Efficiency

As we explained in Chapter 2, semi-strong efficiency considers not only past exchange rate changes but also other public information. Forward exchange rates, currency futures rates, inflation rates, interest rates, information about the country's stock market, or any other information available to the public that could ostensibly reveal the path of future exchange rates can be included in the semi-strong information set.

4.2.1. Forecasts Based on Forward and Futures Rates

Forward and futures rates provide information for good tests of semi-strong form efficiency. If the forward market is a perfect forecast of the future spot market, then

$$S_{t+n} = F_{tn} \tag{5.2}$$

Where S_{t+n} is the actual spot rate at time t+n, and F_{tn} is today's forward rate maturing at t+n.

Because new information arriving between time t and t+n will probably change the spot exchange rate, the forward rate may not equal the actual future spot. The forward rate, then, can at best be described as unbiased—that is, after estimating the regression:

$$S_{t+n} = a + b\,F_t^n + e_t \tag{5.2'}$$

If the regression error, e_t, is random, the forward rate neither overestimates nor underestimates the future spot rate on a consistent basis. If a=0 and b=1, the forward rate is, again, an unbiased predictor of the future spot rate.

Similar arguments can be made in connection with the forecasting prowess of the futures market. There are differences, of course, between the futures and forward markets, so the forecasting effectiveness of the two markets cannot be assumed to be always the same for a currency. Relatively few currencies have organized futures markets, and some minor currencies also have quite limited forward trading. In this case, the forecaster may use the forward rate quotation of another currency, one whose spot movements are highly correlated with the currency of interest.

There exist numerous studies on the forecasting effectiveness of forward and futures markets. Many of the studies verify the unbiasedness of the forecasts supplied by these markets. Others find poor forecasting performance, which they attribute to a number of factors, including the existence of risk premium and market inefficiencies. The principal advantages of using forecasts provided by forward and futures rates are the ease and low cost of acquisition. Major financial publications offer continuous coverage of the markets. One disadvantage is the limited time dimension of the forecasts provided; forward contracts are, at the most, of one-year maturity, while the most active futures contracts are of less than nine months maturity.

5. Mixed Approach

Forecasters may also use combinations of two or more of the above methods. For example, the forecaster may use the technical approach to forecast the USD to GBP exchange rate for the next month, and use the fundamental approach to forecast for the next six to nine months.

VI. Forecasting Real Exchange Rates

Market participants may also be interested in the behavior of the real exchange rate. A US visitor in Argentina, for instance, is more interested in the purchasing power of the dollar than in the change in the peso to dollar rate (the nominal exchange rate). Subsidiaries of foreign firms that have scheduled payments in the local currency have the same concern. Because the real exchange rate is composed of the nominal exchange rate and prices of the respective countries, a real-rate forecast could be formulated using these individual components. Alternatively, the real exchange rate could be forecasted directly.

The analysis of real exchange rates should be an integral part of any effort to learn more about exchange rate behavior in general. Forecasting real rates, besides being a valid task on its own merits, affords great insights about the behavior of nominal rates and prices.

Concept Questions

1. Describe the elements of a fundamental forecasting model.
2. What is the relationship between technical analysis and market efficiency?
3. What is the role of the forward rate in forecasting future spot rates?

VII. Forecasting in a Fixed Exchange Rate Environment

According to some foreign exchange market observers, an advantage of fixed exchange rates is that currency realignments occur infrequently. Currency value adjustments under a fixed rate regime, however, can be relatively large. Both sides of the "fixed versus floating rates" debate agree that forecasting is not superfluous under either system, although there may be a difference in emphasis on forecasting under the two systems. In a floating rates system, the analyst's challenge lies in forecasting the direction, timing, and magnitude of the future change. Under floating rates, some analysts view timing as a lesser challenge than the other two dimensions. In the case of fixed rates, timing is of the greatest importance, followed by the magnitude of the change. In most cases, the direction of the change is generally well anticipated because of the pressures the country is under to devalue or revalue its currency. Indeed, market participants tend to get very jittery as they wait to see whether the country will devalue its currency on Friday or wait until the following Monday or Wednesday. One or two days, especially over the weekend when markets have two days to adjust to the news, may make a big difference in the speculator's pocketbook because of the size of the adjustment.

The decision to devalue or revalue is in the end made by the government; it is based on economic factors, but political considerations cannot be ignored. The forecaster, then, needs to take stock of a variety of macro and micro issues, including:

1. The Economic Situation

The first task is to examine and assess the state of the economy, with particular attention to the external economic sector. The objective is to arrive at an estimate of the equilibrium exchange rate: the rate that would equate the supply and the demand for the currency in the absence of government exchange rate policies. Some of the factors to be examined include the rate of growth in the country's GNP, and inflation and interest rates. Comparable analysis of other countries, particularly major trade and investment partners, is also necessary.

The analysis can be formulated in terms of selected indicators of economic activity, which may offer a quick glimpse into the pressure exerted on the country's currency. Analysts have used some of the following:

- The rate of change in the country's international reserves.
- The ratio of international reserves to imports.
- The ratio of imports to exports.
- The ratio of domestic to foreign money supply growth rates.
- Foreign debt service ratio.
- Import/export ratio.

2. The Difference Between Actual and Equilibrium Exchange Rates

After identifying the factors behind actual and potential exchange rate movements, the analyst must estimate how far away from equilibrium the current level of the currency is. The length of time over which a currency has been "overvalued" or "undervalued" is a factor. Information on similar experiences the country has had may be relevant as well.

3. The Implications of the Differences between the Two Rates

One of the most difficult tasks a forecaster faces is analysis of the impact of allowing the current situation to persist. Will the economy deteriorate? Will the government face pressures from internal and external groups? Should action take place now or later?

4. Policy Formulation

After generating the appropriate information, the government must decide on a course of action, evaluating all alternatives. While currency realignment is one choice, the government also may consider imposing price controls or taking further fiscal and monetary measures. Assistance may be available from international organizations or trading partners. The costs and benefits of each action should be investigated.

5. Policy Implementation and Control

Once the decision on a policy is made, the manner with which the policy is implemented may be of great importance. Lack of communication with other countries, for example, may provoke retaliatory action, rendering the country's initiative ineffective. Forecasters must in this case have drawn up scenarios of policy revisions. A conscientious effort by the country to manage the new level of its currency effectively may establish a more orderly path for the future.

The exact way of approaching a currency recommendation will differ from forecaster to forecaster. Some forecasters must be careful to follow steps such as we have outlined. Others might use devices such as country checklists to reveal the status of country economic and environmental variables, or statistical methodologies such as discriminant analysis to identify countries likely to realign their currencies. Political risk analysis is another possibility. Whatever the benefits of each, the methodologies used have in general failed to deal effectively with the entire set of objectives represented in the outline above.

Forecasting under fixed rates requires perhaps a more thorough understanding and constant monitoring of country developments than forecasting in a floating rate system. The market cannot be relied on to any extent. While the transition to a floating system in the early 1970s was greeted with skepticism by some, for forecasters it instituted an environment where their skills were both in greater demand and supplied with anticipation of greater effectiveness. Forecasting under government action uncertainty has been replaced by forecasting under market behavior uncertainty; for many the latter uncertainties entail far fewer costs.

Concept Questions

1. What are some of the issues encountered when forecasting under fixed rates?
2. State some of the indicators of economic activity that analysts may use to assess the pressure exerted on a currency under fixed rates.
3. State the variables that you think should be included in a forecast of the black market rate.

VIII. Evaluating Forecasts

Evaluation and revision are integral parts of any forecasting effort. They can take the form of looking at a single forecast or comparing a group of forecasts.

The analyst can sometimes improve the accuracy of a single forecast by adding more relevant data or by examining the data more carefully. For example, in-depth analysis may be conducted on the forecast errors. In the case of time series analysis, the model can be revised until the residuals are random. Beyond checking the logic and construction of the model, however, evaluation of individual forecasts is not particularly meaningful. After all, how does one distinguish between the quality of the forecast and the forecast ability of the series itself? As Granger (1980) indicates, it is "virtually impossible to evaluate the quality of a single forecast about some unique event."

Forecast evaluation, then, is more meaningful when multiple forecasts are available. The analyst may rank forecasts with respect to their performance, assess whether these performance differences are indeed statistically significant and then select the best method. Some of the statistics available to evaluate forecast performance include the Sum of Squared Errors (SSE), the Mean Squared Error (MSE), and the Mean Absolute Error (MAE). They are expressed as follows:

$$SSE = (e_t)^2$$

Taking the square eliminates the possibility of negative errors offsetting positive errors while placing more weight on large errors. By taking the average, we generate the Mean Squared Error:

$$MSE = (1/n)\ SSE$$

Alternatively, we can calculate the absolute, rather than squared, differences between actual and forecasted values, generating:

$$MAE = |e_t|/n$$

where e is the forecast error (the difference between the actual and forecasted values), and n is the number of observations.

Similar measures may be generated by analyzing the percentage forecast errors. These include the Mean Percentage Error (MPE) and the Mean Absolute Percentage Error (MAPE). The generation of percentage errors allows for a more valid comparison of the power of a forecasting approach applied to different series. (See Macridakis and Wheelright [1978] for an explanation of forecast evaluation methods.)

Another measure used is the Theil inequality coefficient; it depicts the predictive ability of a model, and is expressed as

$$U = \sqrt{}\ \{[(1/N^*)\ \Sigma_{t=1}{}^{n}(F_j - A_j)^2]/\ [(1/N^*)\ \Sigma_{t=1}{}^{n}A_j{}^2]\}$$

where N* is the number of new observations to be compared to forecasts. A_j represents the N* number of actual values and F_j is the same number of forecasts. The inequality coefficient, U, then, represents the size of the forecast error in relation to the sum of the variability of the actual and forecasted values. The smaller the U, the more accurate the forecast is (Theil, 1978).

Comparisons among forecasts require certain dimensions of these forecasts, such as the forecast horizon, to be similar. Even after identification of a superior forecast, however, the remaining forecasts cannot be completely ignored. The forecaster may have valid reasons to combine related methods, but at a minimum, the divergence in forecasts should be analyzed. Such an approach may help the forecaster understand the data better, use different methods more effectively in the future, and explain methodology selection to the ultimate user of the forecast more convincingly.

The ultimate test of the model is to forecast out of sample observations and respond to changes in the structure of the series. As much as possible, then, forecast evaluation should reflect this dual concern.

Concept Questions

1. Explain the differences among SSE, MSE, and MAE.
2. What does the Theil inequality coefficient show?

IX. Managerial Implications of Forecasting

Accurate forecasting is an essential part of good decision-making. The quality of managerial decisions depends largely on the quality of the information used. Forecasts can be viewed as information about the future. Some analysts would go as far as to say that forecasts are the only relevant information set the manager needs to make decisions.

The significance of forecasts in decision making places a great deal of responsibility on the forecaster to prepare the product and explain it adequately to the manager (assuming a large organization where separate individuals or units perform the various tasks). To accomplish the task, the forecaster must have a good understanding not only of the methodologies employed but also of international finance. Managers also must understand how to evaluate forecasts and how to maximize the benefit from their use.

Foreign exchange rate forecasting especially has come of age since the advent of floating rates and with the parallel, although unrelated, advancements in technology and information systems. Even though much progress has been made through the years, forecasters must strive to improve their performance through continual practice. As firms and markets become more globalized, the need to generate accurate foreign exchange forecasts will only increase. The need for more cooperation between managers and forecasters will also become stronger as the economic environment gets more complicated.

X. Summary

Forecasting currency values is a fundamental ingredient in decision making for practically every participant in the foreign exchange market. A great deal of care must therefore be taken in formulating and implementing forecasts.

To generate the appropriate forecast, analysts must consider a number of characteristics, including the objective of the forecast, the information available, the approach to be followed, and the way the forecast is to be managed. The role of the exchange rate system in formulating the pertinent methodology differs under fixed and floating rates. Finally, forecasters must have an adequate way to evaluate alternative forecasts and to make the appropriate revisions.

Key Terms and Concepts

In the order in which they are presented in the text

Subjective forecasting: Subjective forecasting relies on the particular knowledge of the forecaster, who may generate a forecast based on some unique knowledge or intuition.

Structural and econometric forecasting: Structural and econometric modeling involves the formal examination of the economic environment within which the forecasting problem arises. This environment may be depicted in the form of equations representing the relevant relationships. These equations become part of a structural model. If the model is based on economic theories, it is called an econometric model.

Deterministic forecasting: Deterministic models feature the relationship between the variable to be forecasted and time.

Ad-hoc forecasting: Ad-hoc methods use the history of the variable to be forecasted. The forecast is then derived by formulating a relationship among the past and present and the future.

Time series forecasting: Time series analysis also incorporates the history of the variable. Time series models are representations of stochastic processes.

Market/equilibrium forecasting: This approach generates forecasts using the relationships produced by the parity conditions (Purchasing Power Parity, Interest Rate Parity, International Fisher Effect, and Forward Rate Theory of Exchange Rate Expectations).

Fundamental approach: The fundamental approach is used to forecast exchange rates with fundamental factors. Fundamental factors include macroeconomic factors such as money supply, inflation rates, trade flows, capital flows, and interest rates.

Technical approach: According to technical analysts, disregarding minor fluctuations in the market, exchange rates tend to move in trends, thus revealing a pattern. Changes in the pattern are brought about by shifts in supply and demand.

Market efficiency approach: This approach assumes that foreign exchange markets are efficient in the weak and semi-strong sense. If the market is weak form efficient, exchange rate changes are random. Past changes can provide no useful information regarding future changes. The foreign exchange market has no memory, so patterns cannot be expected to repeat themselves. If the market is efficient in the semi-strong sense, foreign exchange rates reflect all public information, such as forward rates and interest rates.

Forecasting in a fixed exchange rate environment: Under a fixed rates environment, forecasters may first analyze the country's economic situation and then estimate the difference between actual and equilibrium rates and explore the implications of the differences between the two rates in terms of policy formulation, implementation, and control.

Web Exercises

W1. Using annual data from the International Monetary Fund's *International Financial Statistics* for the JPY/USD exchange rate between 1973 and 2018, formulate a forecasting model for the yen. Evaluate and comment on your results.

W2. If you search, you will undoubtedly find websites of technical analysts who provide information about their services and approach. Go to one of those websites (http://www.fxstreet.com/rates-charts/live-charts/) and review the tools used to forecast foreign exchange rates.

Questions and Problems

1. You have just decided to go on a two-month visit to Italy. You will be leaving in about three months. How would you go about forecasting the dollar/euro rate?
2. This chapter includes examples of bilateral exchange rate forecasting. How would you revise these methods to arrive at multilateral forecasts? Give examples.
3. In December 2013, the Fed announced that it will taper its QE activity over the next few months. How would this information help you in assessing the future course of the dollar?
4. ACME Construction is planning to start operations in Switzerland. One of the factors in its decision is the future behavior of the Swiss franc, since ACME's costs and revenues will be in Swiss francs. These revenues, at least in part, will be sent back to the US. How would ACME arrive at the appropriate forecasts (it needs short-term, intermediate-term, and long-term forecasts)?

   Be as specific as possible.
5. ACME is also considering establishing operations in Zagrovia. The behavior of the Zagri, Zagrovia's currency, is a factor determining its decision to locate there. How would ACME go about forecasting the behavior of the Zagri (short-term, intermediate-term, and long-term)?
6. "Although existing empirical models of systematic exchange rate behavior appear to perform little or no better than random-walk models in out-of-sampling forecasting tests based on ex post data, ... there is scope for some optimism that empirical

modeling of exchange rates will someday lead to significantly better than random ex post explanations and will thus provide an informative framework for ex ante policy and conditional forecasting" (Isard, 1987).

Comment on this statement.

7. Explain how each of the following can be used to forecast currency devaluations or revaluations:

    a. The rate of change in the country's international reserves.
    b. The ratio of international reserves to imports.
    c. The ratio of imports to exports.
    d. The ratio of domestic to foreign money supply growth rates.
    e. Foreign debt service ratio.
    f. Import/export ratio.

Selected References

Booth, G. G., J. E. Duggan and P. E. Koveos. 1985. Deviations from Purchasing Power Parity, Relative Inflation, and Exchange Rates: The Recent Experience. *Financial Review,* (May, 195–218.

Edwards, R. D. and J. Magee, Jr. 1958. *Technical Analysis of Stock Trends.* Fourth Edition. Springfield, Mass: Magee.

Giddy, I. H. and G. Dufey. 1975. The Random Behavior of Flexible Exchange Rates. *Journal of International Business Studies,* Spring, 1-32.

Goodman, S. H. 1979. Foreign Exchange Rate Forecasting Techniques: Implications for Business and Policy. *Journal of Finance* 34 (2): 415–27. doi:10.2307/2326981.

Granger, C. W. J. 1980. *Forecasting in Business and Economics.* New York: Academic Press.

Jacque, L. L. 1978. *Management of Foreign Exchange Risk: Theory and Praxis.* Lexington, Mass: Lexington Books.

Luca, C. *Technical Analysis Applications of the Global Currency Markets.* New York: New York Institute of Finance, 1997.

Macridakis, S. and S.C. Wheelright. 1978. *Interactive Forecasting.* San Francisco: Holden-Day.

Neely, C. J. 1997. Technical Analysis in the Foreign Exchange Market: A Layman's Guide. *Review.* Federal Reserve Bank of St. Louis, September, 1997: 23-38.

Neely, C .J. and P. A. Weller. 2011. Technical Analysis in the Foreign Exchange Market. Federal Reserve Bank of St. Louis. Working paper 2011-001B, July 2011. http://research.stlouisfed.org/wp/2011/2011-001.pdf Downloaded 5/15/15.

Nelson, C. R. 1973. *Applied Time Series Analysis for Managerial Forecasting.* San Francisco: Holden-Day, Inc.

Rosenberg, M. 2003. *Exchange Rate Determination: Models and Strategies for Exchange Rate Forecasting.* New York: McGraw-Hill.

Theil, H. 1978. *Introduction to Econometrics.* New Jersey: Prentice-Hall.

Tsay, R. S. *Analysis of Financial Time Series.* New York: Wiley Series in Probability and Statistics, 2012.

Chapter 7

Exchange Risk and Exposure

Nature and Management

Overview of Chapter Material

A defining characteristic of international business is that it operates in a multi-currency framework. Such an environment offers both rewards and risks. To operate successfully, organizations and individuals must devise strategies that reap the maximum rewards while dealing with risk in the most efficient manner.

This chapter describes the risks posed by exchange rate changes and the strategies available to deal with them. It discusses the concepts of exchange risk and exchange exposure, explaining the ways managers can measure exposure and develop strategies for managing it. Addressing the issues associated with risk in general can be decomposed into three stages: identifying risk, measuring risk, and managing risk. The chapter includes treatment of all three stages.

After Studying This Chapter, You Will Be Able To

- Understand the nature and scope of exchange risk and exchange exposure
- Discuss the various types of exchange exposure
- Identify approaches to measuring foreign exchange translation
- Formulate hedging methods internal and external to the firm

Chapter Outline

I. Exchange Risk and Exposure: Nature and Management
II. Defining the Major Types of Exposure
III. Translation Exposure: Measurement and Significance

I. Foreign Exchange Risk and Exposure: Nature and Management

Forecasting foreign exchange rate changes is a necessary and valuable task for international financial managers. In reality, however, most forecasts deviate from the actual outcome. We denote this discrepancy between actual and forecasted exchange rates as exchange risk. Statistically speaking, we represent exchange risk through measures describing the probability that the actual exchange rate at some future point in time will be different from the forecasted value. We should note that exchange risk is present for all firms engaged in international business, regardless of the degree of their involvement.

By exchange exposure, on the other hand, we mean the significance of exchange risk for the individual participant, whether a firm, an investor, or even a government. Exposure, in the field of international finance, then, is a concept analogous to the concept of elasticity in economics; it reveals the sensitivity of an individual situation to exchange rate changes. A US resident traveling through Europe and carrying dollars to be exchanged for the local currency, for example, may be exposed to changes in the value of the euro against the dollar. A European firm doing business in Japan is similarly exposed; it may find itself gaining or losing from changes in the value of the yen versus the euro. Fortunately, foreign exchange market participants have at their disposal a variety of tools that can assist them minimizing or even eliminating their exposure.

1. Exposure as a Regression Coefficient

We can capitalize on the notion that exposure is an elasticity concept to explain its measurement. We can show this as a simple relationship (Adler and Dumas, 1984):

$$\%\Delta A = f\,(\%\Delta B) \tag{7.1}$$

where A is the price of an asset (or liability/net worth) expressed in the home currency and B is the exchange rate expressed in terms of units of home per local currency.

In their pioneering work on exposure to currency risk, Adler and Dumas (1984) suggest that simple regression analysis is a useful tool for illustrating the meaning of exposure. Thus, in regression form, we have

$$\%\Delta A = a + b\,\%\Delta B + e \tag{7.1'}$$

For example, A could be the dollar value of a receivable that a US company is owed from a Japanese importer. The coefficient b indicates the elasticity of A with respect to B (that is, the percentage change in A attributable to a percentage change in B). The percentage change in each of these two variables is calculated over a certain period. If b = 2, then we conclude that a 1% change in the yen/dollar rate will change the firm's dollar value of these receivables by 2%.

Thinking of exposure in this manner helps us to understand better the meaning and measurement of alternative types of exposure.

II. Defining the Major Types of Exposure

This chapter examines the various types of foreign exchange exposure most frequently encountered by multinationals: translation, transaction, and economic. We will describe the nature and significance of each type of exposure and discuss different approaches to their management.

1. Translation Exposure

Translation exposure, or "accounting" exposure, measures the impact of exchange rate changes on the firm's financial statements. Translation exposure arises from the multinational's obligation to consolidate the financial statements of its subsidiaries and express them in terms of the home country's currency. Individual subsidiaries will most likely prepare their own financial statements in units of the local currency. A US-based multinational's Italian subsidiary may have its asset and liability items denominated in euros. The same company's UK subsidiary has its financial statements expressed in British pounds. At the end of the reporting period, however, the multinational must prepare a consolidated statement reflecting its worldwide operations and expressed in a single unit of account, a single currency. For US-based multinationals, of course, that currency is the dollar; the dollar in this case is termed the reporting currency. In "translating" (or restating or converting) its subsidiaries' financial statements into US dollars, the US multinational must take into account any changes in the exchange rate between each currency and the US dollar during the reporting period. These exchange rate changes may have altered the value of the items included in the firm's financial statements. Translation exposure, then, measures the result of these changes.

2. Transaction Exposure

Transaction exposure assesses the gain or loss in the value of a specific transaction that may result from a change in the exchange rate between the time the contract is signed and the time it is finalized. For example, a German exporter agrees today to deliver a machine to his British customer in return for £100,000 to be received in sixty days. At today's exchange rate of €1.4 = £1, the value of the transaction is €140,000. However, if the value of the euro changes to, say, €1.2 = £1 during the sixty-day period, the German exporter will only receive €120,000, a loss of €20,000 from the original value of the contract. The exporter's transaction, then, was exposed to exchange rate risk; its value changed between the time the contract was signed and the time it terminated. Unfortunately for the German exporter, it changed in the wrong direction.

3. Economic Exposure

Economic exposure reveals the sensitivity of the present value of the firm's cash inflows and outflows to changes in the exchange rate. Let us say that Excelsior, Inc., a US manufacturer of electronic appliances, is considering opening up a plant in Malaysia. To assess the desirability of this investment project, Excelsior must first forecast cash flows in terms of the Malaysian currency, the ringgit, and then convert them to US dollars by forecasting the future value of the ringgit versus the US dollar. As we discussed in Chapter 6, however, the actual future exchange rate (as well as the actual cash flows) many times deviates from its forecast. The unexpected portion of any exchange rate change will generate US dollar cash flows different from those originally expected. The value of the investment project and of the whole firm will change accordingly. Economic exposure, then, deals with the impact of unexpected exchange rate changes on sales, costs, profits, cash flows, and ultimately the economic value of the firm.

Concept Questions

1. Distinguish between foreign exchange risk and exposure.
2. Explain how we can measure currency exposure through a regression coefficient.
3. What are the three major types of foreign exchange exposure faced by multinationals? In what ways do they differ from each other?

III. Translation Exposure: Measurement and Significance

The degree of the firm's translation exposure depends on the composition of its financial statements. In measuring the extent of exposure in financial statements, we classify the various items as "exposed" or "non-exposed" to exchange rate changes over the period covered by the financial statement. We will focus on the balance sheet for our discussion of translation exposure. The balance sheet of a foreign affiliate may include assets and liabilities that are either exposed or non-exposed. We classify balance sheet items as exposed if their home currency value is affected by changes in the exchange rate. They are therefore translated (restated in terms of their home currency value) using the current rate, which is the exchange rate in effect at the closing time for the statement. We classify balance sheet items whose home currency value is not affected by exchange rate changes as non-exposed items. Non-exposed assets and liabilities are translated using the historical exchange rate, which is the exchange rate in effect at the time these items appear on the balance sheet. For select items, translation approaches use a weighted average of two rates, rather than one single current rate.

Balance sheet exposure, then, may be illustrated by decomposing total assets (TA) into exposed (A_e) and non-exposed (A_{ne}) assets and total liabilities and net worth (TL) into exposed (L_e) and non-exposed (L_{ne}):

$$TA = A_e + A_{ne} \tag{7.2}$$

$$TL = L_e + L_{ne} \tag{7.3}$$

When exchange rates change during the period of the balance sheet, only A_e and L_e are affected. The difference between these two, $A_e - L_e$, measures the firm's net exposure. It reveals the degree to which the firm must engage in exposure management. The difference between exposed assets and exposed liabilities also reveals the direction of the exposure. If exposed assets are greater than exposed liabilities, the firm has positive net exposure. It will benefit through an appreciation of the foreign currency vis-à-vis the home currency. If, instead, exposed liabilities are greater than exposed assets, the firm has negative net exposure. In this case, the firm will benefit from a depreciation of the foreign currency.

1. Methods of Translating MNCs' Financial Statements

There are several methods used to translate financial statements of multinational corporations. Most often cited are the current rate, current/non-current rate, monetary/non-monetary, and temporal methods.

1.1. The Current Rate Method

According to this method, all assets and liabilities are considered as exposed. Consequently, they are translated using the current exchange rate. In the case of the annual balance sheet, then, the exchange rate in effect on its closing date would be the appropriate rate. Equity items are an exception, and are translated using the appropriate historical rate(s). Theoretically, translation of the income statement should take place using the rate at which each entry becomes part of the statement. In practice, however, this approach may prove cumbersome. An average of the rates in effect at the beginning and ending periods may then be used.

1.2. The Current/non-current Rate Method

The current/non-current rate method is so-named because it treats current and non-current balance sheet items differently. Current (maturing in less than one year) assets and liabilities are translated at the current exchange rate. Assets and liabilities with maturity exceeding one year are restated at the exchange rate at which they originally entered the records of the subsidiary.

The current/non-current rate method establishes a similar procedure for translation of income statement items. Most income statement items are translated at the average rate for the period. When a corresponding balance sheet item, however, is translated at the historical rate, this rate is also used for the income statement item. Depreciation is one example of an item subject to this treatment.

1.3. The Monetary/Non-monetary Method

According to this translation method, monetary assets are defined as claims held by the firm to receive a fixed amount of foreign currency; they include cash, accounts receivable, and marketable securities. Similarly, monetary liabilities such as accounts payable and long-term debt involve an obligation to pay a fixed amount of that foreign currency. Monetary assets and liabilities are translated using the current exchange rate. Non-monetary assets and liabilities by contrast include such "physical items" as inventories and fixed assets and are translated using the historical exchange rate.

According to the monetary/non-monetary method, income statement items are translated in a manner analogous to that applied to their balance sheet counterparts. Sales revenue, a monetary asset, is translated using the average exchange rate over the period. Depreciation and cost of goods sold, on the other hand, are considered non-monetary and are therefore translated at the historical rate.

1.4. The Temporal Method

The temporal method of translation is similar to the monetary/non-monetary method. While in the monetary/non-monetary method, the choice of the exchange rate depends on the classification of the asset or liability as monetary or non-monetary, in the temporal method, the exchange rate used depends on whether the item has entered the balance sheet valued at market or at cost. Inventories, for example, may be translated at the current or historical rate depending on whether they appear in the balance sheet at market (current rate) or at cost (historical rate).

1.5. Contrasting the Translation Methods

The treatment of assets and liabilities under the various translation methods is illustrated through a general example in Table 7.1. The table shows which exchange rate (historical or current) applies to each translation method.

According to the table, the difference between the current/non-current and the monetary/non-monetary approaches lies in their treatment of inventories and long-term debt. The treatment of inventories distinguishes the monetary/non-monetary method from all other methods, while the treatment of long-term debt distinguishes the current/non-current method from all others (Agarwal, 1975).

Besides identifying which balance sheet items are exposed and which exchange rate applies to each item, multinationals must heed to the specific reporting requirements associated with gains and losses from exchange rate changes and to the inflationary conditions encountered in each country of operations. These and other issues were highlighted when United States multinationals were required to switch from the temporal method per Financial Accounting Standards Board Statement #8 (FASB-8) to the current method, which is described in the Board's Statement #52 (FASB-52).

2. From FASB-8 to FASB-52

As we discussed in our coverage of the international monetary system, the period between the signing of the Bretton Woods Agreement in 1944 and its collapse in 1971 was characterized by fixed exchange rates. Multinationals, then, were not overly concerned with the effects of exchange rate fluctuations on their financial statements or cash flows and were

H: Historical Exchange Rate for Assets, Liabilities and Common Stock: 2

C: Current Exchange Rate: 2.5

H'=Historical Exchange Rate for Retained Earnings: 1.5

	Translation Approach				
	Foreign Currency Units	Current	Current/ Non-current	Monetary/ Non-monetary	Temporal
ASSETS					
Cash	2,000	$800-C	$800-C	$800-C	$800-C
Short-term (@mkt)	1,000	$400-C	$400-C	$400-C	$400-C
Accounts Rec.	500	$200-C	$200-C	$200-C	$200-C
Inventories (@mkt)	1,500	$600-C	$600-C	$750-H	$600-C
Fixed Assets	2,500	$1,000-C	$1,250-H	$1,250-H	$1,250-H
TOTAL ASSETS	**7,500**	**$3,000**	**$3,250**	**$3,400**	**$3,250**
LIABILITIES AND NET WORTH					
Current	3,000	$1,200-C	$1,200-C	$1,200-C	$1,200-C
Long-term	2,500	$1,000-C	$1,250-H	$1,000-C	$1,000-C
Common Stock	1,000	$500-H	$750-H	$750-H	$750-H
Retained Earnings	1,000	$667[1]-H'	$50[2]-H'	$450[3]-H'	$300[4]-H'
Cumulative Translation Adjustment		(-$367)			
TOTAL L&NW		**$3,000**	**$3,250**	**$3,400**	**$3,250**

Table 7.1 Example of Translation Approaches.

1 *Retained Earnings are translated at the rate of 1.5.*

2 *The figure is a plug-in number to make TA = TL + NW. The difference between $667 and $50 represents exchange rate losses.*

3 *The figure is a plug-in number to make TA = TL + NW. The difference between $667 and $450 ($227) represents exchange rate losses.*

4 *The figure is a plug-in-number to make TA = TL + NW. The difference between $667 and $300 ($367) represents exchange rate losses.*

not required to use a specific translation method. To bring consistency in financial reporting, in October 1975, the Financial Accounting Standards Board issued its Statement Number 8. The translation framework for financial statements of US-based multinationals has thus been established.

According to FASB-8, the objective of translation is "*to measure and express (a) in dollars and (b) in conformity with U.S. generally accepted accounting principles the assets, liabilities, revenue, or expenses that are measured or denominated in foreign currency*" (Financial Accounting Standards Board, 1975, p. 5). FASB-8 brought consistency to financial statement translation by adopting the temporal method. It generated considerable dissension, however, in its requirement to recognize an MNC's foreign exchange position in the quarterly income statement. There was no provision for reserves. In a period of fluctuating dollar rates, US multinationals showed volatile net incomes and earnings per share. The Board responded by issuing FASB-52 in December of 1981 (Financial Accounting Standards Board, 1981).

FASB-52 is designed to

- *"provide information that is generally compatible with the expected economic effects on an enterprise's cash flow and equity and*
- *reflect in consolidated statements the financial results and relationships as measured in the primary currency in which each entity conducts its business (referred to as its functional currency.)"* (Financial Accounting Standards Board, 1981, p. 4).

FASB-52 combines a number of interesting translation characteristics:

1. It employs the net investment concept and the current rate translation approach. In accordance with the net investment concept, the US firm (the reporting enterprise) has an investment in a foreign entity; this entity's foreign currency earnings benefit the US firm by the US currency equivalent amount of these earnings.

   Translation takes place using the current rate method. Assets and liabilities are translated using the rate in effect on the date of the balance sheet. Revenues, expenses, gains, and losses are in principle translated at the rate in effect when recognized. In practice, however, a weighted average rate that pertains to the period is used. The current rate also applies to depreciation, cost of sales, and amortization of deferred revenues and expenses.
2. It recognizes translation gains and losses separately from current income by accumulating them in a separate component of equity called the Cumulative Translation Adjustment (CTA) account. CTA is a component of the firm's other comprehensive income (OCI), which itself is part of shareholder's equity. At the time these gains or losses are realized, they affect cash flows. If translation gains or losses do not affect cash flows, they are included in equity and reported under net income. Adoption of this approach makes the income statement less sensitive to exchange rate changes than under FASB-8.
3. It recognizes the economic environment in which the various subsidiaries operate by applying the functional currency concept. According to FASB's definition of the functional currency, "*normally it is the currency of the environment in which an entity primarily generates and expends cash*" (FASB, 1981). Once the functional currency has been properly identified, financial statements are translated from the functional into the "reporting" currency, the currency, that is, of the parent. To assure consistency, the FASB has identified certain indicators that govern selection of the functional currency. These indicators include:

   i. Cash flow
   ii. Sales price
   iii. Sales market

iv. Expenses
v. Financing
vi. Intercompany transactions

To implement FASB-52 in the translation of its financial statements, a firm should

- Identify the functional currency of its economic environment.
- Measure all items of the financial statements in the functional currency.
- Use the current exchange rate to translate from functional to reporting if the functional currency is not the reporting currency.
- Distinguish the economic impact of exchange rate changes on net investment from the impact of these changes on individual assets and liabilities that are receivable or payable in currencies other than the functional currency (FASB, 1981, p. 5).

The recognition of the firm's economic environment provides a link between FASB-8 and FASB-52. In translating a subsidiary's foreign currency financial statements into USD, multinationals must ask the following questions:

Are the subsidiary's statements in foreign currency?

a. If Yes, is the local currency the subsidiary's functional currency?
b. If Yes to a, translate to USD using the current rate method per FASB 52.
c. If No to a, is the USD the functional currency?
d. If Yes to c, translate to USD using the temporal method per FASB 8
e. If No to c, translate to foreign/functional currency per FASB 8 (temporal), and then to USD per FASB 52 (current).

4. It treats gains and losses from transactions as part of net income for the period, thus adhering to the requirements of FASB-8. Gains and losses of transactions for the specific purpose of hedging an identifiable foreign currency commitment, however, are booked as a separate component of stockholders' equity. Exceptions are made in the case of "excess hedges" where gains and losses are lumped with net income. Exchange rate gains and losses resulting from long-term intercompany transactions are deferred and placed in a separate component of stockholders' equity. A transaction is considered long term if settlement is not anticipated in the near future. If settlement is planned on some near future date, gains and losses on these intercompany transactions are included in current income.
5. It recognizes economic conditions by making special provision for MNC subsidiaries operating in hyperinflationary economies. A hyperinflationary economy is defined as one with cumulative inflation reaching 100% over a three-year period. In this case, financial statements are translated as if the functional currency were the reporting currency. The subsidiary is therefore treated as an extension of the parent firm, and translation proceeds in a manner similar to that dictated by FASB-8, the temporal method.

Concept Questions

1. Distinguish between exposed and non-exposed assets and liabilities.
2. Distinguish between the historical exchange rate and the current exchange rate used in translating financial statements.
3. What are the four methods of translating financial statements? How would each of these methods treat the translation of inventories?
4. What are the differences between FASB-8 and FASB-52?

IV. Transaction Exposure: Measurement and Significance

We already defined transaction exposure in Section II above. In this section, we will discuss transaction exposure in detail and give another example.

We indicated that when a firm enters into a transaction today that is scheduled to be settled through payment of a certain amount of foreign currency at a certain time in the future, it becomes exposed to changes in the value of that currency. Such transactions include buying or selling of a good or a service on credit and the lending or borrowing of funds for future repayment. For example, assume Low Taste Traders, Inc., of the United States is importing 1000 cases of Vin Du Jour from a French firm. Payment of EUR20,000 is due in sixty days. Given that payment is due in euros, Low Taste will be affected by any change in the dollar/euro rate. Assume that today's rate is USD1.30=EUR1.

The chance that the dollar/euro exchange rate on the due date will be something other than 1.30:1 gives rise to foreign exchange risk associated with the transaction. The magnitude of transaction exposure faced by a specific firm is measured by the amount of assets and liabilities denominated in a certain foreign currency now and due to mature at some point in the future. Of relevance to Low Taste Traders, of course, is the net exposure in euros, that is, the difference between its exposed assets and liabilities on a certain date. In this case, Low Taste Traders also exports Generic Brand American perfume to France. Payment for the latest transaction, 1000 cases, amounts to EUR14,000, which is also due in sixty days. The firm's net exposure is EUR14,000 – EUR20,000 = (minus) EUR6,000. Low Taste has negative exposure in euros; that is, it is due to pay out more euros than it is scheduled to receive in sixty days.

Depending on the direction of the exchange rate change between now and the date of payment, the firm may incur either an exchange gain or a loss. Let us say that the dollar appreciates and the exchange rate in sixty days ends up being USD1.20=EUR1. We can now calculate the exchange gain/loss from the import transaction using a couple of approaches. We can take the difference between the dollar value of the payment when due (EUR20,000*1.20 = $24,000) and the dollar value when the transaction is initiated (EUR20,000*1.30 = $26,000), a gain from the import transaction of $2,000. The gain/loss from the export is similarly computed as $18,200-$16,800, or -$1,400. The firm's net position generates a net gain of

\$2,000-\$1,400 = \$600. Or, we can find the foreign exchange gain/loss by converting the net exposure of minus EUR6,000 into its respective dollar equivalent (and then calculate the difference (\$7,800-\$7,200 = \$600). A third way of finding the exchange gain/loss is to multiply the net exposure of minus EUR6,000 by the change in the dollar value of the euro (\$1.20-\$1.30 = -\$0.10); this, again, gives us \$600. In general, then, the firm shows an exchange gain from net negative exposure if the foreign currency depreciates and an exchange loss if the foreign currency appreciates.

Beyond the above simplified case of somewhat offsetting transactions, the firm may be involved in transactions denominated in various currencies and due at different times in the future. Multinationals with affiliates in many countries face an immensely complicated exposure picture, particularly as each transaction, and its associated exchange gains or losses, is subject to various tax environments, generating varying after-tax results.

Transaction exposure represents "real" gains and losses, affecting the firm's cash flows. It therefore represents a significant type of risk. It is also potentially broad-based, as it affects not only accounts receivable and payable but also any asset or liability denominated in a foreign currency and subject to a future redemption date.

Concept Questions

1. What is transaction exposure?
2. How does transaction exposure differ from translation exposure?

V. Economic Exposure: Measurement and Significance

Firms operating in foreign countries count on those operations for production, sales, and income. As these operations generate expectations of revenues and costs, many of which are denominated in terms of a currency other than the multinational's home currency. To assess the contribution of foreign operations to expected cash flows and value of the entire firm, changes in the exchange rate must also be taken into account. The firm, of course, takes full account of those exchange rate changes that it expects to take place. Exchange rates, however, change in expected as well as unexpected fashions. Economic exposure focuses on the impact of the unexpected portion of the change in exchange rates. These unexpected changes ultimately affect production, sales, income, cash flows, and firm value.

Economic exposure, then, illustrates the consequences of the firm's multinational nature and affects the quality that is central to the financial theory of the firm: its market value. The exact manner in which unexpected exchange rate changes affect firm value depends on many factors, including the international macroeconomic environment, the efficiency of financial markets, the competitive nature of the firm's product and factor markets, and its operational flexibility. For example, if the firm's product prices and costs move with exchange rates in accordance with the Law of One Price, the effect of changes in exchange rates on firm net revenues (and market value) may be insignificant or even zero. If the firm operates in very competitive markets for local products, however, it may not be able to adjust prices to match exchange rate changes, and it will suffer loss of revenue. From the cost side, the ability of the firm to shift input sources may determine the extent to which an increase in local costs (as a result of exchange rate changes) will affect cash flows.

Measuring economic exposure is a cumbersome task. Some say that it is actually an impossible task, since it deals with unexpected changes in the exchange rate. The firm or the analyst, however, can specify certain realistic scenaria showing how hypothetical exchange rate changes might influence cash flows and firm value. In doing so, the firm can at least design alternative strategies to deal with any effects of unfavorable changes in currency values.

VI. Translation, Transaction, and Economic Exposure Revisited

1. Selected Characteristics of Exposure Types

The three ways of expressing exposure to exchange risk differ with respect to a number of characteristics (Srinivasulu, 1981). These characteristics include the time dimension of the exposure, the nature of gains and losses, the source of exposure, the emphasis each approach utilizes, and the ease of measurement.

- Time dimension: Translation exposure by its nature takes a snapshot of the firm's financial statements at one particular time. It pertains to the firm's past operations. Transaction and economic exposure, on the other hand, are forward looking. Transaction exposure extends over the period of the specific contract under consideration. Economic exposure may be short term or long term.
- Nature of gains and losses: Translation exposure deals with paper gains and losses, and because of that, considered irrelevant to the value of the firm by some analysts. As explained below, however, translation exposure may affect the firm's tax liability. Transaction and economic exposures always deal with real gains and losses, which affect the value of a firm's contracts and cash flows.
- Source of exposure: Translation exposure is exposure by fiat, or by regulation. Whether and how a firm is subject to that exposure depends on the particular statements issued by the FASB. Transaction and economic exposures arise from the firm's line of business as they are affected by actual changes in the exchange rate.
- Emphasis: The differences between the three types of exposure may reflect the emphasis each one tends to have. The accounting nature of translation exposure means that it focuses on the content of financial statements and the book value of the items specified in those statements. Transaction and economic exposures emphasize contractual and market values respectively. They are therefore integral inputs in the firm's decision making.

- Ease of measurement: Translation and transaction exposures are relatively easy to measure. Economic exposure, however, is complicated to measure because it deals with unexpected exchange rate changes.

2. Exchange Rate Exposure and Taxes: FASB-52

Taxes are an integral part of just about every decision made by the firm; the hedging decision is not different in this respect. As firms integrate their accounting systems with FASB-52 requirements, the tax implications are usually the following (Coopers & Lybrand, 1994):

a. Translation gains and losses: They are not taxed until realized (through dividend dispersion, liquidation, or other such activities).
b. Realized transaction gains and losses: These are recorded for income tax purposes; however, the firm may meet certain criteria for deferral or for treatment of traded instruments as capital.
c. Unrealized transaction gains and losses: Again, these are not taxed until realized. There are, however, special rules that pertain to gains and losses from forwards, futures, and swaps. Gains and losses from these contractual arrangements are taxed as income.

Since tax treatment of the firm's translation and transaction exposures represents an important input to the hedging decision, financial managers should ascertain the tax impact of their hedging strategies prior to implementing them. US-based multinationals should also be familiar with the relevant sections of Subpart J of the US Tax Code, which deals with foreign currency transactions. Sections 985, 986, 987, 988, and 989 are especially relevant. The key tax issues dealt with in Subpart J pertain to the amount of gains and losses, the timing of recognition, and the origination of these gains/losses. Since these rules change over time, managers and investors must make sure to consult the most recent status of tax treatment of foreign exchange exposure gains and losses.

3. Measuring Currency Risk Using the Value-at-Risk (VaR) Methodology

To resolve some of the challenges encountered in measuring foreign exchange exposure, financial institutions and other firms have resorted to using the Value-at-Risk (VaR) methodology (Dufey and Pan, 1997; Holton, 2014).. VaR can be defined as "the maximum loss for a given exposure over a given time horizon with z% confidence." (Papaioannou, 2006). For example, if the VaR on an asset is $1m at a 95% confidence interval in one year, then we can say that there is a 95% probability that the value of the asset will fall by less than $1m during the year; alternatively, we can state that there is only a 5% probability that the value of the asset will fall more than $1m during the year. The use of VaR extends beyond foreign exchange risk management to the measurement of other risks faced by the firm.

The VaR approach was popularized in the early 1990s by JPMorgan as part of its RiskMetrics™ set of techniques to measure market risk (J. P. Morgan/Reuters, 1996; Zumbach, 2006). To calculate VaR, we need to define

1. The confidence interval to be used in our estimation (usually 95% or 99%).
2. The relevant time horizon (one day, month, year...).
3. The currency unit to be used.

There are a variety of models used to calculate VaR. They include historical data; use of a variance-covariance model assuming a normal distribution of returns; and, Monte Carlo simulation, again assuming normally distributed returns. Let us give a simple example of VaR calculation using the simplest of the three models which utilizes the historical data approach:

Let us assume that Clean Waters, Inc., a US exporter of water filtering solutions, has a ¥100m receivable from its Japanese customer, Tanaka, Inc., due in one month. The exchange rate is ¥100=$1; so, the market value of the exporter's position is $1m. Clean Waters wants to know the one-month VaR with a 5% probability that the loss will be greater than what the VaR estimates. The firm compiles historical data on the USD/JPY exchange rate, and finds that the standard deviation, σ, of the USD/JPY returns (percentage changes) is .400%. Let us assume that past standardized returns (r_t/σ_t) on the USD/JPY exchange rate are normally distributed, VaR is 1.65σ or 0.66%. This means that 95% of the time the exchange rate is not going to fall by more than 0.66%. So, if Clean Waters's position is $1m, it will not lose more than ($1m * .66%) = $6,600 over the next month.

Firms can use the information provided through the VaR methodology to provide more meaningful information to managers, set position limits in terms of the inherent risk, equip traders with information to take positions that maximize return over risk, and provide a means of the effectiveness of decision makers to translate risk into low return volatility. For financial institutions, VaR can assist in reporting the risk position of the institution to regulatory authorities (JPMorgan, 1995).

VaR has had its shares of critics, primarily due to the nature of the assumptions made, such as the normality of returns and the use of past returns to estimate the effect of future phenomena. It is, however, relatively easy to use. We must also remember that individual risk measurements rarely tell us the whole story. Thus, VaR estimates should be confirmed by estimates provided by other methodologies.

Concept Questions

1. Define economic exposure. What are the challenges encountered in measuring economic exposure?
2. What are the characteristics of each of the three exposure methods?
3. What is VaR? How can it be used to measure foreign exchange risk?

VII. Managing Exposure: Hedging and Covering

The strategies that firms use to manage foreign exchange exposure are usually referred to as hedging. When the forward market is used to manage exposure, the strategy is sometimes termed covering.

Hedging is as much of an art as it is a science. The firm must first decide on and formulate the objectives of the hedging strategy. It might express the objective in terms of minimizing losses or generating profits. It may take a short-term or long-term approach. These and other elements of the firm's hedging strategy must be understood by all those within the firm who are involved in the process. The firm's hedging strategy must also include methods of evaluating progress toward meeting the objectives. More importantly, a particular foreign exchange hedging strategy must fit with the overall strategic objectives of the firm. Only then can the firm define foreign exchange exposure appropriately and manage it effectively.

1. Considerations in Choosing Among Hedging Methods

One hedging strategy does not fit all firms. A large, multinational firm will probably face a different set of alternatives than those available to a smaller firm. In selecting among alternatives, Jones and Jones (1987) suggest that a firm must consider:

- The cost of the strategy. Both explicit and implicit costs associated with a particular strategy must be addressed. Explicit costs are those encountered in undertaking the hedge, such as transactions costs or interest rates. Implicit costs are those in the form of forgone opportunities, since hedging may require the firm to tie up funds that otherwise could be used to take advantage of alternative investments.
- The availability of the strategy. The ability of the firm to hedge exposure to certain currencies, especially those of developing nations, may be limited since financial institutions and markets in those countries are not well developed. The firm should not design hedging strategies that are unreasonably difficult or even impossible to implement.
- The time frame of the strategy. When should hedging actually take place? When should the firm terminate its hedging activity? If the firm engages in a specific hedging activity over a long period, hedging costs may increase. If hedging is terminated too early, however, the firm may not take advantage of the full protection available.
- The effectiveness of the strategy. How certain are we that the strategy will fully hedge the firm's exposure? Has the hedge worked in the past? To what extent have circumstances changed since the last time the firm used it? Can the strategy address cash flows from multiple sources?
- Tax considerations. The cost of hedging should be calculated on an after-tax basis. Any comparisons of costs associated with alternative strategies should also be on that basis.
- The degree of centralization of the hedging operation. Should hedging be directed from headquarters or individual subsidiaries? What are the implications of centralization and decentralization for evaluation of managerial performance?
- Governmental restrictions on hedging activities. There may be restrictions imposed by governments on the amount of foreign exchange transferred or the financing activities of foreign firms.

- The simplicity of the strategy. Other things equal, a simple strategy that is communicated to and understood by all involved is preferred over a complicated one that is understood and implemented by a small fraction of the firm's managers.

It is essential that any hedging strategy be viewed within the context of the firm's entire spectrum of operations. The firm's characteristics, environment, and overall plan should provide a direction for its hedging philosophy to become meaningful and consistent. Foreign exchange hedging strategy should be an integral aspect of the firm's strategic management process and should, in turn, incorporate strategic management considerations.

2. Exposure Management: Internal and External (Market-Based) Methods

One convenient way of classifying strategies of exposure management is by the principal locus of the hedging operations. For illustrative purposes, we label hedging strategies as internal or external. Hedging, that is, may be conducted using strategies internal to the firm or it may involve extensive use of the market and other strategies originating outside the firm. It should be noted that the distinction between internal and external strategies is not always clear-cut. For example, strategies involving operations in the money market are here viewed as "internal" but could easily be classified as "external," since the firm has to operate in an outside market. The distinction between internal and external may be further blurred by the use of multiple strategies by the multinational.

2.1. Internal Methods

The following are some of the internal approaches used by firms to protect themselves against currency exposure.

2.1.1. Balance Sheet Hedge

Translation exposure arises from the difference between the stated value of exposed assets and liabilities. So, one obvious way of eliminating foreign exchange exposure is to match exposed assets and liabilities for each currency. Thus, if a United States multinational has an Italian subsidiary whose euro assets exceed euro liabilities, the subsidiary could either increase its euro assets or reduce its euro liabilities to end up with a net exposure of zero, or at least close to zero.

The ability of a firm to eliminate or manage translation exposure depends on the current composition of its balance sheet and its available resources. A large firm with multiple operations in many countries and currencies has a good chance of consolidating its net exposures in the various currencies and thus minimize its overall translation exposure. A smaller firm operating in two or three countries may have net exposure in these three currencies and, therefore, not be able to consolidate its financial statements in a single currency. For this second firm, eliminating or even limiting exposure requires considerable planning and substantial commitment of resources.

Matching assets and liabilities denominated in the subsidiary's local currency to eliminate balance sheet exposure may be not be an efficient way of doing business. One example is a subsidiary with receivables in Swiss francs in its balance sheet. Should it also create payable in Swiss francs if buying from Swiss suppliers is not cost effective in order to eliminate its Swiss franc exposure? Probably not!

Firms may not always plan to eliminate exposure entirely and for all currencies. Instead, they might follow a more limited strategy by taking advantage of available information. Exposure in certain currencies, that is, may be considered acceptable depending on the direction that the currency is expected to take. If the currency is expected to appreciate, the firm might want to position itself so that it will benefit from the appreciation. It would then increase its assets and reduce its liabilities in that currency. Currencies expected to appreciate are usually referred to as hard currencies; those expected to fall in value are termed soft currencies. Examples of exposure management or hedging strategies for hard currencies include the following:

a. Increase the amount of working capital denominated in the hard currency. Take the case of a US firm with a German subsidiary; the firm expects the euro to appreciate. The subsidiary will want to increase its euro cash holdings, its euro-denominated marketable securities, or its euro accounts receivable. The amount of receivables could increase through booking new transactions or by slowing down the collection of receivables currently on the books.
b. Decrease the amount of accounts payable denominated in the hard currency. The German subsidiary will try to limit its euro debts as much as possible to avoid settling at a higher dollar/euro rate.

These and similar strategies are not without costs. Decreasing the amount of receivables in the softer currencies will probably have an effect on sales. Extending the receivable period for the harder currencies will mean forgone interest payments that could have been generated through those funds.

2.1.2. Leading-Lagging

Firms can manage exchange exposure by adjusting the timing of payments to another firm. Payments in terms of currencies expected to depreciate should be delayed as much as possible; receipts in those currencies should be collected as soon as possible. Conversely, firms should accelerate the payment of liabilities involving appreciating currencies, while slowing down the time schedules of receivables. For example, a US firm importing wool from the UK may decide to redeem its pound-denominated debt before the maximum allowable time if it expects the pound to increase in value relative to the dollar. Let us say that the same firm exports sweaters to Canada. Because the Canadian dollar is expected to depreciate, the firm arranges for terms of sale that discourage late payment. The firm has to ascertain, however, the extent to which these terms will affect its sales.

Payment dates may also be adjusted for transactions between affiliates. Affiliates may also be able to forgo interest payments to each other, for at least a period of time (six months according to IRS Section 482 for United States multinationals). The ability to lead or lag payments may be constrained by regulations in the host country. From time to time, these regulations change. Italy, for example, changed its position in 1989, lifting all regulations on import leads or lags.

2.1.3. Currency Netting

Currency netting is used by international firms that operate in many countries and use a variety of currencies to support their operations. Exposure of one subsidiary in one currency may be offset by (opposite) exposure by another subsidiary in the same currency. By the very nature of their business, then, some firms may be in a naturally hedged position. If a US-based exporter has the same amount of receivables denominated in two currencies that are expected to move in exactly opposite directions, the firm may consider itself naturally hedged, because changes in one currency will be offset by changes in the other. The greater the number of currency environments in which the firm operates, the greater the chance that movements of a single currency will be offset by movements of another.

For a multinational, currency netting is also associated with intra-corporate transactions and is accordingly termed bilateral or multilateral. Bilateral netting involves the offsetting of intra-corporate payments and receipts between two related firms. For example, Companies A and B are subsidiaries of Company C, a US-based firm. Company A is located in the UK and owes Germany's Company B the sum of EUR20,000. As a result of a separate trade-related transaction, Company B owes Company A the sum of GBP10,000. Let's assume that the exchange rate is EUR1.20 = GBP1.00. Instead of making two payments amounting to approximately EUR34,000, a single transfer is made from B to A, amounting to approximately EUR2,000. Multilateral netting, on the other hand, involves the offsetting of three or more intra-corporate claims and liabilities.

2.1.4. Diversification of Operations

The potentially adverse effect of changes in exchange rates may be minimized through establishment of cross-border operations. Operating plants in both Chile and Paraguay, which supply inputs to an Argentinian subsidiary, offers the ability to cushion the effects of local currency changes on total labor costs. Enlightened MNCs attempt to diversify operations functions (production, marketing) as well as sources of their financing.

2.1.5. Money Market Hedge

The objective of a money market strategy is to put the firm in a position of receiving payment (or making payment) in terms of the home currency, thus neutralizing the effect of exchange rate changes. A money market hedge creates a foreign currency asset (or liability) that matches the firm's foreign currency liability (or asset) that was created through its business operations.

For example, accounts payable in euros may be hedged by exchanging dollars for euros now and investing the proceeds in the euro money market. These proceeds can then be used to redeem the payables.

Consider the case of a US firm importing automobile parts from Germany. The terms of its most recent import transaction require the firm to pay to its German supplier the sum of EUR1 million in ninety days. The current exchange rate is USD1.30=EUR1 and the ninety-day deposit rate in Germany is 1.00%. The firm would need to deposit EUR909,091 now to receive EUR1 million in ninety days. At the current exchange rate, this is equivalent to USD1,181,812. In ninety days, when the payable is due, the firm pays with the euro received from its German deposit.

Consider the similar case of a US exporter to Germany scheduled to receive payment in euros in ninety days. The exporter may enter the German money market and borrow euros. These euros can be converted into US$ in the foreign exchange market right now, with the dollars invested in the US money market. When the exporter gets paid, the euro debt is repaid and the US investment liquidated.

2.1.6. Pricing Strategies

The firm may also address its exchange rate exposure by adjusting its pricing policy. These adjustments can include

a. Transfer pricing adjustments. Transfer pricing involves pricing relationships within the firm. It is a mechanism used primarily to reduce the tax burden of multinationals. As one foreign subsidiary sells goods or services to a subsidiary located in another country, it may charge a price or follow a billing method appropriate to the exchange rate changes. In effect, the firm takes advantage of pricing for transactions to minimize its overall tax position. Since the government potentially loses revenue as a result of the practice, authorities try to minimize the extent of tax avoidance associated with transfer pricing. There are, of course, limits on the ability of US multinationals in applying transfer pricing policies. Transactions between subsidiaries and the parent company must adhere to the "arm's length" pricing as indicated in IRS Rule 482.

b. Selling point price adjustments. A firm, or an individual subsidiary, may resort to managing exposure through adjustment of its product prices in the foreign market. In 2012, the yen was gaining strength against the dollar; the exchange rate was around JPY78=USD1 (compare this with the JPY124=USD1 rate in August 2015). Sensing a loss of export market share and a profit slump, Toyota raised prices on its exported vehicles. In general, of course, the elasticity of demand at a particular price range will indicate how serious the impact of price changes is going to be on the firm. Differing degrees to which other competitors are influenced by an exchange rate change may also change the competitiveness of the environment and thereby guide any pricing strategy changes. Additionally, depending on its bargaining position within its supply chain, the firm may also put pressure on its suppliers to lower their prices so that its own profit margin can be maintained. In Toyota's 2012 example, the company went beyond raising product prices to protect its profits against exchange rate changes. It also reduced costs and increased overseas production, thus being in a position to more effectively face future currency gyrations.

Selling point price adjustments are sometimes referred to as "Exchange Rate Pass-Through." That is, firms may not wish to "pass through" to their customers the full effect of a currency depreciation (or appreciation). If a US firm exports to Europe, and the euro depreciates by 5%, the firm will have to decide how much of the revenue loss from the euro depreciation it will pass through to its customers. Will it raise its prices by 5%, 2%, or leave them unchanged?

Concept Questions

1. What are the elements of a hedging strategy that a firm must consider before deciding on the appropriate strategy?
2. How can a firm adjust its balance sheet to benefit from the anticipated appreciation of a currency of one of the countries in which it has operations?
3. Explain how a multinational could operate in the money market to protect itself from exchange rate fluctuations.
4. Explain the concept of "exchange rate pass-through." What are the factors firms must consider when deciding on the degree of the pass-through?

2.2. External (Market-Based) Methods

As we have already noted, internal and external strategies of exposure management often have characteristics of both. Here we isolate several external methods of management, where the firm engages in transactions outside the firm.

2.2.1. Forward-Market Hedge

The concept of the forward contract was discussed in Chapter 2. Entering into a forward contract can offer the firm a way to protect itself against unfavorable currency movements. A US importer with a ninety-day EUR100,000 payable to a British exporter may buy British pounds forward at the appropriate forward rate. If the ninety-day forward rate is $1.35=€1, the firm can lock in that rate now and thus be able to consider its specific dollar expenditure in arriving at the exact cost of the purchase. The full implication of this decision, of course, will not be known until the day of execution of the contract. The firm would certainly feel vindicated if the spot rate changes to, say, $1.40=€1, because then the deal would have been much more expensive in dollar terms. If the spot rate turns out to be $1.30=€1, however, the firm would have been better off if it had not entered the forward market; the cost, that is, would have been less by $100,000. The difference between the forward rate and the future spot illustrates the opportunity cost involved in hedging or covering.

2.2.2. Futures Market Hedge

The futures markets also offers firms and individual investors the opportunity to manage their exposure by taking a futures position opposite to their spot market position. Organized futures markets, such as the Chicago Mercantile Exchange, offer the advantages of standardized contracts and a clearinghouse service. Settlement can take place daily at rates defined by the market. Futures market activity is observable to all market participants through publication of each contract's open interest and volume. The bid-offer spread is normally narrow, indicating efficiency of the markets (Géczy, Minton, and Schrand, 1997).

The behavior of hedgers in the futures market has been presented by three principal frameworks: the Traditional Theory, Working's Hypothesis, and the Portfolio Theory (Ederington, 1979; Working, 1953).

The Traditional Theory of hedging assumes that the basis (difference between futures and spot prices) remains the same. In order for the firm to hedge effectively, then, it should make sure that its futures positions exactly offset its spot positions. If the firm is long in the spot market by JPY100m, it should take a short position of JPY100m in the futures market.

Working argues against the basic assumption of the Traditional Theory, suggesting instead that hedgers formulate expectations about the future spot rate. Their hedging behavior, then, is predicated upon the expected relationship between spot and futures. In some cases, this relationship would indicate a need for less hedging than prescribed by the Traditional Theory.

The Portfolio Theory framework combines elements of both Traditional and Working's theories viewing hedging in a portfolio context, rather than in terms of either risk or return. The firm's portfolio of currency flows, then, may consist of both hedged and unhedged components.

Each of the above theories has its own merits. The Traditional Theory suggests a very conservative approach to hedging. Many firms, however, do not hedge their position fully. Instead, they follow a strategy more closely aligned to Working's hypothesis by hedging 60–80% of their exposure. The Portfolio approach also offers a sound hedging strategy as long as the firm is adequately diversified in terms of the currencies in which assets and liabilities are denominated. Smaller firms, with exposure to one or two foreign currencies, cannot achieve the level of currency flow diversification assumed by this theory.

2.2.3. Options

Another strategy available to firms wanting to manage their exchange exposure is to enter the options market, especially when it faces *contingent* exposure. Let us suppose that a US firm is about to submit a bid for a Swiss infrastructure project. The bid is expressed in terms of the local currency, the Swiss franc. The firm's bid is for CHF1b; a decision on the bid will be made in ninety days. If the bid is accepted, the firm will face transaction exposure at the time of acceptance. Its exposure is contingent upon acceptance of its bid. If the firm is not awarded the project, a forward or futures strategy would imply that the firm would still honor its side of the contract. What the firm needs in this case is the right to buy foreign currency, not the obligation to do so. The firm, then, could buy a call option in Swiss francs, thus accomplishing two things: (a) locking in the exchange rate for the bid and (b) not tying up funds in case it does not receive the bid.

2.2.4. Risk Sharing

The buyer and the seller in a traditional commercial transaction may negotiate up front the sharing of any gains or losses from the movement of the exchange rate. Risk-sharing agreements usually go into effect when exchange rate changes exceed a stated threshold, say

5% or 10% from the current rate. Assume an Australian firm is about to buy equipment at a stated Australian dollar price from a US exporter when the exchange rate is AUD0.9000=USD1 or USD1.1111=AUD1. If the rate moves to 0.800 (or USD1.25=AUD1), the US firm will reap exchange rate gains. If the rate moves to 1.000, however, the US loses from the depreciation of the Australian dollar. Concerned about the impact of these potential losses on its overall financial condition, the US firm is considering pulling out of the transaction. Since the Australian firm is eager to buy the equipment, it proposes a foreign exchange risk sharing agreement with its trading partner. So, depending upon the exchange rate at the time of payment, the two firms will share their gain/loss. If the threshold they agree on is 5%, then each firm will absorb the ensuing foreign exchange gain/loss should exchange rates change by less than 5%. If exchange rates change by more than 5%, the two firms will split the gain/loss from these changes.

Risk sharing is similar conceptually to taking an option as it is also a form of exchange risk barter, since both parties must agree to it. In return, of course, an "exchange risk-free" price is determined for the transaction. This method does away with the intermediary. To be workable, of course, the two firms involved must have a relationship that will help generate the necessary trust. The exact manner of sharing is renegotiated periodically.

2.2.5. Swaps

In general, a swap is an exchange of two different types of cash flows. In the financial markets, the two principal types are interest rate and currency swaps. Swaps involving exchange of currencies are classified as foreign exchange or currency swaps, with the former being the larger of the two. A foreign exchange swap involves exchange of two currencies (principal amount only) on a prespecified date at a rate agreed upon at the time the contract is signed. It is followed by reverse exchange of the same currencies at an agreed upon time in the future at a rate determined at the time the contract is signed. A currency swap, on the other hand, involves commitment by two parties to "*exchange streams of interest payments in different currencies for an agreed period of time and/or exchange principal amounts in different currencies at a pre-agreed exchange rate at maturity*" (Bank for International Settlements (BIS), 2013).

Today's swaps evolved from the older parallel and back-to-back loans—two similar instruments. A parallel loan involves four parties: two parent firms and their respective subsidiaries. Assume that an Italian MNC and a Brazilian counterpart have subsidiaries in each other's countries. The subsidiaries are in need of local currency funds, but currency controls make it practically impossible for the two parents to transfer funds to their subsidiaries. The two therefore reach an agreement by which

a. Each parent enters the domestic money market and raises the necessary funds.
b. Each parent transfers the funds to the other's subsidiary.
c. Each subsidiary services the debt extended by the other parent by making the required interest payments and paying the principal in the local currency.

A back-to-back loan involves exchange of funds from one parent to the other. Each parent raises funds in the domestic market and makes the transfer to the other parent. The respective borrowers service the debts.

Parallel and back-to-back loan arrangements are consummated by assuming the parties involved have compatible funding requirements. They are risky by nature because they include separate and discrete agreements. If one of the parties involved misses a payment or defaults outright, the other party is still liable for its part of the arrangement. The potential for generation of substantial search costs to verify creditworthiness and the threat of unilateral default make these loans inefficient. Swaps developed as a way to correct these inefficiencies. They accomplish this by

a. Formulating a single agreement, thus reducing default risk, and
b. Involving intermediaries, thus reducing default risk and search and transactions costs.

The rationale for the financial exchange represented by a swap is similar to that behind an exchange of goods between two parties. Swaps are justified by the comparative advantage a party enjoys in a financial market. An example of the benefits derived from the swap is shown in Table 7.2. Company A has the comparative advantage in the US market, while Company B has the advantage in the German market.

Company		A	B
Borrows			
	EUR	9%	8%
	USD	4%	5%
Receives			
	EUR		9%
	USD	5%	
Cost of Issuing in:			
	EUR	9%	
	USD		5%
Savings from Swap		1%	1%
Net		8%	4%

Table 7.2 The Benefits of a Currency Swap Arrangement.

Comparative advantage is not the only explanation, of course. Differences in taxes or government restrictions on transfer of funds may also be the motivating factor for creation of a swap, although the existence of comparative advantage facilitates the transaction. In exploiting this advantage, swaps offer the benefit of a joint transaction that yields gains that can be greater than the sum of benefits derived from individual efforts.

There are various types of swaps. In such a developing market, new products will probably continue to come along besides traditional instruments, called vanilla swaps. For now, depending on the needs of the parties involved, the rate of interest paid may be fixed or floating. The swap may also have characteristics of both currency and interest rate swaps or may offer amortizing of the principal over the life of the instrument. Swaps can also be used in combination with other products, such as floating rate notes, forward exchange agreements, and options (Marshall and Kapner, 1990; Beidleman, 1992).

The currency swap market began its modern ascent in 1981, when the World Bank and IBM entered into an important agreement. Since then, the foreign exchange and currency swap market has grown substantially. As we noted in Chapter 1, foreign exchange and currency swaps have become the largest component of the foreign exchange market, reaching a daily average turnover of $3.310tr in 2019, an increase of more than 440% from the 1998 figure of $744b (BIS, 2013). The principal currency of the swap market has been the US dollar, although non-dollar swaps have increased in importance.

Concept Questions

1. What are the differences between a forward-market and an options-market strategy of foreign exchange risk management?
2. Explain the various theories of hedging in the futures market.
3. How can a firm share its foreign exchange risk?
4. What are the differences between a foreign exchange swap and a currency swap?
5. How does the concept of comparative advantage apply to the use of swaps?

3. Changes in Translation Approaches and Changes in Hedging Techniques

One of the interesting exchange-risk-related developments of the last few years has been the supplanting of FASB-8 by FASB-52. Did the change cause the firms affected to adopt different hedging strategies?

While in effect, FASB-8 came in for severe criticism on various fronts. Critics maintained that FASB-8 (1) distorted operating margins by translating sales at current prices and translation rates compared to cost of sales at historical cost and translation rates, (2) contributed to the volatility of earnings through its requirement that exchange gains and losses be reported as part of income, and (3) generated inevitable inconsistencies in the valuation of foreign investments, making subsidiaries in countries whose currencies were rising in value seem as if they were falling behind as the local currency debt was translated at the higher current rates while non-monetary assets were translated at historical rates.

Under FASB-8, MNCs felt pressures on their earnings reports and therefore hedged in order to minimize the adverse effects of exchange rate changes on earnings. When FASB-52 came along, the pressure on earnings was relieved somewhat, and some firms responded by reducing their hedging activity. Soon after FASB-52 went into effect, in 1982, Business International took a survey of sixty-five companies as to the effect of FASB-52 on corporate strategies. While the survey was taken very soon after the change from FASB-8 to FASB-52, some interesting insights regarding reaction to the change were provided. The responses dealt with three major areas of firm policy: trade-transaction management, finance and dividend planning, and translation exposure management. With respect to trade-transaction management, companies replied that the implications of the transition to FASB-52 included less use of the US dollar as the common currency of intercompany billing, shortening the terms of intercompany billing, greater use of currency netting systems, and greater centralization of leading and lagging operations. Finance and dividend planning were effected through use of currency swaps for hedging of net investments and review of guidelines for reorganizing the capital structure of foreign subsidiaries and for dividend planning. Management of translation exposure was effected through less use of forward contracts, more local currency borrowing, and revision of policies on hedging of net investments.

VIII. To Manage (Exposure) or Not to Manage?

The world of international business is made up of a large number of currency environments. Participants must learn as quickly as possible how to function effectively within this multicurrency framework. A firm must decide how to define and measure exposure, whether and how to manage it, and how to evaluate its strategy. The benefits of hedging may be both operational and financial (Allayannis and Weston, 2001; Dufey and Srinivalusu, 1984; Philadelphia Stock Exchange, 1986). From an operational point of view, managers must ask the question: What is our core business? How am I going to allocate my resources to get the maximum benefit? If the firm is in the bicycle business, the manager should be make decisions regarding the bicycle business rather than behave as a speculator in the foreign exchange market. Hedging should therefore receive heavy consideration. For many firms, maintaining a position in the foreign exchange market beyond what is necessary to conduct their primary business may also have disastrous results. These disasters can be avoided through a thorough understanding of the costs and benefits of hedging. One of the main principles underlying the quest for greater efficiency in the process is familiar: comparative advantage. The firm should shift its exposure burden to the party capable of bearing it at the lowest possible opportunity cost.

From a financial point of view, hedging can lower taxes and bankruptcy costs. As we learned, hedging may also lead to the smoothing of cash flows, thus enabling the firm to make sound investment decisions.

International financial managers may ask, "Is managing our exposure to exchange risk worth the cost of hedging?" The answer is not a universal and unequivocal "yes." Indeed, some analysts argue that management of foreign exchange risk is unnecessary. Some of these arguments are based on the general framework of the Purchasing Power Parity Doctrine and the Interest Rate Parity Theorem discussed in Chapter 2. Others have more to do with mainstream finance theory extended to international finance. They include the following:

1. The Purchasing Power Parity Argument

If PPP holds, prices move in a manner that offsets the impact of exchange rate changes. For example, if a currency appreciates, local currency costs incurred by a subsidiary will move accordingly. The firm need not be concerned about economic exposure in this case. The problem, of course, is that PPP does not necessarily hold at every given time. Even if PPP does hold at an aggregate level, it may not hold for a specific good on a specific date. The individual firm, then, should not be lulled into a false sense of security even at a time of general PPP validity.

2. The Interest Rate Parity Argument

If a currency is expected to depreciate, according to interest rate parity, interest rates are going to adjust accordingly as a result of arbitrage. Hedging, then, becomes redundant. The counterargument is similar to the one we have noted when any equilibrium condition is invoked as an argument for not hedging. Equilibrium conditions may or may not hold at any particular time. Moreover, as we pointed out in Chapter 2, the interest rate parity framework does not consider risk, nor is it applicable in the case of all financial instruments.

3. The "Modigliani-Miller" (MM) Argument

This traditional argument about the irrelevance of the firm's capital structure brought by the traditional 1958 Modigliani-Miller thesis may also be applied to management of exchange risk. The investor can afford to be indifferent when confronted with investing in two firms, one exposed to exchange risk, the other exchange risk-free. The reason: the investor can achieve the desired level of exposure either by buying shares of exposed firms or by accepting exposure in his/her own balance sheet and income statement. The investor could also enter the currency options market and take a position commensurate with, say, her foreign currency-denominated bonds. In this argument, corporate exposure and individual or homemade exposure are considered perfect substitutes. Opponents of this position, however, also take their arguments from the long-standing MM debate. Individuals, they respond, do not have the same knowledge or ability as a firm to secure low cost hedges. The firm has a comparative advantage in hedging; by using sophisticated market mechanisms to do so, it passes on the benefits to the shareholders.

4. The Efficient Markets Argument

The assumption of semi-strong market efficiency implies that forward market instruments are priced appropriately. Forward market hedging, then, cannot generate excess returns. Of course, even in an efficient market, hedging may still be justifiable. A firm may incur losses in an efficient market as well as gains. Hedging establishes a known and predictable cost/benefit structure.

5. The Capital Asset Pricing Model (CAPM) Argument

The CAPM assigns primary importance to systematic risk. A firm's shares will thus be priced in accordance with this risk. Unsystematic foreign exchange risk, like other unsystematic risk, may be diversified away. Systematic foreign exchange risk, together with properly priced forward contracts, does not change firm value. However, firms may find hedging attractive since it may generate steadier cash flows for the firm.

6. The Managerial Irrelevance Argument

Some would argue that just as exchange rate movements are generated by forces external to the firm and therefore outside the manager's control, evaluation of management performance, then, should not take the effects of foreign exchange rate changes into account. A counterargument, of course, is that exchange rate risk is really a basic risk of engaging in international business. In the case of manager or division evaluation, division managers have less flexibility or even zero flexibility if the firm has adopted a centralized approach to exposure management.

Additional arguments will surface to describe hedging as a superfluous exercise. The final decision to proceed with hedging depends on a number of factors, including the firm's characteristics, its risk appetite, and its environment. The next hedging step may be easier if a mature MNC has had relevant experience. At the same time, a firm just starting out in international business cannot afford to travel its uncharted waters without exchange risk protection.

The environment the firm operates in may be more than an incidental factor. Transition to the floating-rate system of the early 1970s increased the need for and practice of hedging. Since then, the foreign exchange market has shown periods of high volatility. Managers should not be surprised if exchange rates fluctuate widely from one period to the other. Instead, a good manager should be prepared to take positions that minimize the negative effects of currency gyrations.

IX. Hedging Practices and Firm Value

We discussed the various arguments for and against hedging. At this point, we need to ask a couple of very important questions:

1. Why do firms hedge their currency exposure?
2. Does hedging increase the value of the firm?

Although some studies have been conducted to address these questions, the evidence presented have been limited. In answering the first question, Géczy, Minton, and Schrand (1990) conducted a survey of the *Fortune 500* nonfinancial firms found that 41 percent of the 372 firms responding do indeed use currency futures, forwards, options, swaps, or combinations of these approaches to manage their foreign exchange exposure. The survey also revealed that the use of currency derivatives was more likely when firms aimed at lowering the variability of expected cash flows, especially as they were facing new growth opportunities. Firms were also more likely to hedge when they faced financing constraints; the need to hedge became more apparent as a result of the pressure on the firm to meet these constraints.

The relationship between hedging and the value of the firm is in the heart of the hedging decision. After all, firms should only engage in activities that are expected to add value to the entire organization. However, as we saw above, not everybody agrees on the merits of hedging. To answer our second question: does hedging increase the value of the firm? Allayannis and Weston (2001) conducted an empirical study of US non-financial firms. They found that hedging generates a "premium" for the firm, adding almost 5% to their value.

The benefits of hedging should always be considered on an after-tax basis. For this reason, firms should be aware of the tax treatment of their hedges. The decision to hedge can be even controversial at times. Take for example a somewhat notorious example involving Lufthansa. In 1985, the firm ordered twenty 737s from Boeing; payment and delivery were to take place a year later. Half of the purchase price of $500m was covered through the purchase of forward dollars at 3.2DM=$1, which was close to the rate prevailing at the time of the agreement. The other half of the purchase price was left unprotected. At the time of payment, the exchange rate had changed to DM2.3=$1, making exchange protection a very expensive proposition for Lufthansa (DM= Deutsche Mark; the Mark, of course, has not been in circulation since the adoption of the euro). Should the firm have waited before entering the forward market? Should it have entered the options market rather than the forward? Should it have gone totally unprotected?

The definitive answers to exposure questions are known only when all information is available. Decisions, of course, need to be made before all information is in, which is why hedging is both an art and a science.

Concept Questions

1. Do you think that a multinational should take an active role in managing its foreign exchange exposure?
2. Explain the relationship between hedging and firm value.
3. Discuss the implications of the efficient markets argument for management of foreign exchange exposure.

X. Summary

This chapter described the nature and scope of exchange risk and exchange exposure. It examined the various types of foreign exchange exposure—translation, transaction, and economic—and discussed issues pertaining to their measurement and significance. The strategies used by firms to managed foreign exchange exposure were analyzed. These strategies were classified as internal or external to the firm. Internal strategies included the balance sheet hedge, leading-lagging, currency netting, diversification of operations, money market hedge, and pricing strategies. External methods included the forward market hedge, futures, options, risk sharing, and swaps.

Key Terms and Concepts

In the order in which they are presented in the text.

Foreign exchange risk: Exchange risk is the probability that the actual exchange rate at some future point in time will be different from the forecasted value.

Foreign exchange exposure: Foreign exchange exposure is the impact of exchange rate risk on individual market participants.

Translation exposure: Translation, or accounting, exposure measures the impact of exchange rate changes on the firm's financial statements.

Transaction exposure: Transaction exposure assesses the gain or loss in the value of a specific transaction that may result from a change in the exchange rate between the time the contract is signed and the time it is finalized.

Economic exposure: Economic exposure reveals the sensitivity of the present value of the firm's cash inflows and outflows to unexpected changes in the exchange rate.

Exposed items: Exposed items in the firm's financial statements are those items whose home currency value is affected by changes in the exchange rate. These items are translated using the current exchange rate (exchange rate in effect at the closing of the financial statement).

Non-exposed items: Non-exposed items in the firm's financial statements are those items whose home currency is not affected by changes in the exchange rate. These items are translated using the historical exchange rate (exchange rate in effect when the item entered the financial statement).

Net exposure: It is the difference between exposed and non-exposed items in the financial statement. Net exposure indicates the direction of the firm's exposure and the degree to which it must engage in exposure management. With respect to the balance sheet, net exposure is positive if exposed assets are greater than exposed liabilities; it is negative when exposed liabilities are greater than greater assets.

Current rate method: According to the current rate method, all assets and liabilities are considered as exposed and translated using the current exchange rate.

Current/non-current rate method: According to this method, current (maturing in less than one year) assets and liabilities are translated at the current exchange rate. Assets and liabilities with maturity exceeding one year are restated at the exchange rate at which they originally entered the records of the subsidiary.

Monetary/non-monetary method: In this translation method, monetary assets are defined as claims held by the firm to receive a fixed amount of foreign currency; they include cash, accounts receivable, and marketable securities. Similarly, monetary liabilities such as accounts payable and long-term debt involve an obligation to pay a fixed amount of that foreign currency. Monetary assets and liabilities are translated using the current exchange rate. Non-monetary assets and liabilities by contrast include such "physical items" as inventories and fixed assets and are translated using the historical exchange rate.

Temporal method: In the temporal method of translation, the choice of the exchange rate depends on whether the item has entered the balance sheet valued at market (translated at the current exchange rate) or at cost (translated at the historical exchange rate).

FASB-8: FASB-8 was adopted in 1975; its purpose was "*to measure and express (a) in dollars and (b) in conformity with US generally accepted accounting principles the assets, liabilities, revenue, or expenses that are measured or denominated in foreign currency*" (Financial Accounting Standards Board, 1975, p. 5). FASB-8 brought consistency to financial statement translation by adopting the temporal method.

FASB-52: FASB-52, replacing FASB-8 in 1981, is designed to

- *"provide information that is generally compatible with the expected economic effects on an enterprise's cash flow and equity and*
- *reflect in consolidated statements the financial results and relationships as measured in the primary currency in which each entity conducts its business (referred to as its functional currency" (Financial Accounting Standards Board, 1981, p. 4).*

FASB-52 employs the net investment concept, the current rate translation approach, the functional currency concept, and the Cumulative Translation Adjustment Account. It also accounts for the translation of financial statements under hyperinflationary environments and combines a number of interesting translation characteristics:

Value-at-Risk (VaR): VaR is used to measure exchange risk by arriving at "the maximum loss for a given exposure over a given time horizon with z% confidence" (Papaioannou, 2006).

Balance sheet hedge: Balance sheet hedge is a translation exposure management approach, according to which the firm minimizes the difference between exposed assets and exposed liabilities.

Leading–lagging: Management of foreign exchange exposure by adjusting the timing of payments to another firm.

Exchange rate pass-through: Exchange rate pass-through refers to the change in international prices in response to changes in exchange rates.

Currency netting: Exposure of one subsidiary in one currency may be offset by (opposite) exposure by another subsidiary in the same currency.

Diversification of operations: Minimizing the potentially adverse effect of changes in exchange rates through establishment of diversified cross-border operations.

Money market hedge: The objective of a money market strategy is to put the firm in a position of receiving payment (or making payment) in terms of the home currency, thus neutralizing the effect of exchange rate changes. A money market hedge creates a foreign currency asset (or liability) that matches the firm's foreign currency liability (or asset) that was created through its business operations.

Pricing strategies: Firms may address their exchange rate exposure by adjusting their pricing policies. These adjustments may include transfer pricing and selling point adjustments.

Forward market hedge: The firm protects itself against unfavorable currency movements by entering into a forward contract.

Futures market hedge: The futures markets also offers firms and individual investors the opportunity to manage their exposure by taking a futures position opposite to their spot market position.

Traditional Theory of hedging: The Traditional Theory of hedging assumes that the basis (difference between futures and spot prices) remains the same. In order for the firm to hedge effectively, then, it should make sure that its futures positions exactly offset its spot positions.

Working's Hypothesis: It argues against the basic assumption of the Traditional Theory, suggesting instead that hedgers formulate expectations about the future spot rate. Their hedging behavior, then, is predicated upon the expected relationship between spot and futures. In some cases, this relationship would indicate a need for less hedging than prescribed by the Traditional Theory.

Portfolio Theory of hedging: This framework combines elements of both Traditional and Working's theories, viewing hedging in a portfolio context rather than in terms of either risk or return. The firm's portfolio of currency flows, then, may consist of both hedged and unhedged components.

Options hedge: A strategy of managing exchange exposure by entering the options market.

Risk sharing: Risk sharing agreements entail negotiations between the buyer and the seller in a traditional commercial transaction to share any gains or losses from the movement of the exchange rate.

Swaps: A foreign exchange swap involves exchange of two currencies (principal amount only) on a prespecified date at a rate agreed upon at the time the contract is signed. It is followed by reverse exchange of the same currencies at an agreed upon time in the future at a rate determined at the time the contract is signed. A currency swap, on the other hand, involves commitment by two parties to *"exchange streams of interest payments in different currencies for an agreed period of time and/or exchange principal amounts in different currencies at a pre-agreed exchange rate at maturity"* (Bank for International Settlements (BIS), 2013).

The Purchasing Power Parity argument against hedging: If PPP holds, prices move in a manner that offsets the impact of exchange rate changes. The firm need not be concerned about economic exposure in this case.

The Interest Rate Parity argument against hedging: If a currency is expected to depreciate, according to interest rate parity, interest rates are going to adjust accordingly as a result of arbitrage. Hedging, then, becomes redundant.

The "Modigliani-Miller" (MM) argument against hedging: The argument extends the traditional 1958 thesis on the irrelevance of the firm's capital structure to exchange risk management. The investor can afford to be indifferent when confronted with investing in two firms, one exposed to exchange risk, the other exchange risk-free. The reason: the investor can achieve the desired level of exposure either by buying shares of exposed firms or by accepting exposure in his/her own balance sheet and income statement. The investor could also enter the currency options market and take a position commensurate with, say, her foreign-currency-denominated bonds. In this argument, corporate exposure and individual or homemade exposure are considered perfect substitutes.

The Efficient Markets argument against hedging: The assumption of semi-strong market efficiency implies that forward-market instruments are priced appropriately. Forward market hedging, then, cannot generate excess returns. Of course, even in an efficient market, hedging may be still be justifiable. A firm may incur losses in an efficient market as well as gains. Hedging establishes a known and predictable cost/benefit structure.

The Capital Asset Pricing Model (CAPM) argument against hedging: The CAPM assigns primary importance to systematic risk. A firm's shares will thus be priced in accordance with this risk. Unsystematic foreign exchange risk, like other unsystematic risk, may be diversified away. Systematic foreign exchange risk, together with properly priced forward contracts, does not change firm value. However, firms may find hedging attractive since it may generate steadier cash flows for the firm.

The Managerial Irrelevance argument: According to this argument, exchange rate movements are outside the manager's control. Evaluation of management performance, then, should not take the effects of foreign exchange rate changes into account. A counterargument, of course, is that exchange rate risk is really a basic risk of engaging in international business. In the case of manager or division evaluation, division managers have less flexibility or even zero flexibility if the firm has adopted a centralized approach to exposure management.

Web Exercises

W1. Access the most recent Annual Reports of the following firms:

a. Merck
b. General Electric
c. A firm of your choice

Explain how each firm describes its exchange rate exposure strategy.

Questions and Problems

1. Many observers note that the distinction between transaction and economic exposure is unnecessary and consider transaction exposure a special case of economic exposure. Do you agree?

   Carefully analyze the similarities and differences between these two types of exposure.
2. Your summer job with Pronto Pharmaceuticals requires you to make a presentation to management and staff about the firm's translation exposure. You make the statement that translation exposure deals only with "paper" gains and losses, and a tax specialist takes issue. What do you think is the basis of his disagreement with your position?

3. Comment on this statement recently made by the treasurer of a US firm: "Thanks to FASB-52, we can now evaluate the performance of our subsidiaries in a way that makes sense."
4. "Management of foreign exchange exposure is a concern of the private sector. My government has no reason to be concerned about such exposure." Gorbatz Gorbatzo, Slabovia's Finance Minister.

   Do you agree with the minister? Why or why not?
5. As a National Hockey League franchise based in Boston, Massachusetts, do the Bruins face any exchange risk?
6. A Wall Street analyst is reported to have said, "K-Mart's sales are all in the United States. Therefore, the firm does not have to be concerned about exchange risk." True or false? Explain carefully.
7. "We do a lot of foreign business, especially with Canada, but we do not have to worry about exchange rate changes. All our Canadian customers pay us in good old US dollars." James Nelson, Treasurer and CFO, Amalgamated Faucet Co. Do you agree? Explain your answer.
8. Explain carefully the application of the concept of comparative advantage to the practice of currency exposure management.
9. Your summer internship is with Fenwick, Inc., a US firm with substantial operations in Italy. The CFO is concerned about the dollar value of the Italian operations because she has heard that the euro is weakening. She knows that you have taken a course in International Finance at Faber College (which is also her alma mater). She asks you to give her some hedging alternatives. After thinking about it for a couple of minutes, you provide her with the following options:

   a. Reduce the amount of euro receivables by tightening up the terms of credit you have been giving your Italian customers;
   b. Increase the amount of your euro borrowing;
   c. Delay taking care of your payables right away;
   d. Cut down on the amount of euros on hand (cash);
   e. Tell your customers that you will accept payment in dollars only;
   f. Use the forward market as frequently as possible;
   g. Speed up the cash flow from your Italian operations back to the United States as much as possible.

   The CFO thanks you, but she now wants you to explain the advantages and disadvantages associated with each of the above alternatives. She also tells you that, if you do a good job, she will offer you a full-time job. How would you respond to her request?
10. Fenwick also has operations in Thailand, and the CFO's reading indicates that the baht may be appreciating. She is concerned! She just remembered, however, that you have another intern, Biff Andersen, who took two courses in International Finance from Faber. She asks Biff for a report on hedging alternatives. What will he report?

11. "Financial markets do not provide bargains. Foreign exchange gains and losses offset each other over a period of time. What is the sense of hedging?" Comment on the statement.
12. Global Airways is considering a new route to the East Asia. What are the exchange rate considerations Global must be aware of? How can the firm manage its exposure?
13. GM is considering opening a plant in Poland. What kinds of exchange exposure is it facing?
14. Money Market Hedge:

    The Fabulous Yo-Yo company of NYC has an obligation to pay its Russian supplier RUB100m in one year. The current exchange rate is RUB50=USD1, and is expected to stay at the same level for a year. The Russian one-year interest rate is 15%, while the US rate is 5%.

    How can the company hedge its exposure to the RUB using the Money Market?
15. Your firm is considering opening a plant in a country confronting high inflation. What problems does inflation create for your firm's currency exposure? How would you deal with them?
16. The Australian Wheat Board sells almost all of its wheat in US dollars but pays its growers in Australian currency. You are applying for a job with the Board. As part of your interview, you are asked to suggest some exchange risk management strategies. What strategies would you suggest?
17. Assume that your firm, a Canadian-based multinational, is facing the following situations:

    a. Has £100 in assets
    b. Has £50 in liabilities
    c. Has €50 in assets
    d. Has €100 in liabilities

    All assets and liabilities are exposed to exchange rate changes. What are the risks involved for the firm (in terms of the Canadian dollar)? What are the currency hedging strategies available to the firm?
18. HiTech, Inc. is a US firm with a Mexican subsidiary. The subsidiary reports that its balance sheet shows the following items:

    Cash 5,000 pesos; Short term securities at market 3,000; Accounts receivable 1,000; Inventories at cost 3,000; Net plant 3,000; Current liabilities 5,000; Long-term debt 4,000.

    The current rate is 33 Mexican Pesos=US$1. Assume that the historical rate is 20 pesos per dollar. What is the translation exposure according to the current, current/non-current, monetary/non-monetary, and temporal methods?
19. A US importer is to make payment of 2,000,000 Swiss francs in sixty days. The sixty-day forward rate is \$0.8965. The importer decides to cover his exposure through the forward market. Sixty days later, the spot is \$0.8920. Did he make the right decision? What if the future spot rate ended up being \$0.9020?

20. The XYZ Corporation just closed a sale with a customer from Cornovia. The firm will receive COF1,000,000 in three months. After making the agreement, XYZ realizes that there is considerable risk attached to the Cornovian franc and, unfortunately, no forward market. What options does XYZ have in managing its exposure to the franc?
21. Company X and Company Y are both subsidiaries of the Canada-based Company W. Company X operates in Italy, while Company Y is located in the UK. Company X owes 5,000,000 Canadian dollars to Company W. Company Y owes 3,000,000 Euros to Company X, while Company W owes 2,000,000 British pounds to Company Y. Explain how currency netting would take place.
22. The IM LoanShark Co. has a one-day receivable of £100,000. Historical data show that the £/$ return is normally distributed with a standard deviation of 0.25%. Assume that the exchange rate is £0.70 = $1. What is the VaR at the 95% level of confidence? At the 99%?

Selected References

Adler, M., and B. Dumas. 1984. Exposure to Currency Risk: Definition and Measurement. *Financial Management* 13 (Summer): 41–50.

Aggarwal, R. 1975. The Translation Problem in International Accounting. *Management International Review* 2 (3): 67–79.

Allayannis, G., and J. P. Weston. 2001. The Use of Foreign Currency Derivatives and Firm Market Value. *The Review of Financial Studies* 14 (1): 243–76

Bank for International Statements. 2013. *Triennial Central Bank Survey: Foreign exchange turnover in April 2013: preliminary global results.* Basel: Switzerland: Bank for International Settlements.

Beidleman, C. R. 1992. *Cross Currency Swaps*. Homewood, Illinois: Business One Irwin.

Coopers & Lybrand. 1994. *Foreign Currency Translation and Hedging.* New York: Coopers & Lybrand. *Note*: Coopers & Lybrand merged with PWC in 1998.

Dufey, G., and S. L. Srinivasulu. 1984. The Case for Corporate Management of Foreign Exchange Risk. *Financial Management* 4: 54–62.

Duffie, D., and J. Pan. 1997. An overview of value at risk. *Journal of Derivatives 4* (3): 7–49.

Ederington, L. 1979. The Hedging Performance of the New Futures Markets. *Journal of Finance* (March): 157–70.

Financial Accounting Standards Board. 1975. *Statement of Financial Accounting Standards No. 8*: Norwalk, Connecticut: Financial Accounting Standards Board, October.

Financial Accounting Standards Board. 1981. *Statement of Financial Accounting Standards No. 52.* Norwalk, Connecticut: Financial Accounting Standards Board, December.

Géczy, C., B. A. Minton, and C. Schrand. 1997. Why Firms Use Currency Derivatives. *Journal of Finance.* LII (4): 1323–54.

Holton, G. A. 2014. *Value-at-Risk: Theory and Practice.* Second edition. Cambridge, MA: Academic Press. E-book at http://value-at-risk.net.

J. P. Morgan. 1995. *Introduction to RiskMetrics™*. Fourth Edition. New York: Morgan Guarantee Trust Company.

Marshall, J. F., and K. R. Kapner. 1990. *Understanding Swap Finance*. Cincinnati: South-Western.

Papaioannou, M. 2006. *Exchange Rate Risk Measurement and Management: Issues and Approaches for Firms*. IMF Working Paper WP/06/255. Washington, DC: International Monetary Fund.

Philadelphia Stock Exchange. 1986. Lufthansa: Where Options Would Have Made a Difference. *Intermarket*. November 1986, Supplement, 20–22.

PWC. 2012. *Foreign Currency Tax Accounting*. New York: PWC, Tax Accounting Services, October.

Srinivasulu, S. L. 1981. Strategic Response to Foreign Exchange Risk. *Columbia Journal of World Business* (Spring): 13–22.

Working, H. 1953. Futures trading and hedging. *American Economic Review* (June): 314–43.

Zumbach, G. 2007. *The RiskMetrics 2006 methodology*. New York: RiskMetrics Group. Downloaded from www.riskmetrics.com on 8/1/15.

Chapter 8

International Bond and Equity Markets

Overview of Chapter Material

Development of international financial markets is a classic example of the ingenuity of financial market participants. It is also an excellent illustration of the speed and efficacy with which financial flows can enhance the supply of and demand for capital even in the face of national regulatory obstacles.

We have discussed the nature and significance of the largest international financial market: the market for currencies. We now turn our attention to additional components of international capital. These are markets where participants raise external capital internationally, issuing either debt or ownership claims.

This chapter describes the major characteristics of financial markets operating across borders: the Eurocurrency, medium-term note (MTNs), international bond, and international equity markets. They are dynamic and developing markets, where change is more the rule than the exception. A textbook explanation, then, is no substitute for following market developments on a regular basis. The basic information presented in this chapter is intended as motivation for ongoing study of the nature and impact of developing international market mechanisms.

One word of caution: We should not confuse "Euromarkets" with "Euro Markets." The former are the subject of this chapter. The latter refer to markets related to the European Union.

After Studying This Chapter, You Will Be Able To

- Understand the nature of the Euromarkets
- Explain the various types of international bond markets

- Appreciate the importance of the International Equity Market
- Assess the implications of international financial markets for corporate financing

Chapter Outline

I. The Eurocurrency Markets
II. Euronotes and Medium-Term Notes
III. International Bond Markets
IV. International Equity Markets
V. Derivative Instruments
VI. Additional Issues in Global Financial Markets
VII. Summary

I. The Eurocurrency Markets

We distinguish among the major components of Euromarkets in terms of the maturity of the security involved. These components are Eurocurrency, euronote and Eurobond/Euroequity markets. Eurocurrency markets primarily involve short-term instruments, such as bank deposits. Euronote markets include instruments of short- to medium-term maturity. Eurobond and Euroequity markets deal in longterm financial instruments. The markets have similar origin and impact on national financial markets. We describe them in separate sections of this chapter to highlight their diversity.

1. The Evolution of the Eurocurrency Markets

The end of World War II brought the need for reconstruction of the international financial system as countries were rebuilding their economies. The United States emerged as the uncontested world leader, and the US dollar became the dominant currency in international trade and finance. As western economies slowly began to function again, however, the division between the Western nations and the Eastern Bloc widened—a situation exacerbated by the Cold War of the 1950s—so a US-led financial system was not recognized by every country.

Widespread acceptance of the US dollar after WWII and the advent of US international payments deficits of the 1950s resulted in large dollar holdings abroad. As long as expectations about the state of international economic and political relations were stable, internationally held dollars could be recycled in the United States financial system in the form of deposits in US banks.

Expectations regarding the safety and liquidity of dollar deposits held by foreigners changed, however, as the Cold War progressed and other international crises developed, such as the Suez Canal takeover. Deposits began to be shifted to banks or branches outside the United States. For example, the London-based Moscow Narodny Bank and the Paris-based Banque Commerciale du Nord, both owned by the former Soviet Union, became concerned about possible freezing of Soviet assets in US banks. In response, they placed their dollar deposits in London banks. Also, in the late 1950s, Britain imposed restrictions on pound sterling lending to non-residents, thus reducing the international role of the pound. London banks'

British pound dealings were a source of both profitability and international influence. When this source started to diminish in importance, these banks turned to US dollar-denominated deposits. In short order, the Eurodollar became an accepted instrument of international finance.

The development of the Eurocurrency markets has been spurred by a series of US regulatory actions through the years. These include

- The Interest Equalization Tax (IET). Adopted in 1963, this measure was intended to discourage the purchase of foreign securities issued in the United States and thereby stem the flow of capital out of the country.
- The Foreign Credit Restraint Program. Formulated by the Federal Reserve Board, this program's objective was to limit the flow of funds from member banks to their foreign borrowers in the US markets.
- Flow of funds restrictions. In 1968, the US Office of Foreign Direct Investment placed restrictions on funds flowing from US-based multinationals to their foreign affiliates.
- Regulation Q. Adopted during the Great Depression (1933), Regulation Q imposed interest rate ceilings on time and savings deposits at US banks.
- Reserve requirements. Bank reserve requirements limit the extent to which banks can commit funds to income-earning alternatives. They therefore affect the availability and cost of credit.

Some of these regulations were rescinded or relaxed a few years after their enactment, as operations of financial markets triumphed over the narrow objectives of government regulation. The Credit Restraint Program was discontinued after 1974. Regulation Q began to be dismantled in 1973, when interest rate ceilings were removed for large deposits ($100,000 or more). The US financial system, in general, became less regulated in the late 1970s and into the 1980s. Domestic restrictions gave impetus to the formation of extranational structures that gained their own identity and became an economic force in their own right. The operations of international markets and the experience that the world economic and financial community gained through their operations in the 1960s and 1970s became very valuable in the decades ahead.

2. The Creation of Eurodollar Deposits

In general, Eurocurrencies are currencies on deposit with banks outside the country of issue. Euroyen, for example, are yen-denominated deposits outside Japan. During its early years, the Eurocurrency market was almost totally made up of US dollars and German marks. Over time, however, additional currencies with varying attractiveness to market participants appeared, depending on domestic and international conditions. We explain the nature and workings of the Eurodollar market in a simple illustration of how Eurodollar deposits are created in the Appendix of this chapter.

The example shows the way various institutions participate in the Eurodollar market. Since there are no required reserve requirements for Eurodollar deposits, the process described could continue indefinitely. In practice, of course, leakages do occur and the process eventually comes to an end.

3. Salient Characteristics of the Eurocurrency Market

To describe the nature of the Eurocurrency market, we concentrate on some selected characteristics, such as the market's location, size, instruments used, and interest rates paid on these instruments (Sarver, 1988).

3.1. Location

The Eurocurrency market operates in practically all of the world's financial centers. London is considered the principal locus of the overall market, accounting for about one-third of total Eurocurrency deposits. Brussels and Paris are the leading Eurosterling centers. Other European centers are found in Frankfurt, Amsterdam, Zurich, and Luxembourg. The market is active in the United States as well, through deposits at International Banking Facilities (IBFs). Eurocurrency deposits are also made in Tokyo, Hong Kong, Singapore, the Cayman Islands, and other so-called offshore financial centers. Singapore and Hong Kong are centers of activity for the Asian dollar market, which has become an important component of the global financial system.

3.2. Size and Activity

The multinational nature of the market makes it difficult to assess its exact size and the level of its activity. The variety of deposits included and their differing risk/return characteristics also complicate measurement. Through its *Annual Report,* the Bank for International Settlements in Basel is the most widely quoted source of Eurocurrency activity. According to the Bank, cross-border deposits were approximately $29tr (BIS, April 2019).

3.3. Instruments and Rates

The principal Eurocurrency instrument is the deposit, especially the interbank deposit. Instruments also include certificates of deposit, commercial paper, bankers' acceptances, letters of credit, and bank loans. Interbank deposits are made in large denominations, normally per one million currency units, and pay semi-annual or annual interest depending on the maturity.

Eurocurrency Certificates of Deposit (CDs) are negotiable instruments with relatively active secondary markets. They were introduced in 1966 at the London Branch of Citibank. Most CDs are still issued in London and are denominated in yen, sterling, and US dollars. Dollar CDs have minimum denominations of $25,000 but are usually traded at much larger amounts (multiples of $1m). Eurocurrency lending represents the other side of the market, that is, the uses of funds. Loans are usually provided in multiples of $1m. Maturities can reach fifteen years, but rates may be changed every six months. Lines of credit may be arranged for the shorter-term loans. Overdrafts are normally not available.

3.3.1. LIBOR

The rates applicable to Euroloans are quoted in terms of deviation from the London Interbank Offered Rate (LIBOR), which is an arithmetic, or trimmed, average (excluding the top and bottom 25% of the submitted rates) of the rates considered appropriate for borrowing by major London banks. LIBOR was created by the British Bankers Association and was first published in 1986. Similarly, rates in Frankfurt are called FIBOR and in Hong Kong HIBOR. The deposit rate is referred to as LIBID (London Interbank Bid Rate), while the average of the two is the LIMEAN. There are 150 LIBOR-related rates around the world: for 10 currencies, 15 maturities each. In the US, the rate is calculated by collecting information from 16 banks.

A noteworthy aspect of the Eurocurrency markets is the relationship between LIBOR and LIBID. The difference between them is generally smaller than the difference between offer and bid rates in the domestic market, which is taken as an indication of the greater relative efficiency of the Euromarkets. The offer and bid difference is expected to be smaller in the case of the major currencies, dollar and sterling, as compared to that for the other currencies.

LIBOR may be thought of as the "best" rate at which loans can be extended; it is the rate banks used to lend to each other. The rate charged for a specific loan, which is called the margin or the spread, may be .75% to 3% above LIBOR; the actual rate, of course, depends on many other factors particular to the borrower, the loan, and the environment. Thus, LIBOR has been used as the basis for such diverse transactions as mortgages and student loans. It also affects the pricing of derivative contracts, including swaps and futures. The British Bankers Association went so far as to term LIBOR "the most important number in Finance."

3.3.2. The LIBOR Scandal

This diverse and ubiquitous use of LIBOR and its self-reporting methodology was behind some traders' request as early as 2005 to Barclay's bankers to manipulate its self-reporting of its borrowing rates. Between 2005 and 2009, Barclay's sometimes under-reported, other times over-reported, and still other times reported its rate as unchanged (despite the fact that it had changed). In addition to Barclay's, a number of other global financial institutions were involved in the plot to manipulate LIBOR: They included Deutsche Bank, UBS, RBS, and Rabobank. By 2016, banks had paid about $9B in fines. Perhaps the most important price paid as a result of the revelation of such large scale fraud was in the deterioration of trust in the global banking and financial system (Council on Foreign Relations, 2016).

To reclaim public confidence in the system, in 2014, the Intercontinental Exchange (ICE) took over administration of LIBOR from the British Banker's Association and even changed the methodology of compiling interest rate information from banks (Wyman, 2018). The international financial community is also searching for alternatives to LIBOR, especially since the UK's Financial Conduct Authority announced measures that would in reality terminate the formulation of LIBOR. In the US, the Federal Reserve Bank of New York assigned the task of finding a LIBOR replacement to the Alternative Reference Rates Committee (ARRC). The Committee recommended the secured overnight financing rate (SOFR) as LIBOR replacement. SOFR is based on repo interest rates for overnight Treasury-backed transactions in the Bank of New York Mellon's repo system or cleared though the Fixed Income Clearing Corporation. Other countries' central banks and various international financial institutions have also arrived at their own preferred alternatives. LIBOR's future, and that of its possible replacements, is still to be determined.

Concept Questions

1. Explain the nature of the Eurocurrency market. Describe its characteristics.
2. How can a Eurodollar deposit be created? How does creation of Eurodollar deposits differ from creation of domestic deposits?
3. What developments contributed to the evolution of the Eurocurrency markets?

II. Euronotes and Medium Term Notes (MTNs)

Euronotes are instruments of various maturities, from relatively short term to medium term, offered on underwritten or non-underwritten basis. Once dominated by banks, the Euronote market has seen stiffer capital requirements on these notes, thus reducing bank activity to a point where today fewer than half of the outstanding notes are held by banks.

Euronotes may be issued through note issuance facilities (NIFs) and revolving underwriting facilities (RUFs). These facilities are used especially by borrowers offering instruments of relatively lower quality. NIFs use a mechanism called a tender panel. The panel is a group composed of bankers, brokers, and dealers that bid for an issue in an open auction format. Awarding of the bids takes place in sequential order, starting with the most competitive bid. NIFs specialize in dollar notes, although in recent years options in local currency have appeared. An interesting example is an issue lead-managed by Citicorp on behalf of Enterprise Oil, a UK oil company. Options included: 1) issuing the notes in dollars to the tender panel; 2) asking the panel to make a term loan in sterling; 3) falling back on the sterling standby credit. Eurocommercial paper is simpler to issue, as there is no tender panel. Instead, an investment bank is used as the appointed dealer to sell the paper on a best-efforts basis and to maintain an orderly secondary market. About two-thirds of outstanding Euronotes are classified as Eurocommercial paper, with their most common maturities being 90 to 180 days.

Euro medium-term notes (EMTNs) were first issued in 1986. They have since become an important component of the market. Their maturities range from under a year to ten years, although in theory they can extend to the length desired by borrowers and lenders. Other characteristics of EMTNs, such as size and currency, can also be structured to fit the needs of the issuers. By the end of 1990, one-third of the outstanding EMTNs were in currencies other than the US dollar. Furthermore, market liquidity is guaranteed by the dealers. The market also competes effectively in terms of cost with other markets offering similar products. Underwritten EMTNs, for example, are very similar to Eurobonds. Yet, customized documentation for a eurobond can be ten times more expensive than that for an analogous MTN. For all these reasons, the EMTN market is expected to maintain its strength in the years ahead.

The MTN market remains an important component of the international financial market. It is a relatively inexpensive source of funds provided on terms that are adjusted to market conditions. It has grown in importance because of its flexibility in accommodating lender and borrower maturities. The market is continuous, conducted by brokers or dealers on a best-efforts (non-underwritten) rather than firm-commitment (underwritten) basis. Underwritten EMTNs, however, were popular during the first part of 1990s, with some large offerings, with the Kingdom of Spain's ECU250 million issue heading the list.

Concept Questions

1. Define and explain the importance of Eurocommercial paper.
2. What are Euro medium-term notes? When were they first issued? What is their role?

III. International Bond Markets

The global bond market has two principal components: the domestic bond market and the international bond market. The domestic bond market features bonds issued by a domestic entity (public or private), it is denominated in terms of the home currency and sold in the home market. The international bond markets have traditionally been classified into two categories: foreign bonds and Eurobonds (O'Malley, 2015; Sfez, 2014; Thau, 2011) . According to the original classification, foreign bond markets include bonds issued by a foreign entity in another country's market and denominated in that country's currency. For example, US dollar-denominated bonds issued by a German firm in the United States are considered foreign bonds. These bonds would be underwritten and sold by a group (syndicate) of US financial institutions. Eurobonds initially included bonds issued by an entity outside its own country but denominated in the issuer's currency. A US dollar-denominated bond issued by a US firm outside the United States is considered a Eurobond. The market has evolved to the point, however, that Eurobonds are also distributed internationally, including in the country of origin. US firms whose dollar bonds are syndicated internationally, then, are considered to be participating in the Eurobond market.

International bonds are used to raise funds by a broad spectrum of borrowers. They include national government, international institutions such as the IMF, the World Bank and the Asian Development Bank, and multinationals. The international bond market generates more than half of the total amount of funds raised in international capital markets. A number of factors influence the size and composition of international bond markets. They include the macroeconomic environment, and especially interest rates and foreign exchange rates, international tax provisions, developments in world financial markets, and the general attitude and behavior of various market participants.

The Mexican crisis (1994), Russian crisis (1992), Asian crisis (1997–98), and European crisis (2009–?) have directed a great deal of attention to bonds issued by national governments and denominated in a foreign currency. These bonds fall under the classification of "sovereign debt." The default risk associated with these bonds depends on the ability of the issuing government to generate tax revenues. Developing countries, therefore, often have to pay a significant risk premium to be able to borrow in the global capital market.

1. The Foreign Bond Market

Foreign bonds differ from domestic bonds in terms of the regulatory constraints they face in each country of circulation. That is, foreign bonds may be subject to different taxes and different requirements regarding registration, disclosure, and ownership. The most active foreign bond markets are in Swiss francs, US dollars, euros, Japanese yen, and British pound sterling.

Some of the foreign bond markets have acquired casual descriptive names: Yankee bonds are issued in the US by foreign entities. These bonds must be registered with the Securities and Exchange Commission. Bulldog bonds are foreign bonds issued in London; Rembrandt bonds are issued in the Netherlands; and samurai bonds are issued in Japan, to name a few. Other international bonds may not fall neatly in the foreign bond or Eurobond category. For example, sushi bonds are dollar bonds issued by Japanese firms for placement in Japan. Heaven-and-hell bonds are Eurodollar bonds, but with a currency option. Recently, we have seen the development of the dim sum market, CNY-denominated bonds issued primarily in Hong Kong.

2. The Eurobond Market

According to many market observers, the international nature of the syndicate is the distinguishing feature between Eurobonds and foreign bonds (Bowe, 1988). As markets become more integrated, however, the distinction between different types of bonds has been blurred.

The first Eurodollar bond issue took place in July 1963. The issuer was Autostrade, the Italian State Highway Authority, which borrowed $15m by issuing this new kind of international debt security, called Eurobonds. The Autostrade issue exemplified the principal characteristics of Eurobonds: bonds issued in bearer form, and coupon payments made without withholding tax. The specifics of the issue included

Number of Bonds:	60,000
Face Value:	US$250
Coupon Rate:	5 1/2 %
Payment of interest:	Annual (July)
Lead Manager:	Warburg & Co.
Co-Managers:	Banque de Bruxelles, S.A.
	Deutsche Bank AG
	Rootterdamsche Bank N.V.
Listing:	Luxembrourg, London
Form of issue:	Bearer

A few days after the issue of the Autostrade bonds, on July 18, 1963, the Interest Equalization Tax (IET) came into existence in the US. The IET, which added a 15% tax to the purchase price of non-domestic bonds, along with other capital controls imposed by US authorities, diverted funds from the New York market and gave additional impetus to the Eurobond market. Like the Eurodollar market, the Eurobond market managed to circumvent US regulatory restrictions by changing instrument characteristics to accommodate market participants. For example, a withholding tax imposed by the US government on interest paid by US issuers of Eurobonds to nonresidents was followed by the establishment of offshore subsidiaries in places such as the Netherlands Antilles. Withholding taxes can also be neutralized by special bond provisions that aim at compensating the lender for the tax paid. When, in 1984, the United States eliminated the withholding tax at the source, the maintenance of subsidiaries for the purpose of getting around the withholding was no longer necessary. Some of these subsidiaries were kept nevertheless, obviously serving other purposes.

The abolition of the IET and other controls failed to abate interest in the Eurobond market. During the first five years of its existence, 1963–1967, the market hosted the issuance of $4.8b of Eurobonds. The number increased to $17.5b, $47b, and $119b over each of the next three five-year periods (1968–1972, 1973–1977 and 1978–1982). In 2009, the market reached an all-time high of annual issues at $4.5tr. Issues declined during the ensuing financial crisis, but rebounded to $4tr by 2013, the market's fiftieth anniversary (Glover, 2013). The Eurobond market has had appeal to borrowers because it allows them access to a new group of investors and subjects them to less stringent disclosure requirements than those encountered in some domestic markets, ultimately exposing them to lower borrowing costs. For investors, the market's appeal lies primarily in the bearer form of the instruments and the lack of withholding tax. Individual investors may be all sorts of well-off professionals, characteristically termed "Belgian dentists," in any part of the globe. Institutional investors include banks, pension funds, insurance companies, quasi-governmental units, and sovereigns.

The development of the international swap market gave an extra boost to the market by enabling global investors to utilize their comparative advantage and gain access to borrowing structures that best suited them, including lower interest costs and the choice of fixed or floating rates.

2.1. Eurobond Interest-Rate Structures

Eurobond issues are structured in a variety of ways with respect to interest rate. One of the traditional distinctions is between fixed and floating rate issues.

2.1.1. Fixed-Rate Structure

Fixed-rate bonds are the most common form of Eurobonds issued. Also referred to as straight bonds, these bonds are usually unsecured and of maturity of seven to ten years. They have a fixed rate of interest, payable annually, and are registered on a European stock exchange, most likely London or Luxembourg. Most trading activity, however, takes place over-the-counter.

2.1.2. Floating Rate Structure

In 1970, the Italian state utility ENEL was about to issue $125 million in bonds at an interest rate specifying a rollover feature to protect against interest rate uncertainty. Interest rates for the issue were set at 3/4% above LIMEAN (the average of LIBOR and LIBID) and were to be reset at predetermined periods. Many other such issues, called Floating Rate Notes or FRNs, have surfaced since then. The rollover period is usually six months, although some issues have a threemonth rollover. Rates are set at 0.125% to 1.25% above LIBOR or SIBOR (Singapore Interbank Offer Rate). The US Treasury Bill rate has also been used as a benchmark. FRNs most often specify a minimum below which the rate will not fall. A special kind of FRN, called the perpetual FRN, has also circulated. As the name implies, it does not have a maturity date.

FRNs come in relatively smaller denominations ($1,000 to $10,000) than other comparable bonds. Corporate borrowers and financial institutions have found this market an especially convenient source of funds. The market for FRNs nearly collapsed in 1987 as investors became wary of changes in interest rates, and prices fell in both FRNs and perpetual FRNs. The market rebounded in 1988 and continued to experience a substantial increase in activity in 1990 and then again in 1992, when floating rates appeared to offer more of a hedge against interest rate risks. The market has also floundered during the recent financial crisis, as uncertainty hit this component of the international bond market the hardest.

2.2. Issuing Eurobonds

The issuance of a Eurobond is spearheaded by the managing underwriter, or lead manager; in ENEL's case, it was Morgan Stanley, with Nomura as the colead. The lead manager and the issuer establish the specifics of the financing proposal, including the size and timing of the issue, the coupon rate, maturity, price, and fees. The co-managers are expected to help with the placement of the issue in their respective domestic markets. The lead managers of the issue will interact with the other underwriters in a manner dictated by the syndication approach followed. There are two basic underwriting approaches: the European and the American. In the European approach, the lead manager alone sets a price that reflects the bid it has made to come to terms with the issuer. In the American-style syndication, the lead manager is appointed as the agent in accordance with an agreement signed by all underwriters, and bonds are sold only at the agreed-upon price. Deal managers in this case take an allocation of bonds that is commensurate with what they estimate they can place with investors.

The American approach eliminates the need for the issuer to sell the deal to the lead manager and for the lead manager to sell it subsequently to the rest of the syndicate. Some market observers credit American-style syndication with revitalizing the fixed-price reoffering market when it was suffering from excess competition and poor profitability.

Another component of the underwriting task is the selling group. Unlike underwriters, selling group members do not assume any market liquidity risk. The underwriters, that is, guarantee the issuer the agreed-upon price. The sellers merely receive a selling commission for the bonds they sell. Underwriters may also serve, of course, as members of the selling group.

We can use a simple example to illustrate how the various parties are compensated in an example of a $1,000 Eurobond issued at par. If the issuer is to receive $980, $20 is the flotation cost or gross spread to be divided among the lead manager and the co-managers, with the lead manager probably receiving about half or more. After paying the issuer $980, the manager will sell the issue to the underwriters for, say, $985 and subsequently to the selling group for $989. Thus,

Gross Spread: 1000 − 980 = 20 (100% of spread)
Management Fee: 985 − 980 = 5 (25% of spread)
Underwriting Fee: 989 − 985 = 4 (20% of spread)
Selling Concession: 1000 − 989 = 11 (55% of spread)

Besides these fees, there are expenses incurred for printing, listing, advertising, and for other services rendered. The total fees, commissions, and expenses will depend on the characteristics of the issue, including the currency of denomination, maturity, and size.

The managing and underwriting industry offers an interesting study in the dynamics of industrial organization in an industry that has been subjected to many changes at the top, the most noticeable one recently being the increasing influence of the Japanese financial firms.

2.3. Eurobond Products

The market has given rise to a number of new products during the last few years. The characteristics of these products are similar to those of the US bond market. Eurobond issues have included zero coupon bonds, convertibles, and asset-backed bonds.

2.3.1. Zero Coupon Bonds

As in the US bond market, the Eurobond market includes zero coupon bonds or zeros. These are fixed-rate bonds; investors buy them at discount and redeem them at face value at maturity. The advantages of zeros depend on several factors, including any difference between the applicable capital gains tax and the ordinary income tax rates.

2.3.2. Convertibles and Equity Warrants

Convertible bonds pay the usual coupon, but may be exchanged for another asset. The first convertible by a US firm was floated by Monsanto in 1965. The assets into which conversion may be made include financial or real assets. Convertible issues may also carry a currency option if they are denominated in a currency other than the investor's. Currency convertibles basically offer the investor the option to receive interest payments on the principal in an alternative currency. The rate of exchange may, in turn, be fixed or floating depending on the terms of purchase and the anticipated volatility of the two currencies. Equity warrants work much the same as a call option vis-a-vis the stock. They allow the investor to redeem the Eurobond for equity during a specified period of time at an agreed-upon price, called the exercise price.

The advantages of convertibles and warrants for the issuer include a reduction in interest payments and some increased marketability of the issue. For the investor, the convertible likewise offers protection in the event that a particular market takes an unfavorable turn. Bond interest payments may be subject to more favorable tax treatment than equity proceeds.

The specific costs and benefits for issuers and investors, of course, depend on many factors, including the terms of purchase and market conditions.

2.3.3. Asset-Backed Eurobonds

The securitization of Euromarkets has been in the making since the mid 1980s. Securitization refers to the creation of readily marketable securities backed by financial instruments that are not as readily marketable. Such instruments include consumer loans, auto loans, and credit card receivables. Eurobonds backed by such instruments are termed asset-backed. For example, Standard Credit Card Master Trust issued a 10-year note in August 1993. Goldman Sachs was the lead underwriter, with Citicorp providing the assets from credit card loans. In the same month, Anglo Leasing PLC packaged $165 million of leases through Anglo Financing No. 1 PLC, a Special Purpose Vehicle (SPV). SPVs are created for the purpose of buying assets in order to securitize them. The lead manager of the issue was Kleinwort Benson Ltd; the maturity of these notes was 6.4 years (Pugley, Meidelmann, Teitelbaum, Schaan, and Van Zant, 1993).

Another interesting issue involved the Brazilian agricultural commodities processor Sanbra-Sociedade Algodoeira do Nordeste Brasiliero. Sanbra entered the market in 1992 to borrow $70 million through an issue of 3-year bonds. The issue was priced at 95.772; it paid a quarterly coupon of 10% and has an estimated annual yield of 11.75%. It was leadmanaged by Merrill Lynch. To conduct the deal, Sanbra International Finance (SIF), a Cayman-based financial entity was established. SIF then issued the bond on the basis of its export contracts. Bunge, the Swiss-based grain trader, committed to buying soya meal and pellets from Sanbra. The cash flows servicing the deal, then, for the payment of the principal and interest, came from outside Brazil.

Other assets used to back Eurobonds have included sterling Collateralized Mortgage Obligations (CMOs), World Bank bonds, mortgages, and high-yield securities. Protection to investors is provided in some cases by companies such as Financial Security Assurance, which will insure the deal and receive in return a premium as well as control over its structure.

2.3.4. "Floaters"

Some Eurobond issues have been characterized as perpetual floaters, since they do not have a stated maturity date. Some issues are termed reverse floaters, since coupon payments decline when interest rates rise. Eurobonds whose interest rates are capped at a pre-agreed level are called capped.

In general, the Eurobond market has been a continuous source of innovation and a strong competitor to national bond markets. The free flow of capital has enabled the Eurobond market to bypass the limitations of national bond markets and made it the largest international capital market in the world.

2.4. A Final Word on Euromarkets and Eurobonds

The success of the Euromarkets has not gone unnoticed by national authorities, who view these markets as siphoning tax revenues (lack of withholding tax), promoting tax evasion (bearer form), and compromising their control over their monetary policy (lack of regulation). The EU, for example, has considered a transactions tax on bond trading. Both the EU and the US have been trying to identify tax evaders. The Foreign Account Tax Compliance Act (FATCA), enacted in 2010 in the US, requires foreign financial institutions and certain non-financial institution's banks to disclose the names of American citizens with accounts over $50,000. The penalty for non-compliance by foreign institutions is a 30% withholding tax and possible ban from operation in US markets.

It remains to be seen whether these efforts by the EU and the US will have an impact on the growth of the Euromarkets in general and the Eurobond market, in particular. These markets have faced such challenges throughout their history, but have so far persevered. Will they continue to do so?

3. Sovereign Debt

Sovereign debt is issued by national governments in a foreign currency. Bonds issued by these governments are principally general obligation bonds; that is, they are backed by the issuing country's tax revenues. Should the government's taxing authority deteriorate due to non-performance of the domestic economy, sovereign bond holders are at risk of not receiving periodic payments or principal repayments. Although sovereign default does not occur often, some recent well-publicized defaults (Argentina, Russia, and Greece) have made investors more cautious when deciding to enter the market.

4. The Emergence of Sukuk Bonds

The resurgence of Islamic financial services has given rise to Sharia-compliant bonds called Sukuk. Sukuk are "*certificates of equal value that represent an equal interest (proportional to the investor's interest) in the ownership of an individual asset (both tangible and intangible) usufruct, services, or investments in particular projects or special investment activities.*" (Asian Development Bank, 2011, p. 18). Sukuk are similar to conventional bonds in that payments to Sukuk holders depend on the ability of the issuer to make them. And, similar to conventional bonds, Sukuk prices fall when interest rates rise. However, Sukuk structures differ from conventional bonds in order to comply with Islamic principles and concepts. Some Sukuk contracts represent ownership claims on the underlying asset and the cash flow and proceeds from that asset. Other Sukuk contracts represent rights to cash flow from the asset, but not the asset itself. Still other represent rights to pre-agreed proportion of profits or losses.

Issues of Sukuk bonds have been primarily offered in Malaysia and the Gulf States. Malaysia is the single largest market for Sukuk. Sukuk issuance, however, has expanded to the United States, Europe (especially London and Luxemburg), and other countries in the Middle East and Asia. Some of the sovereign issuers have included the governments of Malaysia, Pakistan, Bahrain, Qatar, and Dubai. Corporate issuers have included Standard Chartered Bank (Malaysia), the Nakheel Group (UAE) and the Dubai Ports Authority. Sukuk may be issued in the local currency, or in US dollars, or in another currency. For example, in 2011, Malaysia issued its first Renminbi-denominated Islamic bond.

The differences between conventional corporate bonds and Sukuk make the latter a good candidate for further portfolio diversification (Cakir and Raei, 2007). Compared to conventional bonds, Sukuk have a more limited secondary market and overall liquidity. The prospect of further development of the Sukuk market, though, seems bright as the pools of borrowers and investors are becoming larger.

Concept Questions

1. What are the two major categories of international bond markets? How do they differ from each other?
2. What is the significance of the international bond market in terms of funds raised in international capital markets?
3. Explain the distinction between fixed-rate and floating-rate Eurobonds.

IV. International Equity Markets

Like the bond markets, equity markets operate throughout the world in many different forms. The last few years have eliminated all doubt about the existence of a global economy. Consider the events surrounding the crash of October 1987, the Persian Gulf crisis of 1990–91, and the Subprime crisis of 2007–2009. New York was not the only financial center. Tokyo, London, Hong Kong, Sydney, and Singapore were also impacted, albeit to different degrees. The formation of the EU has affected all markets, including equities. Large multinationals, especially those domiciled in the United States, have sold stock on a worldwide basis for a long time, even though their domestic capital market is substantial in size. Some multinationals, however, are in domestic markets that do not have the capacity to satisfy their capital requirements. Changes in some domestic environments, moreover, have forced changes in capitalization needs. The privatization movement in European and Latin American countries, for example, has brought with it the need for new funding. International developments, such as financial integration, have already affected and will probably continue to expand the international equity markets. Finally, the Lehman Brothers collapse uncovered the extent to which international financial markets are interrelated.

The international market for equities may be discussed in terms of three components: Euroequities, international share placement, and world stock exchanges.

1. Euroequities

The Euroequities component of the market refers to placement of international tranches of new issues in markets outside the issuer's home country. Bell Canada Enterprises, for example, issued one of the first Euroequities in 1975 by listing simultaneously in Amsterdam, Brussels, Frankfurt, London, Paris, and Zurich. Activity in the market was diminished as a result of the recent crisis, but Euroequities represent a viable financing option for multinationals.

2. International Share Placements

International share placement refers to special arrangements made to facilitate investment in equities by non-residents. A US investor has a variety of ways of participating in the international equity market:

- Shares of stocks. Stock of companies domiciled in countries whose securities laws are similar to those of the United States can be sold in the US. These include Canadian, Israeli, and Philippine companies.
- Fund shares. Access to international investments need not be through shares of individual firms. Investors instead may buy shares in a variety of mutual funds based in the US and invest throughout the world, including

  a. country funds, which specialize in single-country investments;
  b. regional funds, which invest in specific geographic area, such as the Pacific Basin;
  c. international funds, investing in all countries outside the United States;
  d. global funds, which invest in any country including the United States; and
  e. bond funds, which specialize in fixed-income securities in foreign countries. Bond funds may have a special orientation, such as global or international.

The funds have important advantages for investors seeking access to foreign markets and for securities markets in search of recognition and liquidity

- American depositary receipts. The American depositary receipt (ADR) is the most widely accepted way of buying into a world company for a US investor, institution, or individual. The ADR is a receipt issued by a bank verifying that foreign company shares have been placed on deposit with the bank's branch. The purchase of the ADR thus eliminates the need for physical transfer of the shares. Payments and receipts are made in US dollars, thus eliminating exchange rate risk for domestic investors.

The first ADR appeared in 1927. It was introduced on behalf of Selfridge Stores, which became part of Sears Holdings p.l.c. by Morgan Guaranty, then the Guaranty Trust Company. By 1961, 150 companies had issued ADRs. By 2012, there were 2,000 ADRs representing companies from 70 countries (www.investor.org). They are listed on the New York or NASDAQ or traded over-the-counter. ADRs registered with the SEC qualify as listed securities for US pension funds. (See www.adr.com; the site, sponsored by J. P. Morgan, contains very useful SDR information.)

ADRs may be sponsored or unsponsored. Sponsored ADRs are issued by an American depository bank at the firm's request. The issuing bank distributes information about the company to ADR holders. For the issuer, the benefits of sponsorship include a potentially bigger investor pool, greater control over the shareholder base because of the use of a single depositary, and more flexibility in structuring an equity strategy by offering the firm improved access to the American capital markets. For the investor, sponsorship may bring the benefits of lower share costs, more information about the company, and US dollar transactions (buying shares, receiving dividends, selling shares).

Unsponsored ADRs are issued at the request of brokers. To establish an unsponsored ADR, the depository bank needs a letter from the company verifying that it has no objection to the issuance of the shares. An exemption from registration for the company under Rule 12 g3-2(b) of the SEA of 1934 is filed by the depository. An F-6 registration statement is filed with the SEC. Following that step, the depository may make the announcement regarding ADR availability. For the sponsored ADR to materialize, the firm notifies the depository of its intention to issue the ADR and works with it to get an exemption from the SEA. An agreement is then signed between the issuing firm and the depository, followed by the issue of an F-6 registration statement. After taking care of printing details, the certificates are ready for distribution.

There are currently three levels of ADRs. Level 1 is traded over-the-counter, while levels 2 and 3 are listed on US exchanges; the two higher levels denote higher level of regulation and more rigorous disclosure. ADRs have been imitated to some extent by Institutional Depositary Receipts (IDRs), Continental depositary receipts (CDRs), and European depositary receipts (EDRs), which are traded outside the United States. EDRs for the most part have been issued by a small number of Japanese companies listed on the Luxembourg Stock Exchange. The most recent development is the development of the Global depository receipt (GDR) market, which circulate outside the US. The characteristics of ADRs and GDRs are shown in Table 8.1.

ADRs					**GDRs**
Type	**Level 1**	**Level 2**	**Level 3**	**Rule144A**	**Regulation**
Where Found	US only	US only	US only	US only	Global/Outside US
Description	Unlisted in US	Listed	Listed	Private Placement to US Qualified Institutional Buyers	Listed Outside US
Shares Offered	Existing	Existing	New	New	New
Where Traded	Over The Counter Rule 12g3-2(b)	NYSE, NASDAQ	NYSE, NASDAQ	PORTAL Trading System	Outside US
Registration	Form F-6	ADRs: Form F-6 Company: Form 20-F Full SEC Registration	ADRs: Form F-6 Company: Form 20-F Full SEC Registration	No SEC Regulation	Local regulations apply
Disclosure	Per local market	Annual/Interim Reports	Annual/ Interim Reports	No Disclosure requirement	Local rules apply

Table 8.1 Characteristics of ADRs and GDRs.

ADRs					GDRs
Type	**Level 1**	**Level 2**	**Level 3**	**Rule144A**	**Regulation S**
Advantages	Low Cost; easy execution No US SEC registration	Access to US; Visibility	Level 2 plus raising capital	Easiest, most cost effective; no US SEC registration	Access to markets outside the US; no US SEC registration
Disadvantages	No exchange trading Lower liquidity Cannot raise capital	Full SEC Registration and Disclosure	Full SEC Registration and Disclosure	Qualified Institutional Buyers only (own/manage $100m +)	Institutional Investors mostly

Table 8.1 *(Continued)*

Adapted from:

Bank of NY Mellon: www.adrbnymellon.com Downloaded 7/15/2015

Citi: www.citiadr.idmanagedsolutions.com Downloaded 7/15/2015

J. P.Morgan: www.adr.com Downloaded 7/15/2015

http://topforeignstocks.com/foreign-adrs-list/ Downloaded 7/15/2015

3. World Stock Exchanges

Investors can also participate in international markets by buying and selling shares in stock exchanges all over the world. Although investing in markets of other countries enlarges the scope of opportunities and allows for diversification across national borders, it is subject to currency and other risks not associated with domestic investing. Information about foreign markets also may not be as readily available as it is domestically. In addition, world stock exchanges are governed by various sets of regulations. For example, since its founding in 1992, the Shanghai Securities Exchange (SSE) limited the participation of foreign investors by offering two types of shares: A-shares, open only to Chinese investors, and B-shares, open to both Chinese and foreign investors. The market, however, has been gradually opening up. In 2014, the Chinese government announced the Shanghai-Hong Kong Stock Connect Program. The program allows foreign investors to buy shares on the SSE, while also allowing Chinese investors to access stocks listed in Hong Kong. Markets may also differ with respect to the distribution and tax treatment of earnings, the degree of required disclosure, the types of companies allowed to trade, settlement period, and the conduct of trading. Many markets still allow trading on the exchange floor, while others have switched or are in the process of switching to computerized trading. Trading hours may also vary, with some exchanges allowing as few as two or three trading hours per day. Trading hours on the most active exchanges can be for six or seven hours. As global trading approaches a twenty-four-hour schedule, however, exchanges may revise floor trading practices and hours of trading.

Equity markets have also included differential trading arrangements for shares issued by particular firms. One example is Indonesia, where in 1987 capital market reforms included the creation of a parallel market where shares of high-risk firms are listed. The

European stock markets were also known for their second-tier, or Unlisted Securities Markets (USM), and third-tier over-the-counter (OTC) markets. These niche markets that appear from time to time in various exchanges are examples of market innovation. They can cater to the needs of small- and medium-size growth companies and have a simpler regulatory structure than their main-tier counterparts. For example, a company may float a relatively small portion of its equity and still be allowed to list in a second-tier market. The existence and operations of these markets raises a number of questions regarding their role in the process of financial market integration. If they are not able to maintain their special characteristics, a very important economic sector may be underfunded and underutilized.

Multinationals may list their equities in more than one exchange. Cross-listing offers some advantages for companies, since it gives them access to a larger network of capital financing. On the other hand, for multinationals from emerging markets, listing in a developed market exchange may involve providing additional information on their financial statements in order to adhere to more rigorous disclosure requirements.

V. Derivative Instruments

We have discussed the nature of forward, futures, options and swaps and their importance for participants in the foreign exchange market. These contracts are part of a group of financial instruments known as derivatives, since they are linked to or derived from an underlying instrument, such as currencies, equities, or bonds. Derivatives have provided market participants with new ways of dealing with uncertainty and of taking advantage of opportunities. The trend toward integration of financial markets has encouraged creation of derivatives based on international markets. Some examples are futures and futures options on Eurodollars (traded in the International Monetary Market and the London International Futures Exchange), futures on Japanese government bonds (traded on the Chicago Board of Trade), options on the Tokyo Stock Exchange Index (traded on the Chicago Board of Trade), and futures on many other stock exchange indices.

The market for derivative instruments has become an integral part of world financial markets and has extended the horizon of the international financial manager. The importance of derivatives has increased along with global economic uncertainty; in addition, competition for financial products has become more intense and the technological infrastructure more sophisticated.

Concept Questions

1. What are the various components of international equity markets? Define each component.
2. Discuss the nature and importance of ADRs.
3. What are derivative instruments? Give some examples of such instruments.

VI. Additional Issues in Global Financial Markets

Creation of the Eurocurrency markets is an excellent example of market innovation. The market contributes to the development of a flexible environment where participants meet on an "even playing field." It helps breach barriers erected by protective governments and facilitates enhanced competition and a freer flow of capital.

Financial markets will become even more global as macro and structural issues have necessitated (Pavel and McElravey, 1990). The process is strengthened by galloping advances in technology and fueled by intense competition for market share. In fact, all these factors go hand-in-hand. Countries need funds for economic development purposes. If they intend to rely on private funds, they must allow for the development of an active secondary market. To accomplish that, governments must show a liberal attitude toward capital flows, which means balancing maintenance of market and national integrity with minimization of barriers to market access.

Critical to competition among financial centers is establishment of the appropriate technological infrastructure—both in terms of telecommunications and data processing. Financial globalization of these networks has proceeded with impressive speed, moving faster at the wholesale (bank to bank or bank to multinational) rather than retail level. The effects at the customer level seem to be mainly indirect, as prices of financial services and interest rates are impacted by the influences of global economic and financial conditions. As globalization advances further and institutions such as banks and investment firms continue to cross national borders, direct customer access to suppliers will also tend to increase.

Obstacles to financial market globalization still exist. Countries still impose capital controls. Two types of controls are worth mentioning. One type constrains the flow of securities, thus differentiating between the treatment of domestic and foreign assets. The other type discriminates against foreign residents by limiting the extent to which they can participate in the domestic financial markets. Countries are trying to resolve these control issues by discussing principles of mutual recognition and home currency control.

Certainly attempts to achieve financial integration have benefits. A study by Price Waterhouse shows that financial market integration does indeed bring welfare gains to participants. Whether regional integration movements, such as EC 1992, provide "optimal" gains, however, is still debatable. In whatever case, market integration, regional or global, is a process that seems irreversible once begun.

VII. Summary

This chapter presents an overview of international financial markets and examination of the Eurocurrency, international bond, Euronote, and international equity markets. Developments in these markets have been closely paralleled in world economic developments in general. They provide a valuable outlet for the international investment community as well as a significant source of funds for the private and public sector. International financial market operations have reached practically every corner of the world. The success of present and future movements toward economic integration undoubtedly will depend to a great extent on how well financial markets perform their functions.

Key Terms and Concepts

In the order in which they are presented in the text.

Interest Rate Equalization Tax: A tax levied by the US on the returns gained by US citizens on foreign stocks and other financial assets.

Foreign Credit Restraint Program: Formulated by the Federal Reserve Board, this program's objective was to limit the flow of funds from member banks to their foreign borrowers in the US markets.

Flow of funds restrictions: Restrictions on funds flowing from US-based multinationals to their foreign affiliates placed by the US Office of Foreign Direct Investment in 1968.

Regulation Q: Adopted during the Great Depression (1933), Regulation Q imposed interest rate ceilings on time and savings deposits at US banks.

Reserve requirements: Bank reserve requirements limit the extent to which banks can commit funds to income-earning alternatives. They therefore affect the availability and cost of credit.

Eurocurrencies: Eurocurrencies are currencies on deposit with banks outside the country of issue

Eurocurrency Certificates of Deposit (CDs): Negotiable instruments with relatively active secondary markets in the Euromarkets.

London Interbank Offer Rate (LIBOR): An arithmetic average (excluding the top and bottom 25% of the submitted rates) of the rates considered appropriate for borrowing by major London banks. LIBOR is thought of as the "best" rate at which loans can be extended; it is the rate banks used to lend to each other.

Secured Overnight Financing Rate (SOFR): Viewed as the LIBOR replacement, SOFR is based on repo interest rates for overnight Treasury-backed transactions in the Bank of New York Mellon's repo system or cleared though the Fixed Income Clearing Corporation.

Euronotes: Instruments of various maturities, from relatively short term to medium term, offered on underwritten or non-underwritten basis in the Euromarkets.

International bond markets: Include foreign bonds and Eurobonds. **Foreign bond markets** include bonds issued by a foreign entity in another country's market and denominated in that country's currency. **Eurobonds** are bonds issued by an entity in the currency of its country in another country's market.

Autostrada: Italian State Highway Authority, issuers of the first Eurobonds in 1963.

Sovereign debt: Bonds or other debt instruments issued by national governments in a foreign currency.

Sukuk bonds: According to the Asian Development Bank, Sukuk are *"certificates of equal value that represent an equal interest (proportional to the investor's interest) in the ownership of an individual asset (both tangible and intangible) usufruct, services, or investments in particular projects or special investment activities."*

Euroequities: The Euroequities component of the market refers to placement of international tranches of new issues in markets outside the issuer's home country.

American depositary receipt (ADR): The ADR is a receipt issued by a bank verifying that foreign company shares have been placed on deposit with the bank's branch.

Sponsored and unsponsored ADRs: The sponsored ADR is issued by an American depository bank at the firm's request. Unsponsored ADRs are issued at the request of brokers.

Questions and Problems

1. Explain the importance of the Eurodollar market for US and European investors and firms.
2. How has the Eurodollar market affected the US financial system? Has there been any change through time?
3. Assume that you are an investor considering opportunities in the Eurobond market. You find out that Austria recently floated a large issue. How would you decide whether to participate in this issue?
4. A number of regional integration arrangements have been proposed during the last few years, the most notable being the European unification movement. Explain the implications of these arrangements for financial markets. What are the benefits of such arrangements? What are the obstacles? What are the concerns?
5. Look at a copy of today's *Wall Street Journal*. Identify a foreign or international market. How would you go about investing in that market?
6. Why would an individual consider investing in a zero coupon bond? A convertible bond? Why would a borrower consider issuing a convertible bond?
7. Assume that your firm is in need of funds. How should you as a financial manager go about selecting a source from the following?

    a. domestic bonds
    b. foreign bonds
    c. Eurobonds
    d. borrowing in the Eurocurrency market

    Explain the factors that you considered in reaching your decision.
8. Considering what you have read in this chapter and elsewhere, what is your expectation for the future of the Eurobond market? What about its dollar and euro components? Explain the reasons for your conclusion.
9. What are NIFs? How do you explain their existence and development?
10. Look at today's *Wall Street Journal*. Find the futures and options instruments pertaining to the Eurodollar market. Who would use these markets?
11. "Even though the variety of international mutual funds offers the opportunity to invest in more than a single company or country, they may not offer complete diversification."

    Comment on the above statement.

12. Consult a recent issue of the *Wall Street Journal* or the *Financial Times*. Locate an announcement of a recent issuance of a Eurobond or foreign bond. Comment on its characteristics.

Selected References

Asian Development Bank. 2011. *Malaysia Bond Guide*. Tokyo: Waseda University.

Bank for International Settlements. *Annual Report*. Various years. Basle, Switzerland.

Bank for International Settlements. 2015. *Statistical Release*. Basle, Switzerland.

Bowe, M. 1988. *Eurobonds*. Homewood, Illinois: Square Mile Books/Dow Jones-Irwin.

Cakir, S. and F. Raei. 2007. Sukuk vs. Eurobonds: Is There a Difference in Value-at-Risk? *IMF Working Paper WP/07/237*. Washington, DC: International Monetary Fund, October.

Council on Foreign Relations. 2016. Understanding the LIBOR Scandal. October 12, 2016. Accessed at http://www.cfr.org/united-kingdom/understanding-libor-scandal/p28729. Downloaded October 20, 2018.

Glover, J. 2013. Eurobonds as Refugees from Tax Men Turn 50 in $4 Trillion Market. *Bloomberg*, June 24, 2013. Accessed at: http://www.bloomberg.com/news/articles/2013-06-23/eurobonds-as-refugees-from-tax-men-turn-50-in-4-trillion-market. Downloaded July 10, 2015.

J. P. Morgan. 1990. *American Depositary Receipts: J.P. Morgan; The Market Leader*. New York: Morgan Guaranty Trust Company of New York.

O'Malley, C. 2015. *Bonds without Borders: A History of the Eurobond Market*. Wsr Sussex, UK: Wiley.

Pavel, C. and J. N. McElravey. 1990. Globalization in the Financial Services Industry. *Economic Perspectives*. Federal Reserve Bank of Chicago 14 (3): 3–18.

Pugsley, J., N. Elliott, C. Middelmann, H. E. Teitelbaum, R. Schaan, and E. Van Zant. 1993. Asset-Backed Eurobonds Arrive in Force, Led by SCCM's $750 Million Global Issue. *Wall Street Journal, Europe*, Brussels, August 30, 1993, 21.

Sarver, E. 1988. *The Eurocurrency Market Handbook*. New York: New York Institute of Finance.

Sfez, F. 2014. Changes in organizational patterns of the Eurobond market: an historical analysis. *Society and Business Review* 9 (1): 85–97.

Smyth, D. 1988. *World Wise Investor: International Opportunities in Today's Markets*. New York: Watts.

Thau, A. 2011. *The Bond Book*. New York: McGraw-Hill.

Wyman, Oliver. 2018. Changing the World's Most Important Number: LIBOR Transition. Accessed at https://www.oliverwyman.com/our-expertise/insights/2018/feb/libor-rate-transition.html. Downloaded 5/21/19.

Concluding Comments

We have noted that the international monetary system is a reflection of the status of international economic and political relations. The world came to this realization in the most dramatic fashion when relations practically collapsed in the three decades during and between the two World Wars. Success of the international monetary system at any time is based on cooperation among participating countries.

Without adequate international cooperation, fixed exchange rates may not provide the necessary level of liquidity for the system to function; retaliatory policies can bring the system to a standstill. There is a need for cooperation during times of floating rates, when the market must be left alone to function efficiently. Future functioning of the international monetary system, then, depends on the extent to which countries can appreciate and realize the benefits of international cooperation.

There are plenty of good examples of structures enhancing international monetary cooperation. The IMF would not exist had it not been for the willingness of so many countries to cooperate. More recently, the Plaza Agreement of September 1985 and the Louvre Accord of February 1987 serve as examples of cooperative efforts. The Plaza meeting of the Group of Five (the G5 countries of Britain, France, Germany, Japan, and the United States) resulted in policies to foster international trade, reduce protectionist measures, and bring down the dollar. The 1987 Louvre Accord attempted to stop the fall of the dollar and bring about greater currency stabilization. Of course, the mere signing of an agreement does not necessarily mean that countries will adhere to a policy, although expectations continue to bid that a continual dialogue can only bring positive results in the long run.

Cooperation is much more difficult to attain during times of economic hardship. The financial crisis did not provide an environment conducive to such cooperation. And, as the US–China trade war showed us, trade wars are not over and nor are currency wars. The instability we have witnessed in the global economy after the crisis has somewhat abated, but it remains a threat to the system. History has offered us numerous lessons but, steeped in economic nationalism, countries are unwilling to learn from them.

Globalization of finance, along with rapid technological progress, has produced additional developments, complications, and controversies. The emergence of China as a major economic power and the ascent of India and Brazil have brought havoc to the existing global economic order. China's currency is increasing in importance in international trade and finance. Chinese holdings of huge amounts of international reserves are both a stabilizer and a threat to the system. It is perhaps ironic that the solution to some of the problems facing a global system built in the West could come from the East.

At the same time, European countries are still arguing amongst themselves about the approach out of the crisis. When it is all said and done, the European Union will be hailed as either the greatest economic union of the last two centuries or an example of the damage that nationalism-based arrogance by a few countries can create.

Systems of any kind, of course, are as good as the people running them. In this regard, the international financial system has been badly served by the actions of some of its high-profile participants. The first part of the twenty-first century has featured seemingly endless investigations on illegal behavior surrounding trading in the foreign exchange market and the setting of LIBOR. Thus, the integrity of the system has come into question. Similarly, doubts have arisen regarding the system's effectiveness. Frequent national and international crises and cross-country squabbles have revealed the dearth of innovative solutions to financial problems being brought forward by international agencies and institutions. The search for ways to improve the functioning of the international system must be continuous and persistent. A strong global economy requires a strong international financial system. As students of the system, we wait anxiously for what comes next.

Respectfully,
Peter E. Koveos
George C. Philippatos

Appendix 4.1 European Union Timeline: 1945–2020

Year(s)	Event(s)
1945	WWII ends
1948	Congress at the Hague: European Union of Federalists
	European Constitution rejected by UK
1949	UK devaluation
	Other countries follow
	European bilateralism/non-convertibility
1949	European Payments Union (EPU) clearing house
1951	Treaty of Paris
	European Coal and Steel Community
	Belgium, France, Germany, Italy, Luxembourg, and Netherlands
1957	Convertibility Returns
	EPU dissolved
	Treaty of Rome
	European Economic Community (EEC) or Common Market
1960	European Free Trade Association
1961	Austria, Denmark, Norway, Portugal, Sweden, Switzerland, UK
	Britain, Denmark, Ireland apply for EEC membership
1963	de Gaulle vetoes UK membership
1967	Creation of Single Council and European Commission
	UK devalues currency
1968	European Community Customs Union

Year(s)	Event(s)
1973	First Enlargement
	Denmark, Ireland and the United Kingdom
1974–1975	Salazar overthrown (Portugal);
	Franco dies (Spain)
1979	European Monetary System/European Currency Unit
	Exchange Rate Mechanism: Band created
	UK does not join
1980	Second Enlargement
	Greece
1984	Jacques Delors becomes President of European Commission
1985	First Schengen Agreement signed; borders of agreeing member states opened
1986	Third Enlargement
	Spain, Portugal
1987	Single Market/European Act into force
1989–1990	Berlin Wall falls
	Reunification of Germany
1993	Maastricht Treaty signed
	Monetary Union
	European citizenship
1992	UK pulls out of ERM
1993	Maastricht Treaty into effect
	Completion of single market
	Social Chapter
	Maastricht Treaty
	Movement of goods, services, labor, capital
1995	Further Enlargement
	Austria, Finland, Sweden
	Schengen Agreements
	Elimination of national borders
1999	Treaty of Amsterdam
	Eastward Expansion approved
	Euro comes into existence

Year(s)	Event(s)
2001–2002	Euro becomes the European Currency
	National Currencies replaced by euro notes and coins
2004	Ten new countries join the EU
	New Constitution
2006	Turkey EU bid stalls
2007	Two new countries join the EU
	Romania, Bulgaria
2008	Global financial crisis
2009	Treaty of Lisbon
	Creation of modern institutions/working methods
	Charter of Fundamental Rights
2016	UK votes to exit from EU
2017	UK Prime Minister May invokes Article 50 of the Lisbon Treaty
2019	Following repeated, but failed, attempts to put together an approved Brexit plan, Prime Minister May resigns (May 2019)

Generated from:

www.europa.com/about-eu-history Downloaded 11/28/13

BBC News-A timeline of the EU www.news.bbc.co.uk/hi/world/europe Downloaded 11/26/13

Friedrich, Klaus. International Economics: Concepts and Issues. New York: McGraw-Hill, 1974

Appendix 4.2 European Union Crisis Timeline: 2009–2013

Year(s)		Event(s)
2009		
	December	Greece announces debt of €300bn (113% of GDP); EU limit 60%
		Greek debt downgraded
2010		
	January	Greece's budget deficit revised at 12.7%; 4x Euro limit
	February	Greece announces austerity measures
		Portugal, Ireland, Spain join Greece on list of countries under watch
	March	EU, IMF establish €22bn safety net for Greece
	April	EU announces €30bn loan fund
	May	EU, IMF announce €110bn bailout package for Greece
	November	EU, IMF announce €85bn bailout package for Ireland
		Ireland passes austerity budget
2011		
	February	European Stability Mechanism (permanent bailout fund) established: €500bn
	May	EU, IMF provide €78bn bailout fund for Portugal
	June	Greece announces new austerity plan; rumors of EU exit
	July	Greece austerity measures approved
		EU agrees to new Greek loan tranche of €12bn
		Second bailout for Greece: €109bn
	August	ECB announces program to buy Italian and Spanish bonds
	September	Spain passes constitutional amendments on budget deficits
		Italy passes €50bn austerity measures
		Greece holds talks with Troika (EU, IMF, ECB)
		Italy's Standard & Poor's rating cut from A+ to A
		Eurozone private sector shrinks for first time in two years

Year(s)		Event(s)
	October	Markets decline as decision to lend to Greece is delayed
		Bank of England adopts QE to stimulate economy
		ECB announces new emergency loan measures
		Markets react positively to Franco-German accord on crisis resolution
		Dexia Bank (Franco-Belgian) receives bailout
		EU approves €8bn Greek bailout averting default
		EU reaches "three-pronged" agreement to solve debt crisis
2012		
	January	Standard & Poor's downgrades France, eight other countries and the European Financial Stability Fund
	February	Greece agrees to demands of international lenders
		Greece passes new austerity bill; cuts €32mn from budget
		EU sector shrinks
	March	EU jobless record hits new high
		Second Greek bailout (€130bn)
		Eurozone rescue fund doubles to €1tr
	April	Italian, Spanish borrowing costs increase
	May	Bankia, Spain's fourth largest bank, asks for bailout
	June	Spain to ask for €100bn loan; country's borrowing costs highest since 1999
		Greece elects pro-austerity party
2013		
	December	Ireland announces bailout exit

Adapted from: BBC News. Timeline: The Unfolding Eurozone Crisis. 06/13/12. www.bbc.uk/news/business-13856580;

Appendix 5.1 Exchange Rate Dynamics

Additional Factors and Approaches

Throughout Chapter 5 we assumed that autonomous changes in particular variables generate a consequent change in currency values. This, of course, is unrealistic. Economic environments are dynamic; variables are not only influenced by circumstances in an environment, but they in turn affect their environment. Exchange rates are influenced by prices, money, and incomes, to mention a few variables. Exchange rates also have an impact on these and other variables. They may, then, have an impact on decisions made by individuals and governments and on the distribution of income.

Examples of the impact of exchange rates may be discussed in terms of currency adjustments (revaluation or devaluation), currency substitution, and the fundamental equilibrium exchange rate (FEER).

I. Currency Changes and Adjustment

Analysis of the impact of changes in the exchange rate follows three main approaches:

a) The elasticities approach examines the impact of devaluation on the various sectors. If devaluation is followed by appropriate changes in the quantity of imports and exports, a country's trade balance may improve. Changes are appropriate if the sum of the elasticity of domestic demand for imports and foreign demand for exports is greater than one. This is known as the Marshall-Lerner condition (Lindert and Kindleberger, 1982).

The net effect of the devaluation on the trade balance is usually illustrated under different assumptions about supply and demand elasticities in both home and foreign markets. Thus, if the trade balance, T, is denoted as

$$T = P_x X - P_m M \text{ or } T = V_x - V_m, \tag{5.28}$$

where

$P_x X = V_x$, the value of exports before devaluation, and

$P_mM = V_m$, the value of imports before devaluation

then, by taking the elasticity of T with respect to the change in the exchange rate, r, Lindert and Kindleberger (1982) show that we get

$$E_T = (dT/V_m)/(dr/r) = (V_x/V_m)[(d_x + 1)/((d_x/s_x) - 1)] = (s_m + 1)/((s_m/d_m) - 1) \quad (5.29)$$

where

s_m, s_x are supply elasticities for imports and exports respectively, and

d_m, d_m are demand elasticities for imports and exports respectively

if $s_x = s_x = \infty$, ET>0 when |dx + dm|>1

The significance of the values of the elasticity coefficients has led to their use as arguments in the fixed vs. flexible rates debate. The size of the assumed elasticities, of course, will vary with time. In the short run, the elasticities may remain low. This phenomenon may give rise to a J-curve behavior of the trade balance; the trade balance initially deteriorates but ultimately improves. Empirical studies on the Marshall-Lerner condition vary in their results. A study by Rose (1991), for example, does not find evidence for rejecting the hypothesis that the Marshall-Lerner condition does not hold.

b) The absorption approach addresses macroeconomic variables. At equilibrium,

$$Y = C + I + G + (X - M) \quad (5.30)$$

where Y = gross national product, C = consumption expenditures, I = gross private domestic investment, G = government expenditures, X = exports, and M = imports. Rearranging,

$$(X - M) = Y - A \quad (5.31)$$

where A is the domestic absorption of goods and services (C + I + G). Currency devaluation will improve the trade balance (X − M) if its impact on output, Y, is greater than that on domestic expenditures, A.

c) The monetary approach examines the impact of devaluation through its effects on the money market. By increasing the prices of traded goods, devaluation reduces real money supply and thereby leads to adjustments in the demand for real balances. Ultimately, spending and income are affected.

II. Currency Substitution

Adjustments in currency holdings (substitutions between domestic and foreign currency) facilitate the transmission of monetary shocks from one country to another (Canto and Nickelsburg, 1987). The following testable relationship is generated:

$$\log (M/P)t = a + b(\log Y)t - c(\log I)t - d(\log X)t + g (\log (M/P))t - 1 + Ut \quad (5.32)$$

where M is the domestic money stock, P is the domestic price level, Y is real income, I is the domestic nominal interest rate, and X is the expected return from foreign currency holdings. The signs preceding the coefficients are those predicted by the theory. According to Batten and Hafer (1984), empirical evidence has not in general shown that currency substitution in fact decreases the degree of independence of national monetary policies during floating rates.

III. The Fundamental Equilibrium Exchange Rate (FEER)

The FEER is defined as "the exchange rate that is consistent with both internal and external balance simultaneously" (International Monetary Fund, 2008; Williamson, 1994). Internal balance implies full employment at stable prices; external balance is defined as a balance of payments state that is sustained over a three-to-five-year period. Identifying internal balance depends on the difficult talk of arriving at the level of full-employment output. For the system to be in internal and external balance simultaneously, then, external balance implies internal balance as well. The International Monetary Fund's (IMF's) model arrives at the FEER by following two steps:

Step 1: express current account balance as a function of the real exchange rate, as shown in (4.33):

$$CA = ntb + nfa = q^{REER}, y^*_d, y^*_f) \quad (5.33)$$

Where CA is the current account balance composed of the net trade balance (ntb) and net foreign assets (nfb); y^*_d, is the full employment output of the domestic economy; y^*_f is the full employment output of the foreign economy and FEER is the real effective exchange rate.

Step 2: solve for the equilibrium exchange rate by assuming that the equilibrium capital account is exogenously determined. External balance, then, implies CA= −K*; K* is the equilibrium capital account. By substituting in (5.33), we get

$$q^{FEER} = f(K^*, y^*_d, y^*_f)$$

The IMF uses its FEER model to assess the need for appropriate exchange rate adjustments. Other scholars have also used the FEER concept through their own approaches. In a recent finding, for example, Cline (2014) employs the FEER to show that the major international currencies (US dollar, euro, UK pound sterling, Japanese yen and Chinese renminbi) are indeed close to their fundamental equilibrium levels. His conclusion is that there is no need for major currency realignments at this time. This is an important conclusion given the accusations of exchange rate fixing directed at Japan and China by their international trade and investment partners.

Concept Questions

1. What is the Marshall-Lerner condition? What is its importance?
2. Under what conditions is devaluation beneficial according to the elasticities approach?
3. What is the implication of currency substitution for the degree of independence of national monetary policies?

Appendix 8.1. The Creation of Eurodollar Deposits

An Example

Assume that Daedalus, A. E., a Greek manufacturer of hot air balloons, has just been paid in US dollars for delivering an order to a US customer. The customer transfers the necessary payment to Daedalus from an account at a New York bank. This is shown on Table 7A.1 in the form of the traditional accounts, where the A column stands for assets and the L column for liabilities. For purposes of simplicity, only changes in each column are noted.

1. The US importer's account at New York bank decreases by $20; the amount is transferred to the Greek exporter's account with the same bank.
2. The Greek exporter's deposit account at New York bank increases by $20.
3. Daedalus decides to transfer the deposit to an interest earning account at a Paris bank. At this point, a Eurodollar deposit is created. To create its Paris account, the exporter draws the funds from its existing New York bank account, thus adding to the Paris bank's account with the New York bank. Notice that the original US-dollar deposit is still with the New York bank.
4. The Paris bank's account at the New York bank increases; its liabilities also increase as the Greek exporter's time deposit account increases.

The new funds give the Paris bank the opportunity to search for income generating outlets. One probable outlet is the interbank loan market. The Eurodollar market is primarily an interbank market; these banks are called Eurobanks, and they own more than four-fifths of the Eurodollar liabilities. On the other side of the market, the borrowers include large corporations and political entities. The denominations involved on either side of the market are very large, making the market essentially a wholesale enterprise.

5. The Paris bank lends its US dollars (from the New York bank account) to a London bank. Its loan account increases, but its dollar deposit decreases by $20.
6. The London bank's deposit account at the New York bank increases by $20; its loan liabilities also increase by $20.

7. The New York bank's ownership of deposit liabilities of $20 shifts from the Paris bank's account to the London bank's account.
8. The London bank lends its US dollars from its New York bank account to a British importer who has bought computers from a US supplier. The British importer deposits the funds with the New York bank and now has a loan liability of $20.
9. The London bank's deposit account at the New York bank decreases by $20; its loans increase by $20.
10. The New York bank's deposit accounts are adjusted to reflect the shift of $20 from the London bank's account to the British importer's account.
11. The British importer pays for the computers by writing a check on his New York bank account. The British importer's inventory increases by $20.
12. The US exporter now has a $20 deposit account at the New York bank, while his inventory decreases by $20.
13. The New York bank's deposit accounts are adjusted to reflect the payment by the British importer to the US exporter.
14. When the computers are sold, the British importer pays back the loan. His inventories decrease and his loan obligation is met.
15. The London's bank loan portfolio decreases by $20, while its reserves increase by $20.
16. The London bank repays its loan from the Paris bank.
17. The Paris bank accepts the repayment and closes its loan account with the London bank.

This simple example shows the way various institutions participate in the Eurodollar market. Since there are no required reserve requirements for eurodollar deposits, the process described could continue indefinitely. In practice, of course, leakages do occur and the process eventually comes to an end.

CPSIA information can be obtained
at www.ICGtesting.com
Printed in the USA
LVHW060150090122
708058LV00002B/15